THE IRRELEVANCE OF
CONVENTIONAL ECONOMICS

THE IRRELEVANCE
OF CONVENTIONAL
ECONOMICS.

—

THOMAS BALOGH

LIVERIGHT PUBLISHING CORPORATION
NEW YORK

Library of Congress Cataloging in Publication Data
Balogh, Thomas, Baron Balogh, 1905–
   The irrelevance of conventional economics.
   Includes bibliographical references and index.
   1. Economics.   I. Title.
HB71.B29 1982   330   81-20773
ISBN 0-87140-646-2   AACR2

Liveright Publishing Corporation
500 Fifth Avenue, New York
New York 10110

Printed in Great Britain by
Butler & Tanner Ltd
Frome and London

Contents

Acknowledgements   ix

1 Introduction: Hubris and After   1

   1. Changing theoretical fashions   1
   2. The neoclassical triumph   3
   3. The quantified apotheosis   6
   4. Humility and self-criticism   8

2 The Nature of Economic Problems and Relationships   12

   1. Introductory   12
   2. The basis of economic advice   13
   3. Schedules, curves and reality   17
   4. The false lever   21
   5. Escape routes   23

3 A Story of Irrelevance   29

   1. The historical context   29
   2. The neo-orthodox stance   32
   3. Interwar landscape: imbalance and the
      Keynesian revolution   38
   4. A return to the womb   42
   5. The point of weakness: inflation   47
   6. Counter-revolution and schism   48
   7. The Keynesian failure   50
   8. The revival of neoclassical macro-monetarism   53
   9. The revival of neoclassical micro-economics   56
   10. The growing fissure   61

4 Evaluating Policy   64

   1. Welfare and economic welfare   64
   2. The criterion of excellence   66
   3. Welfare and economics   68
   4. The conflict of criteria   73
   5. Kinds of criteria   75

5 The Individual and the Group   78

   1. The individual as consumer   78
   2. The discontinuity of economic progress   87
   3. The bias against collective needs   89
   4. The change in the urgency of needs   92
   5. The individual and the group   95

6 Production: Freedom and Efficiency?   105

   1. The mirage of optimum production   106
   2. The quality of decision   113
   3. Oligopoly   118
   4. Short run and long run   121
   5. Excess capacity   124
   6. Profiteering   126
   7. Risk and corporate management   128
   8. Further limitations   130
   9. The managerial revolution   131

7 Full Employment and the Distribution of Income   141

   1. Classical gloom   141
   2. Neoclassical cheer   142
   3. The Marxist vision and the orthodox defence   143
   4. The international distribution of income   148
   5. Stagnation and inflation   150

8 Backwards to Monetarism   158

  1. The failure of Keynesian management   158
  2. The backslide into monetarism   159
  3. The nature of inflation   163
  4. The meaningfulness of the quantity theory   168
  Appendix: Professor Friedman and statistics   178

9 The International Aspect   183

  1. International trade in the modern world   184
  2. The irrelevance of orthodoxy   185
  3. The meaningfulness of the two-commodity model   186
  4. The impact of decreasing costs   188
  5. The money aspect   190
  6. Managing the transfer   193
  7. The neoclassical model adopted by monetarists   195
  8. The asymmetry of the system   197
  9. The political background   199
  10. Prevalence of oligopoly in manufacture   199
  11. The determinant factors   201
  12. Indeterminacy   203
  13. Monetarism and inflation   205
  14. Confusion   206
  15. Liquidity   208
  16. Are existing precautions sufficient?   209
  17. Conclusion   211

Notes   213
Index   255

Acknowledgements

My grateful thanks are due to Peter Balacs, who bore with friendly interest a great burden, and to Paul Streeten, alas no longer at Oxford, who did so much to help me towards anti-conventional views, as did Keith Griffin. I am specially indebted to Hugh Stretton, who saved me from my increased impatience and read, and helped in finishing, this book. He gave generously his time and collaborated in revising the final draft. I benefited from my great friendship with Dick Crossman, so prematurely taken from us. One would long to have his analysis of Thatcherism (which goes a long way towards vindicating his ideas). I have discussed these topics since the early fifties with Peter Shore. Aubrey Jones and I spent many hours arguing about the ways in which Britain is governed. I admired and learned much from Frank (Lord) Kearton. Finally, I must thank Harold Wilson for giving me the chance to study the bureaucracy and politicians from inside the machine.

I have received help from the Woodrow Wilson Foundation of the Smithsonian Institution. They are quite outstanding in making research smoothly stimulating. Queen Elizabeth House, Oxford, and the Economics Department of the University College, London, were kind enough to allow me to work in their offices, despite pressure on space. They were agreeable years and I am duly thankful. Miss Morris MA was indefatigable in the pursuit of materials. My colleagues at Balliol helped me before and after I became Emeritus. Finally, the SSRC and the Leverhulme Trust enabled me to have research and secretarial help. I am of course entirely responsible for the results of my work.

CHAPTER ONE

Introduction: Hubris and After

1. Changing theoretical fashions

It has been my fate not only to restart my career several times over – both geographically, beginning in Hungary then Germany then Britain, and professionally, between private banking and academic life, as government adviser in a number of countries including in the end my own, and as Minister of State – but also to live through two devastating world wars, the second of which was caused mainly by economic folly. Being present at the destruction of the Austro-Hungarian Empire moreover gave me an evil foretaste of things which might not be avoided even in Britain, with its matchless historical record for political adaptation, in the event of serious economic breakdown. All these experiences lead me to repudiate conventional economics and the policy advice flowing from it.

The following chapters are based on lectures at Oxford and elsewhere. They draw upon numerous articles and the introductions to my earlier collections of writings.[1] In this introductory chapter I shall sketch the violent changes in mood and fashion that have beset economics and economists during my lifetime, and some of the fluctuations and failures of economic policy to which their advice has contributed. I wish to explore the causes of these misfortunes, and especially of the incorrigible tendency of my profession to irrelevance. The central thesis of this study is that the weaknesses of almost all current approaches to applied economic problems are due partly to a failure or refusal to recognize the actual nature of economic relationships; partly to a restricted view of what are conventionally regarded as economic relationships to the exclusion of other vital influences; and partly to the inadmissible methods of analysis to which this narrow view gives rise. The rest of the study consists of a reconsideration of economic doctrines and problems from the viewpoint of a more realistic approach.

The most depressing aspect of my work has been the failure of the so-called 'mainstream' economics, whether neoclassical Keynesian or monetarist, to contribute to the progress, happiness and contentment of the world. Even the odious lessons which ought to have been taught by the Great Depression and its bloody consequences seem to have been forgotten. There was indeed an exciting moment, a brief period after the publication of the *General Theory*, when the proto-Keynesians, and in particular Joan Robinson[2] and Nicholas Kaldor,[3] on its basis, developed ideas which promised practical and appropriate applications of theory to actual historical situations and institutions. But it was not to be. Conventional modes of thought regained first academic, then political, dominance. This was facilitated by the fact that even Keynes himself never accepted the international implications of his analysis.[4] To make matters worse, his theory and method of analysis were almost immediately frozen back into a mechanical equilibrium system, mainly by some of his own followers. (Though of course its forms have varied with time and place, I have followed some of its leaders in calling that school of thought 'neoclassical Keynesian' in the following chapters.) It proved to be unable to deal with the policy needs of the most menacing present-day phenomenon, inflation. The pure or monetarist neoclassical counterattack therefore had a relatively easy task and took to it with relish. As we shall see, since 1970 or thereabouts we have regressed towards pre-Great Depression economics. I do not believe that it is mere coincidence that we have at the same time suffered a deep and distressing depression of the 1930s type. A definite reversal of this awful trend is as yet not certain - though there are scattered signs that the neoclassical monetarist school feel themselves to be on the defensive. The most encouraging aspect of the present situation is the fact that at least five schools of economic theory have grown up each bewailing the ignorance and limited intellectual capacity of the others.

This acidulous tilting at each other is not altogether regrettable. It means that those who have to take decisions are not confronted with a solid phalanx of opinion, as statesmen often were before the Second World War. The quarrelsome voices of the diverse experts often enough cancel out, and common sense prevails. Yet the history of the last eight or ten years suggests that we have been near to a serious breakdown of our economic system partly because of the basic dogmatism of our profession. Even in the postwar period of Keynesian triumph and unparalleled expansion, the mixed economies experienced a disturbing trend. Each recovery was less successful and left more unemployment behind than its predecessor, until finally the upheaval of 1971-5 showed a frightening similarity to the prewar cycles. In the United Kingdom the troubles since 1979 are worse, and even more obviously and directly linked to policies derived from dogmatic theories.

Since I was hotly opposed to the various 'pure' schools, only a series of unlikely coincidences enabled me to obtain and hold an academic post. In the furious drive towards 'rigour' my scepticism about 'positive theoretical' economics based on (sharply differing) monocausal systems was taken as savage illiteracy, or at best as controversy for controversy's sake, and I was condemned to be a non-person whose objections to the quick-changing orthodoxies could be left unanalysed and unanswered. Moreover the dogmas do change frequently, despite pretensions to building a 'cumulative' science. The fluctuations in world economic fortunes have had dramatic effects on the spirits of the economic profession, whose changes of mood have been almost as violent as the changes in their proposed nostrums for our ills. Each major blunder which cannot be explained away by mathematical manipulation or by resort to new explanatory factors leads to painful soul-searching and self-criticism, and much corrective publication.

Yet withal there is a quick return to normal; failures are forgotten, and thinking returns to familiar grooves, however shamefully wrong it has proved in practice. The self-criticism turns out to be a sham, a device to blunt the edge of the attacks which provoked the contrition. It is one of the more unpleasant characteristics of the economist's profession that old untruths are suddenly dished up as new discoveries. Particular fallacies are revived; so are methods of analysis which experience has discredited as irrelevant or misleading. The process is often accompanied by claims of theoretical advance and originality.[5]

2. The neoclassical triumph

Academic economics has had two centuries of chequered existence. It went through traumatic trials resulting from the repeated crises of the second quarter of the last century. Those were the hungry decades which produced Marx. But by the end of the century the monolithic unity of the profession had been restored by the victory of neoclassical optimism based on what was believed to be the objective scientific demonstration of the optimal working of the market mechanism. It was an international achievement. From Vienna came Menger, Wieser and later Böhm-Bawerk. From Lausanne came Walras and Pareto, and from Cambridge, Marshall, followed by Pigou. In America there was J. B. Clark. Realities of industrial growth, and the decisive raising of mass standards of living above bare subsistence, helped the marginalists' united counterattack to defeat Marxian economics. Unhappily other heretics too, such as Veblen, Hobson and Abbati, were banished along with the Marxists from the sanctuaries of Academe.

The next century seemed at first to be prosperous, and so accordingly did the new economic consensus. Then as now it was affirmed that most progress would be achieved by least government. The central bank could do the little necessary to maintain stability;[6] the market, through the price mechanism, would do the rest, provided only that monetary and fiscal excesses were avoided. Indeed the similarity between the conservative wisdom of half a century ago and that of today is not only bewildering but, in view of its consequences in the 1930s, ominous.

But that professional consensus was shattered by the unemployment of the 1930s, which it could neither explain nor remedy. That crisis provoked the Keynesian revolution, which is explored at length in following chapters and need not be described here. Keynes attacked Say's Law, orthodox ideas of the labour market, orthodox ideas about the determinants and effects of aggregate demand, and the orthodox blindness to many critical effects of time and uncertainty on economic behaviour. His work was nevertheless conservative in intent: a revolution only in the sense that it demonstrated that the modern economy had no automatic balancing mechanism, but needed some deliberate public management.

What followed from that has depended ever since on which 'Keynesians' you ask. From the beginning, Joan Robinson and some others perceived that success with 'managed full employment', though deeply desirable, would in turn create a new and critical problem of inflation. In a broader way, what the world called the 'Left Keynesians' and it might be truer to call the 'planning Keynesians' developed two other implications. First, the

4

necessary central management of the national economy would take more than the gentle, indirect management of aggregate demand by fiscal and monetary means that the neoclassical-Keynesian majority of the profession hoped for. Second, the Keynesian revolution would lose its force and usefulness if it was assimilated to the old conception of *science*: if it was frozen into a closed, determinate theoretical system which purported to model the main economic relationships in a formal and determinate way. Understanding that danger, Robinson, Kaldor and a few others proposed an open-ended analysis of the determinants of economic activity, one which saw economic activity always in its social and political context, alert for the uncertainties and continuous historical changes to be expected from that environment. They also saw the need for some direct as well as indirect methods of economic management: for example incomes policy, and some uses of public ownership and of direct physical controls.

Unhappily however these were not the dominant intellectual consequences of Keynes' work. From both sides of the Atlantic came elaborate 'reconciliations' to produce what its authors called the neoclassical Keynesian synthesis (or 'consensus economics' or 'mainstream economics'). They accepted from Keynes the need for some management of aggregate demand. But first, they believed that could be done by a few easy, indirect, global[7] controls. Second, they believed Keynes' contribution could be reconciled with almost all of the neoclassical micro-economic doctrines, including those which purported to justify the existing distribution of income as the due reward of everyone's productive contribution. And third, they retained intact the old dream of a formal science, a closed, deductive science appropriate only to a closed, determinate, mechanical economic system. Into such a frozen formal system the neoclassical Keynesian synthesis was quickly transformed.

For a time, the new optimism seemed to be amply justified. For a quarter of a century after the Second World War most of the economically advanced Western countries had steady growth. The overall rate of increase of real income accelerated as compared with the prewar years, even in countries such as Britain which had a comparatively sluggish record. (Monetarists depict postwar Britain as a 'socialist failure', by comparing its rate of growth with those of West Germany and Japan. If each country's postwar performance is compared instead with its prewar performance, the *laissez-faire* argument collapses.) More remarkable, the impressive growth came with an unprecedented achievement of continuous full or nearly full employment. There were stop-and-go cycles, but they were so different in degree from the violent fluctuations of the preceding century or more that they were not regarded as being of the same kind.

Accordingly, economists claimed at last to have conquered the besetting evils of the system of individual enterprise, and to have reconciled wealth, freedom and even some improving equality. How had the miracle been achieved? By rigour and quantification: measurement, together with as many equations as there were unknowns, would capture reality and enable objective and positive advice to be given to political leaders.

3. The quantified apotheosis

Thus economic science was thought to have come of age. It could produce testable hypotheses, and soon therefore 'policy menus' providing a reliable basis for scientific, quantified 'trade-offs', that is in English 'choices'. Decision-makers could henceforth pick and choose from a 'menu' of alternative policies, all proven reliable by well-tried scientific methods. The consumption function, the accelerator, Okun's 'law' of the relation of income to employment, the Phillips curve, linear programming, or what have you, had at last raised the economist to the level of the physicist, indeed of the cybernetician. Social science, but especially economics, had at last become a real science.

Take Paul Samuelson – an outstanding liberal-neoclassical-Keynesian – enthusing (in a now rather strange-sounding manner, somewhat like an economist on the couch) to a British audience in 1962. His Stamp lecture[8] clearly discloses the immense importance which economists attach to 'scientific' status, a motive which has played an important role in the recent development of economic thought.[9] He tells us that economists are as good as physicists, even those connected with one of its most modern branches, cybernetics. Just to prove the contention, a whole series of theorems is rattled off, each accompanied by the twinning, tripling, or even quadrupling of names: to achieve the desired effect, moreover, names of the classics are coupled with those of friends. There is in one seat of learning, say, the Ricardo-Marx-Kindleberger-Solow Theorem, in another the Hume-Fisher-Friedman-Schultz Equation:

> Linear programmers tell firms how each week to mix their chicken feed and dog food (the Stigler least cost diet problem); how each month to ship most cheaply from plants to customers (the Hitchcock-Kantorovich-Koopmans transportation or assignment problem); how each minute to distribute the power load among alternative generating stations in a network; how each season to vary stocks (Whitin-Arrow-Bellman dynamic and stochastic programming). The most esoteric discounting methods of Irving Fisher have, through the work of George Terborgh and others, revolutionized the practice of capital budgeting in large and middle-sized firms.

In this way, not only professional solidarity but institutional loyalty is established; the cognoscenti are differentiated from the plebeians who know nothing of the significance of the views thus christened; the insiders are distinguished from those outside; an aura of scientific achievement settles over the profession. Samuelson again, in the same lecture:

> By temperament some scientists are simply not good decision-makers. I may illustrate by the case of an illustrious mathematician, my MIT colleague, Norbert Wiener. He is a good example because no-one doubts the originality of his contributions to Barach-Wiener space; the Wiener-Brownian motion; Fourier analysis and ergodic theory; generalized harmonic analysis and Komogoroff-Wiener-Shannon information theory, cybernetics; and Wienerism generally . . . Wiener is not a good chessplayer . . . Good decision-making is neither like chess nor like creative mathematics.

If Samuelson rejoiced at the apotheosis of pure and mathematical economics, the late A. M. Okun, a former chairman of the President's Council of Economic Advisers, was not less exultant about the success of the new applied science:[10]

> As of this writing (November 1969), the nation is in its one-hundred-and-fifth month of unparalleled, unprecedented, and uninterrupted economic expansion. The persistence of prosperity has been the outstanding fact of American economic history of the 1960s. The absence of recession for nearly nine years marks a discrete and dramatic departure from the traditional performance of the American economy.

4. Humility and self-criticism

How long ago it seems that my protests and J. K. Galbraith's against this sort of academic scientology were dismissed as journalistic attacks from beyond the pale of accepted knowledge! But all that has changed. Here is Professor Phelps-Brown uttering a warning:[11] 'Economists' studies should be field determined, not discipline determined.' We have heard dissatisfaction expressed not only by three presidents of the British Association and the Royal Economic Society, surely the embodiment of the British academic establishment, but also from the height of the profession in America. They have all recently voiced their discomfiture about the state of our profession.

Professor Leontieff,[12] who has been one of the most fertile minds in the mathematical field, has criticized recent developments:

Enthusiasm for mathematical formulation tends to conceal the ephemeral substantive content of the argument behind the formidable front of algebraic signs; hence, by the time it comes to interpreting conclusions the assumptions on which the models are based are easily forgotten – but it is precisely the empirical validity of these assumptions on which the usefulness of the exercise depends. The growing stockpile of increasingly complicated (but soon forgotten) models, reflecting a preoccupation with imagined rather than observed reality, is seen to have led to a distortion in the system of values whereby economists as a profession assess the scientific performance of their own output.

The younger economists seem to be now quite content with the situation in which they demonstrate their prowess and advance their careers by building more and more mathematical models and devising more and more sophisticated methods of statistical inference without ever engaging in empirical research.

(This is a bit hard on the 'younger' economists. *Homines economici* as they are, in contrast to almost everyone else, they follow the path that most easily and quickly leads to tenure and full professorships. It is their misguided elders on Appointments Boards who ought to be censured.)

Professor Solow, whose severe strictures on Cambridge (England) new and old[13] now seem strangely misplaced, discovers rather late in life that 'one advantage the physicist has over the economist is that the velocity of light has not changed over the past thousands of years, while what was in the 1950s and 1960s a good wage and price equation is no longer so.'[14] Yet he still does not see the absurdity in this field of taking coincidental 'fits' as discoveries of stable relations. He still hankers after the *'ceteris paribus'* basis of analysis when, as we shall see, *grosso modo* changes make this illegitimate.

Deprecatory noises have also come, even more surprisingly, from one of the chief representatives of the mathematical school in this country, Professor Hahn of Cambridge, in his presidential address to, of all things, the Econometric Society:[15] 'It cannot be denied that there is something scandalous in so many people refining the analyses of economic states which they give no reason to suppose will ever, or have ever, come about.'

He concludes more than a little naïvely: 'The study of equilibria alone is of no help in positive economic analysis; yet it is no exaggeration to say that the technically best work in the last twenty years has been precisely that. It is good to have it, but perhaps the time has now come to see whether it can serve in an analysis of how economies behave.' It seems both a late and a lighthearted repentance, from someone who has spent his life propagating absurdities. Also it was shortlived, as we shall presently see.

The mulish reluctance of the profession to admit the fact that structural changes have rendered the economic system indeterminate and unstable is quite comprehensible, if scientifically reprehensible. For instance, Professor Walters (then at the London School of Economics, now at the right hand of the British government), one of those Friedmanites whose monetary explanations have exploded in their faces, admits:

> The desperation with which professional economists (and others) have sought remedies and the variety of policies suggested are some indication of the quandary in which economists find themselves. Not since the early 1930s has there been such uncertainty and disappointment with the standard policy prescriptions ...

But he continues:

> Yet clearly one should not give up the ghost! The most distinguished monetarist, Milton Friedman, has indeed recently suggested a tentative theory of the adjustment process explicitly incorporating the division of changes in money income between changes in the price level and changes

in real output. But he does not specify the determinants of the division between changes in output and prices; nor does he specify the time path.[16]

This may reflect Professor Friedman's audacity, but as 'a theoretical framework for monetary analysis' it is not very convincing.[17] Indeed, it is interesting to note that Professor Friedman himself has sometimes, if briefly, appeared to join the ranks of the penitents.[18]

Professor Heilbroner summed up the outlook: 'Economists are beginning to realize that they have built a rather elaborate edifice on rather insubstantial, narrow foundations.'[19] In his opinion, economics must resume its original name, 'political economy', and draw on political science, sociology, and psychology as well as on its own traditions. The result would be an eclectic theory that 'asks questions economics doesn't ask and answers some questions that conventional economics asks in a rather unconventional way'.

Considering that Myrdal, Galbraith and myself have been attacked and disparaged for thirty or forty years for holding views which economists are now 'beginning to realize', this formulation is welcome, however late. Nevertheless it would be foolish to think that the battle for realistic political economics has been won.[20] The repentance of the orthodox that seemed to begin a decade ago has not gone far, or always in sensible directions. Ten years after the Presidential Address quoted above, Professor Hahn was not only defending algebraic General Equilibrium Theory still, he was threatening to give it another generation of life by replacing the old Walrasian General Equilibrium algebra with a new Keynesian General Equilibrium algebra. As to that new algebra:

> When we have it, the present theoretical disillusionment with Keynes will, I conjecture, be reversed. If we think of an economy in non-Walrasian equilibrium with involuntary unemployment, it would seem that Keynesian policies would once again come into their own.
>
> ... It is therefore not at all clear that from the vantage point of such an achieved theory, General Equilibrium analysis will not be seen as a stepping stone rather than a *cul de sac*.[21]

Professor Hahn condemned growth models in 1964,[22] 'unreal' analysis in 1970, some other sins in his Inaugural Lecture in 1973; in 1980 he condemned 'textbook misuses' of his style of analysis and its longstanding assumption of 'no involuntary unemployment'. But none of that has been allowed to interrupt the continuing output of algebra with no conceivable relevance to real economic life or real economic problems. Like all too many of the profession he steadfastly reverts to type after all misgivings, like a Sicilian peasant after confession.

I conclude that there is still a need for full and patient explanation of the reasons why that sort of economics does not work.

CHAPTER TWO

The Nature of Economic
Problems and Relationships

In my view every economic fact whether or not it is
of such a nature as to be expressed in numbers, stands
in relation as cause and effect to many other facts, and
since it NEVER happens that all of them can be expressed
in numbers, the application of exact mathematical
methods to those which can is nearly always waste of
time, while in the large majority of cases it is positively
misleading; and the world would have been further on
its way forward if the work had never been done at all.

Alfred Marshall[1]

1. Introductory

Why is fashionable economics, of whatever school, so stubbornly
irrelevant to reality, with such detrimental effects on policy-making? Is the persistent failure of attempts to use closed, determinate
systems and models inherent in the subject matter of economics,
as no less a patriarch than Marshall suggested? I believe so. But
most of my profession cannot bear to believe it, because they would
so hate the consequences of believing it. It would condemn economists to ploughing too uncertain and 'unscientific' a row. It would
also mean that some unwelcome critics had been right about them
for generations past.

In order to be fully scientific, a determinate system must be
created. It is here that problems arise. While training in economic
reasoning remains necessary, the complexity of factors of potentially major influence on developments makes economic flair, what
the Germans call *Fingerspitzengefühl*, the most important qualification for economic advisers.[2] This complexity is, in my opinion,
not only or primarily the consequence of lack of data or of the
sophistication of statistical method and manipulations – though as
we shall see, both play an important part in misdiagnoses. It is
rather the character of economic problems, the continuous change

12

in environment, and, in consequence, the paucity of observations in sufficiently similar circumstances, the multitude of factors – all these render model-building largely irrelevant. This kaleidoscopic character of economic relationships makes economic development a limitless and often unique series of historical events. Experience and general knowledge (or the cooperation of experts familiar with the non-economic aspects of the situation) are essential for practical usefulness.[3] Keynes put the limitations of economics in his inimitable way:

> It is a great fault of symbolic pseudo-mathematical methods of for-malizing a system of economic analysis ... that they expressly assume strict independence between the factors involved ... whereas, in ordinary discourse ... we can keep 'at the back of our heads' the necessary reserves and qualification.... Too large a proportion of recent 'mathematical' economics are merely concoctions, as imprecise as the initial assumptions they rest on, which allow the author to lose sight of the complexities and interdependencies of the real world in a maze of pretentious and unhelpful symbols.[4]

2. The basis of economic advice

The contrast, indeed chasm, between the trend in conventional 'pure' economics and the practical needs of the policy-makers has widened sharply. As the structure of production and consumption became ever more complex, the requirements of the 'science' – in the sense of its being able to propound a system capable of pro-ducing determinate answers and automatic balancing adjustments – became increasingly difficult to fulfil. This forced its votaries to adopt ever more simple basic assumptions; meanwhile, however, the manipulation of data based on statistical and econometric tech-niques became breathtakingly complex, as the professional jargon of teuto-pseudo-abstractions burgeoned – abstractions whose re-lation to reality was increasingly shaky.

Consequently there has been an increasing impatience with, and disdain on the part of the profession for, the grievous limitations imposed upon them by the complexity of human behaviour and feeling which we have tried to set out. The growing dependence of 'economic' factors or forces on *individual decisions*, and therefore on the historical setting and socio-economic structure, has been especially aggravating. As the coverage of statistical information grew and as its quality improved, albeit in a fragmented and necessarily uneven fashion,[5] the yearning after 'tested', impersonal, general and quantified rules or 'laws' increased. The temptation to cut through or circumvent the constraints became overwhelming. However, one of the disagreeably important characteristics of economic phenomena is their potential self-justifying nature. Provided the brainwashing is sufficiently intensive, reactions to change may themselves also alter, thus justifying nonsense claims.[6]

Could the political element, the pretensions of modern sociology and psychology, not be ignored when giving economic advice? Could no robust commonsense procedure, preferably quantifying and resembling the natural sciences, be applied? The rush towards mathematical economics and econometrics, especially on the part of the more conservative and mathematically not very adept,[7] shows the strength of this yearning, the sociological implications of which we shall consider in the final section of this essay.

The inductive method of arriving at policy advice starts out with an apparently modest scientific reticence. Led by Milton Friedman,[8] its more extreme votaries assert that the assumptions on which a hypothesis rests are of no importance. What matters is whether the conclusion or prediction to which it leads corresponds with ascertainable developments. Thus we had economists putting forward an ever-increasing number of hypotheses on important relationships in a form which could be 'tested'. The test is the correctness of the 'prediction' based on the assumed validity of the hypothesis about the relationship. If the prediction 'worked', in a very special sense of that word, that is if it was 'consistent' with the empirical findings, the hypothesis could be claimed to achieve the status of a general 'law'. The usefulness and logic of the hypotheses need no analysis. The battle-cry is that they 'work'.

Over very large areas of economic analysis this is a wholly insufficient procedure. Predictions based on hypotheses might work for the wrong reasons, i.e. they might depend on factors which do not enter the hypothetical argument and whose later disappearance would then lead to falsification.[9] The chances of the right answer coming out for purely fortuitous reasons are very considerable – e.g. in different historical situations or different countries the same sort of change (or measure) might have totally different effects.[10]

Professor Streissler, who wrote perhaps the most telling critical survey of economic forecasting,[11] quoting Sir Karl Popper,[12] averred:

> It is a commonplace of long standing that exact forecasts are impossible in economics. This has been most forcefully stressed by Sir Karl Popper. He once said:
> 'Long-term prophecies can be derived from scientific conditional predictions only if they apply to systems which can be described as *well-isolated, stationary and recurrent*. These systems are very rare in nature; and modern society is surely not one of them.' (Italics added.)
> Strictly speaking the same impossibility theorem is true for short-term economic forecasts as well.

It may be commonplace to Professor Streissler: it is certainly far from being so to most practitioners of this new black magic.[13]

It is, moreover, extremely difficult and very often impossible to establish whether the repercussions of a change represent a stable relationship between two variables, one of which can be assumed or shown to be 'independent' or explanatory, or a change in the relationship which might have existed or seemed likely to exist at a particular moment in the past.

Implicitly or explicitly, of course, a 'model' or image of the economic system must underlie all empirical attempts at establishing such relationships. The empirical testing of hypotheses or theories will almost inevitably involve drastic simplification, the creation of 'ideal types' and the reduction of postulated relationships to simple, mathematically manageable form, if possible even to the extreme of linearization. This is a practically inevitable procedure in any science. And if we are confronted, as in the case of the natural sciences, with an (in principle) unlimited number of observations, whose replicability may be ascertained through experimentation, this is also a legitimate procedure. Indeed, the simpler the explanations, the more general are their applicability.

Economics is not in this sense a 'science'.[14] It might be called – if this protected the *amour propre* of its practitioners – scientific in the sense that it is a training in orderly methods of analysing certain types of problems, mainly involving choice between various actions or policies. But it is also an art, a professional art maybe, of distinguishing between and combining a vast number of factors and their probable effects, some unquantifiable, and, as we have seen, of weighing them upon the basis of some scale of moral or political values. In my opinion, therefore, the difficulties in the way of using economic 'systems' or models to arrive at determinate and quantified answers to macro-, and indeed to large-scale micro-, economic problems are innate and insuperable.

Even when the simplified assumptions of the neoclassical revival, a semblance of perfect competition and increasing costs, still bore some relation to reality, the instability of the monetary system presented an insurmountable obstacle to developing a truly comprehensive theoretical system. This was shown by the total failure to integrate general equilibrium with monetary and trade cycle theory at the end of the nineteenth century. Now that vast concentrations of economic power on both sides of industry assume an ever-increasing importance, methods based on statics, including comparative statics, and the conventional procedure of assuming that 'other things remain equal' are totally illegitimate.

Hence the desperate resistance of the profession to any suggestion that atomistic competition and what it implies can no longer be regarded as operationally valid for the present state of the industrial economy. In criticisms of Galbraith, efforts were made to establish that oligopolistic markets dominated by giant firms were of limited importance, being less than a quarter of private business activity or less than a fifth of total national income.[15] This response neglects the impact of these markets, and of the existence of price leadership or management, on other competitors and middlemen and indeed on the rest of the economy. It would take a very other-worldly individual to accept that large and potentially destructive competitors do not have such influence. But then any argument based on firm 'consensus' economics is good enough to disarm dissent – especially if the dissent menaces, as it obviously does, the determinate neoclassical system, however modified to absorb a few Keynesian arguments.

Without sociological investigations not only of people's motivations but also of the compatibility of existing social and political institutions, it was assumed that the economic system could function smoothly and thus supply the needed impetus for continued growth and an improved distribution of income. No one asked whether the necessary supply of managerial ability and entrepreneurial eagerness would in fact be forthcoming, provided that sufficient (material) incentives were given. Enterprise and decision-making capacity were taken *wholly* for granted, as were the legal institutions. Above all, it was assumed that the misleading certainty of the response of *homo economicus* to market forces, acting within the framework of a simplified and distorted image of the techno-economic system, represented reality and could be used for practical purposes. But without the necessary sociological basis, such models are incapable of describing secondary, medium- or long-run repercussions: at best they are essentially short-run. Moreover, their empirical validity for productive purposes is seriously limited by their dependence on observations of the historical past.

3. Schedules, curves and reality

Even such relatively simple relations as demand and supply ('schedules') for a single homogeneous commodity may involve staggering difficulties. The only observations we have, after all, relate to price, demand and output at different historical points of time. How they are connected with each other, if they are so connected, is a Gestalt in the beholder's eye. Provided the commodity is unimportant quantitatively, no doubt the secondary effects of changes in price or quantity can be neglected. But can general progress, can advertising campaigns be ignored, which interlock the level of demand to the cost of supply? And what will be their effect in time, and of time itself?[16]

The avowedly straightforward theoretical determination of price by the intersection of the two lines expressing the hypothetical possibilities of the effect on price of changes in supply and demand - possibilities which are supposed to be independent of one another - does not turn out to be so simple. The shape of the curves allegedly crossing at the observed points might in fact be so intricate as to defy mathematical handling. Their shape and position will in all probability change in time. And they are by no means necessarily independent from one another - if they are important, quite the contrary. Indeed they might be better represented by discontinuities rather than smooth curves. They are most unlikely to be linear. If they exist at all, that is to say if we could, over an appreciable period of time, confidently predict the response of the dependent variable to a change in the independent, how long will their shape or position remain undamaged? Thus, even in unsophisticated cases, the cumulative effect of further simplifications might lead to major errors.

It might be permissible in a strictly static system to treat changes in demand for a commodity as being generally inversely related to changes in its price, and to assume that the reaction to change will tend to restore 'balance'. Even this is questionable, however, when the so-called simplifying assumptions are dropped, and quality, service, persuasive forces and all the other factors are taken into account – as in modern conditions they must be. In this case all determinacy vanishes, even if the existence of 'inferior' goods (goods which supply a need less well than others but on which an appreciable part of income is spent) are dismissed because they are now rare in the Atlantic area. But in real life a decline in price may cause panic selling and drive the price still further down, or the reverse.[17] In a great number of important instances the change in stocks has outweighed the 'normal' flow. The concentration of economic power has had an important impact in this respect. The fluctuations of the exchange rate is another example. They had little to do with current account. By provoking conventional responses, the hot money flows did untold harm.

When it comes to important and complex factors, mainly the large aggregates – such as wages, exports and imports, or national income and its components, savings, investments, etc. – these simplifications are totally illicit. The demand for and supply of imports and exports are not independent of each other;[18] nor can the 'wages rate' be considered as an equilibrium market-clearing price determined by the interplay of independently given supply and demand. The demand for labour is a derivative of the demand for commodities and therefore of total expenditure. The assumption of a determinate and stable 'under-employment equilibrium' seems inconsistent. This means that each situation will represent a disequilibrium leading to the next (but still unstable) position – all influenced by the historical past and the present setting.

Shifts in, and alterations in the shape of, the 'curves' depicting these hypothetical situations – if such 'curves' (especially smooth ones) existed meaningfully at any moment at all – would be the rule and not the exception at each important change. In the first place the only observed and observable facts are the points at which these assumed, or alleged, curves cross.[19] The curves themselves

18

would need to reflect the relationship of two or more variables to each other at other (non-observed) points, a relationship which must be stable enough in time to be relevant over a reasonably long period. We have seen that this is in fact improbable.

There is, secondly, the impossibility of measuring certain qualitative, including psychological, factors that codetermine the outcome of economic processes, which – as Alfred Marshall has already pointed out – renders overall quantification dangerously misleading.

There are further grave complications. The distinction between moves *along* and shifts *of* these 'curves' is logically false. Every point on the curves presupposes that that specific relationship (e.g., in the case of demand curves, the quantity demanded at each price) not only has prevailed long enough to enter the memory of all concerned but that external circumstances have not changed since, so as to alter anticipations. Thus moves from one point of the 'curve' to another are logically impossible. There are different points according to each different history and hence memory of past relationships.

The only way to get round this difficulty is to assume that people have no memories. Hence the ubiquitous use of the proviso 'other things being equal'.[20] But we have argued that in almost all relevant cases this proviso is failing in logic and hopelessly misrepresents the actual world. This is the last deposit of the completely static, unchanged and unchangeable neoclassical system, implicitly demanding perfect or at least the best possible foresight, or its replacement by the best possible expectation. Hence the invention of the so-called REH or ratex (rational expectation hypothesis), which asserts or assumes that people act on the best *possible* assumptions. As we have seen there are grave logical contradictions in this assumption. We shall return to this important and neglected point.

This characteristic of economic factors is especially important when it comes to building 'large' models. All equations which do not rely on individual judgement are derived from historical observations. The more such relations are involved, the greater the risk of failure because of the increasing probability that the final results will be seriously and cumulatively affected. In periods of tranquillity, no doubt, such 'models' worked, but then under such conditions continuity of development can be reasonably assumed;

not so at turning points, whether spontaneous or externally induced, when primitive methods work better.[21]

Whenever new psychological and sociopolitical factors arise these need to be taken into account by re-estimating the relationships, in preference to relying on the stability of (often worn) past relationships. The 'primitive' approach enabled, indeed forced, the expert to involve in his forward estimate not only all available data but also his estimate of varying consumer, business and governmental intentions and reactions. Testing in the sense that we try to see whether prediction is justified by the outcome is therefore inapplicable. Indeed it was as we saw the prophet of the neoclassical liberal school, Popper, who flatly condemned the methodology adopted by Friedman and his acolytes. Over time or under different conditions the modelled relationship can change its intensity and even its direction as new or neglected factors come into play.[22] Policy measures therefore might have completely unexpected results.[23]

However complicated and sophisticated, mathematical manipulations are usually quite inadequate to establish the *direction of causation*.[24] Practical policy recommendations of a quantitative character have to take account not only of stable relationships, but also of reciprocal and reversible relationships. The formal mathematical models have no means of judging when their 'strategic' variables, which are subject to conscious control or manipulation, may react on themselves or work in reverse. For example exports and imports have behaved under similar policy treatment in startlingly different manners at different times and in different countries.

It is sometimes argued[25] that with increasingly refined methods and improved statistical material, economics will eventually be able to do what some present practitioners of forecasting necromancy claim for their current products. I hold this to be fundamentally mistaken. While the use of statistics and statistical methods is obviously helpful, ultimately they can be utilized only on the basis of judgement drawing not only on logical but on empirical knowledge, on experience and help from other fields of social knowledge and analysis.

4. The false lever

For the system to be determinate it has to be anchored to some factor or relationship which is assumed to be stable, or changing only imperceptibly, much like Archimedes' fixed point from which to move earth and heaven. Otherwise the path of adjustment following a shock, change, or impulse will escape regularity, all certainty being buffeted and altered by exogenous factors or indeed by changes in the system or relationship itself. It was the great merit of the proto-Keynesian approach that it left the system open-ended. As such, however, it had fatal defects because it was not really as 'scientists' would have it, a 'system'.

Thus the neoclassical revivalists of the Walrasian system secured its clarity and stability by assuming that goods exchanged directly against goods and that factor prices were determined by the inter-action of factor supply and demand, the latter determined by the derived demand for goods and the marginal contribution of factors to output. Balance is attained by means of the self-righting nature of the model, which in turn results from assuming constant or increasing costs. The possible disturbing impulses caused by money, credit and banking were separated from the main body of the doctrine; so were periodic fluctuations in activity.

As the conception of the Walrasian model was – quite rightly – rigidly static and repetitive, so it was consistent. Unfortunately it could not readily be used to analyse dynamic problems. This required that a new trick be introduced to make it applicable to current policy making. Thus was the 'rational expectations hypo-thesis' (REH) substituted for that of 'perfect foresight' supplied by the original static model. This hypothesis states that rational economic agents will endeavour to form expectations of relevant future variables by making the most efficient use of all information provided by past history. This has, as Professor Modigliani states, a number of remarkable implications: *ex post* errors in price expec-tations cannot be avoided, but they can only be short-lived and random. In particular, there cannot be persistent involuntary un-employment above the natural rate. As the best possible decisions are assumed to have been taken, it follows that all government intervention in the economy is destabilizing. The 'rational expec-tations hypothesis' turns out to be a roundabout and learned reas-sertion of the original Say-Walrasian static system coupled with a primitive quantity theory thrown in where disturbances are exclusively related to changes in the money supply which are disproportionate to those in 'real' output. Yet even Modigliani seems to consider that the incorporation into Friedman's model of this hypothesis would deal a fatal blow to the already 'badly-battered body of Keynesianism'.[26] In fact it is a quite implausible contrivance which has been and is being disproved by the history of economic fluctuations. So far from rational expectations being the norm, undue optimism and pessimism alternate and cause untold harm. As Modigliani himself showed in the same article, recent monetary history does as little to conform to these conclusions as do the pre-Second World War cycles. At this point neoclassical monetarist economics becomes based on the fallacy of affirming the consequent, a fallacy because there are usually many different and possibly conflicting propositions from which the result might follow.

Experience of commodity and stock markets[27] is entirely disregarded; but the rational expectation hypothesis is politically appealing (and certainly so motivated) since it adds support to the argument against government intervention in the economy. If monetary factors are introduced, this is usually by way of a simple quantity theory, based on the constancy of the velocity of circulation (arbitrarily defined).

The relationship between the 'real' and the 'monetary' sectors is not as the monetarists would wish it, solid and stable. Each, of course, interacts with the other; but the outcome is determined by social and institutional factors. More especially, recent, or more distant but traumatic, historical experience will dominate psychological anticipations and hence short-term (mainly monetary) and the longer-term (mainly 'real') variables.[28] The starting point from which any reaction or change occurs, and the short-term path followed, thus play an important, indeed overwhelming, role in determining the outcome.[29] Some neo-Keynesians have postulated stability in private sector financial transactions, implying a given net rate of acquisition of financial assets. They were thus able to gain a decisive *point d'appui* for their demand management recommendations, claiming that the government, through its control of budgetary policy, could thereby control the balance of payments. This idea collapsed within two years.

In their model of investment and income, consumption and

savings are linked in a rigid equation system. Investment is determined by the rate of interest, which is itself linked to the demand for liquidity and to banking policy. The tacit assumption is that the marginal efficiency of capital is ultimately determined by 'real' factors such as the stock of capital technology, etc. But in reality, psychological factors of optimism and pessimism are quite powerful enough to defeat that mechanical style of prediction, time and again. Unfortunately, at full employment in an oligopolistic system there is no practicable way of increasing real savings to cover increased investment, which leaves inflation as the only means of restoring balance. The ratio of savings to income, which was supposed to increase steadily with increasing income, has proved to be more unstable than the variable consumption it is supposed to explain. This instability is due to the ever-increasing importance of consumers' credit (and premature repayment), the use of vast idle money resources, and immense accumulations of consumer durables, which can offset – and more than offset – changes in the budget, in taxation, or in monetary policy. Thus expansionary policy, e.g. budget deficits, can be offset by increased saving, and/ or increased repayments of debt, due perhaps to apprehension about future recession, however ill-informed. On the other hand increased interest charges can, provided they are numerous, be offset against taxes or shifted on to the consumer.

The very number of these varying attempts at mechanistic explanation and prediction demonstrates at one and the same time the striking similarity between the various conventional approaches to macro-economic problems, and their crippling inability to accept the limitation imposed on economic analysis by the complexity of modern society, the increasing concentration of economic power and the ever-increasing importance of single decisions and complex motivations. All of these attempts, even if they have produced a good 'fit' to the data for a short time, have lacked explanatory power in the longer run.

5. Escape routes

Economists have two favourite methods by which difficult and, in my opinion, quantitatively insoluble problems can be treated with great rigour – at least formally.

The first involves the postulation of the existence of a function or of a factor which in practice cannot be measured but which looks formally precise.[30] The so-called social welfare function belongs to this category of circumventive devices. It can be given unlimited generality. All factors influencing people can be included. What is never clear is how exactly it should be used to answer any practical question. It certainly reflects political value judgements which alone ought to prevent its quantification.[31] Another device is to admit that a vital factor or relationship, e.g. the stock of capital, is in principle not measurable, and evade this problem by using some other related factor or item, e.g. the volume of steel embodied, as a proxy and use it with other quantifiable factors in the model.[32]

The second approach takes a set of observations of the magnitude of certain economic factors taken over a period and postulates that these can serve as the basis for establishing a permanent relationship. From this set a wonderful array of curves is derived, characterized by their mathematical, or at least geometrical, simplicity, showing the relationship between pairs of variables, including complex aggregates like inflation and employment.[33]

We have discussed the reasons for distrusting this approach to the behaviour of large aggregates over appreciable lengths of time. Experience has shown that the number of interacting variables may well be so large that the observations obtained will not show any systematic relationship between the most plausible and presumably potent variables, because of the effects of changes in numerous but less obvious and less important or less quantifiable factors. This was certainly the case when in 1974 and again in 1977–8 the dollar was decried as overvalued, and forced to devalue by massive direct investment abroad, and an even vaster movement of hot money out of the US. A similar process hit Britain in 1976.

One of the earliest of these inexcusable theoretical devices is the Marshallian reciprocal demand curve of foreign trade. This gives us a picture of what a country is willing to pay for its imports in terms of its own exports. But in the case of large aggregates which affect the country's economic situation, it is not possible to foretell what sort of effects may flow from large changes (e.g. a very large harvest) by way of consequential changes in relative prices. (Britain had a good dose of this in the 1951 crisis, when imports surged ahead due partly to increased stock-building and partly to changes in prices.)

This is clearly shown by F. Y. Edgeworth's treatment of Marshall's 'static' geometry of reciprocal demand curves, which implicitly recognized one complication, although it failed to realize the decisive importance of the consequential limitation of the value of the curves. Edgeworth compared reciprocal supply-demand curves with the hands of a clock which are activated by a mechanism behind its face. 'A movement along a supply-and-demand curve of international trade should be considered as attended with re-arrangements of internal trade; as the movement of the hand of a clock corresponds to considerable unseen movements of the machinery.' This simile brings out clearly that both Marshall and Edgeworth thought of the relationship between a causal initial change and the resulting new 'equilibrium' as something given and enduring. The clock can only go at a predetermined pace and move the hand a predetermined way.

The authors of such constructs often claim that they depict equilibrium relationships only when all adjustments have been made and the balances of the system have been re-established all round. This implies a basic unreality because, once the balance has been disturbed, it is unlikely that the system will return to the original position. When for instance the late Harry Johnson and Professor Baghwati say:[34] 'the answer to the problem of how the elasticity of demand (supply) affects the extent to which the shift in demand (supply) alters the price and the quantity exchanged depends on the precise way in which the shift is defined,' has this statement any meaning at all?

The analysis is based on 'other things being equal'. But, as we have seen, this is wholly illegitimate. If the final position is historically observed the proposition is trivial; if it is not, demand and supply cannot be assumed independent from one another, and the final equilibrium position – which of course need not be reached in principle, and will probably never be reached in fact – cannot be legitimately derived from a schedule and its elasticity because they cannot be assumed to be unchanged if the shift is – as it often will be – sufficient to affect income. Thus the initial relationships change and their change cannot be predicted from the data which neoclassical authors postulate because – even if we admitted the initial existence of stable schedules – the process of readjustment will change them.

Thus it will depend on the historical circumstances what the eventual position of the ultimate balance appropriate to the unique 'shift or change' will be. A one-sided upward shift in demand will produce not merely a change in the terms of trade but in all probability, at least initially, a deficit in the balance of trade phenomena which are excluded from the ambit of this approach. The path of the adjustment through time will also depend on the impact of the psychological atmosphere (particularly if political influence or reciprocal bluff are practised). It cannot derive from the initial position and the initial relationships. What happens in the end (and eventually) is in the lap of the gods.

The relationship between the initial change in the balance of payments and consequential developments is, of course, of an entirely different and much more tenuous character; it will also depend on the historical factors and position, which will determine anticipations, i.e. the reactions of the countries, producers, etc. involved. This is of decisive importance. If this mechanism is a 'clock' at all it is a very peculiar one, in which the movements of the hands necessarily influence the working of the 'machine', and in which it is equally possible that the 'off-scene' happenings will have varying effects on the working of the hands with each change in the situation or psychological climate. The *ex-ante* schedule and its elasticity are not necessarily relevant, since these might (and probably will) change as a result of developments through time. It is wholly illegitimate in any case to assume a priori that they do not change. The *ex-post* schedule, on the other hand, depends on the historical sequence of events (e.g. the influence of the level and urgency of demand in each country), and their effect on expectations, all of which will influence capital accumulation and, thereby, the competitive power of the country. If there is a causal relationship between the initial and these further changes or impulses, these latter can no longer be ignored as being of a second order of importance.

If this is the case it is illegitimate to talk of countries A and B without specifying their economic and social characteristics, their size and endowment (including international reserves), and without specifying the relationship which is to be analysed. A given reciprocal demand curve would thus only be applicable *ex-post* to a single change. This is implicit theorizing with a vengeance. The contribution to general economic insight of this type of analysis is trivial. Historical situations and developments are unique. The interrelation between initial change and effect will vary accordingly.

The concept of the shifted curve and its elasticity *after* the change is even less legitimate than guesses at *ex-ante* magnitude as a basis for policy formation. What we know is the position which has been established after a change; whether this was a movement on a curve or a shift of a curve is not verifiable. The curves are figments of the imagination which, as we have said, might be helpful in certain cases where supply and demand are independent from one another and income effects can be neglected. Even then, a knowledge of the historical background and the institutional setup is needed, for otherwise the reaction to change cannot be gauged, especially in the field of large aggregates such as imports and exports, or labour. If by a shifted curve one means a new schedule established after balances were attained after readjustment, then the falsity of this type of theorizing is revealed when the pseudo-mathematical veil is stripped from the pseudo-mathematical jargon.

An analysis of the impact of a sizeable change in demand cannot be conducted in terms of comparative statics. The *process* must be described, the problem lifted out of the framework of timeless balance. It will be determined by the impact of the balance of trade deficit or surplus, and the consequent income changes and policy decisions, on the two countries' foreign trade. It will be necessary to know the size of the countries, the fraction of their trade with one another, their attitudes to employment and prices, their gold reserve position, their capacity within these limitations to implement any policy, and the range of policy instruments at their disposal, e.g. physical controls, tax mechanisms. All these factors will determine which of the countries can bluff and which will have to give in if it is bluffed, because of short reserves, or inability to influence the incomes of its trading partners.

All this moreover will happen between countries in process of growth.[35] To talk about stable situations and 'elastic' G-demands is a turn of phrase by which the writers conceal from themselves the nature of the problem: for the new equilibrium position will be codetermined by the path taken by the readjustment, and not deducible from the initial position and the initial change without further assumptions. The problem is one of income effects due to changes in investment or growth, the introduction of new methods of production and new products, which may well carry the system – at any rate for a time – away from equilibrium. There will be employment effects and terms of trade effects which will impinge on each other and which may start cumulative movements which in their turn may well overshoot the 'equilibrium' position. If the country in which this happens is the dominant one (e.g. if it is bigger and has large liquid reserves) it can impose readjustments on its partner, and can carry the latter with it away from the old towards a new position which might or might not be an equilibrium position in the traditional sense. These secondary changes are far from negligible, and they are all capable of causing further shifts. As changes are continuous and adjustments take time, no position of 'eventual equilibrium' will in actual fact ever be reached, or is necessarily existent even in principle. The system may be in continuous disequilibrium 'chasing': the series of consequential adjustments lead towards or away from a steadily receding and changing 'equilibrium' position.[36] What is happening is history. History never reaches equilibrium, it merely moves slower or faster, and in frequently changing directions.

CHAPTER THREE

A Story of Irrelevance

The achievements of economic theory in the last two decades are both impressive and in many ways beautiful. But it cannot be denied that there is something scandalous in the spectacle of so many people refining the analyses of economic states which they give no reason to suppose will ever, or have ever, come about. It probably is also dangerous. Equilibrium economics, because of its well-known welfare economic implication, is easily convertible into an apologia for existing economic arrangements, and it is frequently so converted ... It is an unsatisfactory and slightly dishonest state of affairs.

Frank Hahn[1]

1. The historical context

One of the most remarkable features of the development of economic theory over the last hundred years, and especially since the Second World War, has been the insistent craving to purge it of all political, social and moral content. This process has not been confined to the West (in this context, mainly Britain and the United States) but has to a certain extent occurred also within the Soviet sphere.[2] The distillation which remains is an allegedly *wertfrei*, that is objective, body of theory, proliferating under the name of positive economics. More recently the principal development has been towards dressing this arid theoretical framework with the trappings of empirical social relevance, as evidenced by the attempts to measure and predict economic relationships and phenomena by the application of statistical tools supposedly akin to those of the physical sciences.

Economic reality having been circumscribed within the mathematical limits of some arbitrary system of equation, it is hoped that the 'discipline' of economics will finally be accorded the ultimate accolade of scientific status, and hence its practitioners the respectability of scientists. Thus would the economist be redeemed from the consideration of matters which one of the wittiest of their number, the late Professor Sir Dennis Robertson, once dismissed as being better suited to the divinations of prophets or priests.[3] What in fact happened was that these ambitions reduced the history of economic 'science' into a tale of evasions of reality, into attempts to derive general rules from a few arbitrary and unprovable assumptions while asserting that this procedure, which at best might lead to a logical system of choice, legitimizes the offer of determinate counsels to policy-makers.

This professional failure is so actually and potentially damaging to democratic prospects that it is critical that its causes be understood. In some respects they can best be understood historically. It is hard to review the modern history of economic theories, and then in following chapters subject them to critical analysis, without some repetition, but readers are nevertheless asked to be patient with this historical chapter. Only so can we see how the conservatism and the misconceived 'scientism' of the profession have interacted, time and again through the last hundred years, to keep the mainstream of economic theory irrelevant or wrong about the main problems – the historically changing problems – of economic life.

The flavour of the classics
Matters were not always so bad. Whether or not we agree in detail with the views held by the great classical economists, there can be no doubt that they approached their field of inquiry in the right spirit: not for them the evasions and scientism of present-day discussion. It was self-evident to them that if economics was to mean anything at all it would have to be *political economy*.[4] The notion that they should spend their time constructing models whose only criteria should be consistency and elegance, but which could have no relevance to the world in which they lived, would have struck them as absurd. The *raison d'être* of their political economy, so far from its being divorced from the historical and social realities of the day, lay precisely in its application, there and then, to the fabric of everyday life.

The impact of progress
The birth of classical political economy towards the end of the

eighteenth century followed shortly in the wake of that momentous watershed in history, the establishment by the human race through science and technology of its practical domination over the natural environment. The preceding two thousand years or more had left Western man neither much more numerous nor technologically much advanced. Within a mere two hundred years, however, a new and hitherto inconceivable change was to occur. Initially founded on the work of individual genius, animated by intermittent flashes of insight, and then gathering greater stimulus from systematic and collective research, man's capacity to exploit his physical environment and harness its elemental forces to his purposes was unrecognizably transformed. The vicious stranglehold of primitive stagnation, abject poverty, debilitating sickness and ignorance was to be finally broken, the stultifying incubus of primitive fears and magical superstitions thrown off, thereby unleashing the productive force of man's long dormant ingenuity. But – at least initially – this explosive dynamism was confined mainly to a small group of 'North Atlantic' countries.

The face of the earth, little changed since the invention of the plough and the wheel, was transformed. Capital accumulation and science together induced technical progress and created vast new industries. New urban growth was made possible and the globe shrank under the combined impact of immense capital works and individual human genius. A frantic drive was initiated to catch the custom of the fast-increasing new multitudes with money to spare. From a cheap press and cheap clothing, a steady progress was made towards mass luxuries to seduce all to ever-increasing expenditures. Spending – not only among the privileged few – became increasingly and over an expanding field connected with extravagance and ostentation or imitation, rather than with need. New status symbols arose, available to all who could afford them, and which could not be disregarded if the class differences of former times were to be maintained.

The irrelevance of economics

The economy, however, seemed at the same time to be beset with increasing social tensions, owing to the periodic emergence of unemployment which had nothing to do with the primeval inability to produce wealth for lack of knowledge or skill or equipment. It became apparent to all and sundry whose common sense was not dulled by dogma that the new poverty, the new suffering, were not due to the limitation of supply: rather there was a periodic failure to exploit existing physical possibilities to the limit. The defect was connected with the maldistribution of income, social tensions, and ultimately with the fluctuations in demand which resulted from instability and uncertainty, acting on an increasingly elastic monetary system and exaggerated by violent changes in psychology.

Yet during this period of unparalleled social and economic upheaval, with demand increasingly following the dictates of fashion and social ambition, with general economic activity subject to violent cyclical fluctuations, and with inequality between nations visibly widening, what did economics have to contribute? In the face of constant change, economic theorising was restricted to the analysis of price and income relationships. This, as we shall see, could be done successfully only within an essentially *static* and *timeless* framework, within which, against all evidence to the contrary, not only consumers' tastes and needs but also resources were assumed as given and as automatically fully employed.

2. The neo-orthodox stance

The modern history of economic theory is a tale of evasions of reality. Faced with the challenge of these vast changes and vital problems for over a century, it reacted by denying their existence in order to be able to produce a 'scientific' system, a smoothly-functioning self-balancing model. This was originally done on the plea of eliminating the 'veil' of money and analysing a system which was limited to the production and exchange of a specific number of goods (usually two: one producer or capital good and one consumer good), which would be created usually by two, and at most four, factors of production: capital and labour, with land and entrepreneurship possibly slipped in later.

Subsequently – during the counterattack on Keynes – the effects of monetary disturbances were dismissed as of merely short-term significance and self-adjusting, provided the State refrained from meddling with matters it could not understand. To make this model 'work' it had to be assumed that, as the demand and production of any product increased, so did its cost and price, and that no single unit either on the supply or on the demand side could influence prices, which were signals which all must obey.

This theory represented a combined attack on Marx. Begun in the 1870s and still going strong between the two world wars, it considered the labour market to be very much as any other market; as, say, that for turnips. The behaviour, both of the employer and employee, was not studied in an actual historical and traditional setting and framework; it was analysed within a theoretical construction, in which both employers and employees were assumed to act in a 'perfect' market, in terms of goods that is, a market which neither party could deliberately influence. This means that, if 'real' wages were to rise above the *'real'* productivity of the worker (that is 'his' marginal product), he would be dismissed, as his continued employment would diminish profits. There would always be a 'market-clearing' *real* price.

Say

In particular, economists continued to accept one of the most extraordinary theses in the history of economics. Say's notorious 'Law' of Markets, set out in his *Treatise* of 1803:

It is worth while to remark, that a product is no sooner created, than it, from that instant, affords a market for other products to the full extent of its own value. When the producer has put the finishing hand to his product, he is most anxious to sell it immediately, lest its value should diminish in his hands. Nor is he less anxious to dispose of the money he may get for it; for the value of money is also perishable. But the only way of getting rid of money is in the purchase of some product or other. Thus, the mere circumstance of the creation of one product immediately opens a vent for other products.[5]

The slipshod formulation of the 'Law' renders a fair interpretation difficult. It seems clear, however, that it rests on a basic fallacy. In the first place, it is implicitly assumed that the price of all products will always be affected by risk in the same way. If this were not so, there would be some goods which would be held in preference to others in times of changing risk and uncertainty; these goods retained being either more essential, or usable for a greater variety of purposes and/or more easily stored. But if this *were* so, the hoarding of goods or money, that is, speculation for a rise in their price, or accumulation merely for reasons of precaution, can no longer be ruled out; and the so-called law breaks down. (This problem still haunts economic 'science' in the persistence of the dichotomy between 'real' micro-economics and 'monetary' macro-economics.) More particularly, the law assumes that *both* sellers and buyers are *equally* determined to change their holdings of goods or money, whichever they happen to hold. This is obviously absurd, since it would result in a simultaneous scramble from goods to money and vice versa. No such desperate fluctuations in the velocity of circulation of money (which could certainly lead to a breakdown of any monetary economy) have been observed, except in the case of wartime or postwar cataclysms. The most charitable interpretation of the thesis would be to assume that Say was unconsciously, and rather imperfectly, anticipating Professor Hicks' demonstration that competition and perfect foresight are incompatible with the existence of money: but that theory could certainly not serve as the basis for a static and even less for a dynamic analysis of macro-equilibrium.[6]

Thus despite vehement and continued attacks by writers such as Sismondi, Lauderdale and, much the most important, Malthus, in face of which Say began to modify his view,[7] the assertion that aggregate supply could not outrun demand, that 'supply creates its own demand,' became entrenched dogma, the *pons asinorum* for succeeding generations of orthodox economists. It was not analysed how total money demand was determined and how it acted on supply. Thus, the all-important dogma was that to every apparent failure of demand for some goods there corresponded an excess of demand for (deficiency of supply of) some other goods; that there *may* be partial overproduction in certain sectors, but that there could not be general overproduction, i.e. insufficient demand, in the economy as a whole. Unemployment, then, was the result of undue interference with the natural forces in such markets. In the absence of such unnatural meddling, the economic system would automatically return to full employment. But dirigisme, government intervention or 'interference', such as public works or budget deficits, would only intensify any imbalance and depression. This was the thesis defended by Chicago and the London School of Economics in the 1930s. As we shall see, the failure of Keynesian doctrine and policy to deal with the problem of inflation has led to a vigorous revival and temporary triumph of this approach.

But goods do not in fact exchange against goods. Somehow

money and monetary institutions had to be allowed for, had to be incorporated into the schemes and a substitute found for perfect foresight. Thus was born the quantity theory of money whose revival has as we shall see already caused so much mischief and may well cause more. While relative prices – that is the exchange rates between goods – and the real remuneration of capital and labour were all thought to be determined by 'real' factors – that is technical and physical factors which (except for harvests) were assumed to be relatively slow-changing – money prices and incomes were thought to depend on the quantity of money in existence.

Provided 'money' remained 'neutral' all was well. That is, neutral in the sense that, whatever happens to the quantity of money, *relative* prices will not be affected – i.e. movements in the price level are strictly proportional to changes in the money supply. It was precisely this that Keynes denied: prices would not rise in proportion to a given increase in money supply, since part of the latter would find its way into idle balances (liquidity preference); this, together with its attendant impact on interest rates, invalidated the 'neutrality' assumption. Thus it was and is illicit to draw conclusions about the possible effects of an increase in the supply of money without determining *how* the increase comes about and *whose* money balances are involved. (Open-market operations by the Bank of England, for example, will, in the first instance, only increase the money balances of people who happen to be holding bonds.) But as soon as Keynes split the stock of money into M_1, M_2 and M_3, the apparent simplicity of the concept of the velocity of circulation (V) was lost. It is by no means accidental that Professor Friedman has been obliged to resort to helicopters from which to distribute impartially his fresh supplies of money: one would be intrigued to learn what fiendish device he would suggest for the opposite purpose.

Tergiversations

How have the more sterile neoclassical concerns survived so long? The stubborn attachment to a traditional theory which, in contrast to much of the applied institutional analysis, was irrelevant to the problems of reality, is rather difficult to comprehend. On being challenged on any particular point most economists would of course disclaim that, *qua* economists, they give objective advice. They would argue that the unequal incidence of any policy measure on different members of the community, the 'interpersonal non-comparability of utility', would by itself prevent any 'scientific' answer from being given; and would then cheerfully assert their special privileged role as professional guardians of, and spokesmen for, *efficiency* considerations on the basis of the status quo, i.e. politically opting for it, as if this did not imply a positive attitude to existing inequality and privilege.

Alternatively they would maintain that the theory could only help to discern long-run tendencies, forgetting that the long-run results of development largely depend on what happens in the short period. Or they would claim that the theoretical construct serves merely as a first approach, to be refined later, despite the fact that the nature of the subject matter might itself make such refinement impossible, a suspicion deepened by some six score years of failure. Finally, they often say that the whole exercise of classical and neoclassical economics is didactic in purpose, an essential mental discipline without which practical insight is not possible.

The positivists would assert, in other words, that *in its own terms* pure economic theory is clear, consistent and intelligible, and generates its own standards of excellence. However, they would then leave the gossamer purity of their models and descend with alacrity, like so many lusty Olympian gods, from their lofty heights into the marketplace to take a vigorous part in any sociopolitical brawl that there was going, and to apply their methods to a reality with which their assumptions were inconsistent. The 'austere standards of excellence' seem oddly incongruent with the uses to which the theories concerned are put. The fact that such theories 'survive' attack is no proof of their value. As the example of Say's law shows, blatant fallacies leading to inappropriate, indeed catastrophic, policies can survive if a sufficient part of the profession is committed to them. Practical failures can always be explained away by asserting that the (unsuccessful) remedy was not administered with sufficient force.

Economics as politics

There can be no question but that economists at all times have aspired, quite rightly, to elucidate and to help in solving the great practical questions of their day. Indeed, nothing less would do. There is, for example, that famous rhetorical passage, a moving plea of the last great English economist of the 'old' neoclassical tradition, the late Professor Pigou, to the budding economist:

> I would add one word for any student beginning economic study who may be discouraged by the severity of the effort which the study, as he will find it exemplified here, seems to require of him. The complicated analyses which economists endeavour to carry through are not mere gymnastics. They are instruments for the bettering of human life. The misery and squalor that surround us, the dying fire of hope in many millions of European homes, the injurious luxury of some wealthy families, the terrible uncertainty overshadowing many families of the poor – these are evils too plain to be ignored. By the knowledge that our science seeks it is possible that they may be restrained. Out of the darkness light! To search for it is the task, to find it, perhaps, the prize, which the 'dismal science of Political Economy' offers to those who facc its discipline.[8]

And his frank avowal of his ambitious designs: 'The goal sought is to make more easy practical measures to promote welfare – practical measures which statesmen may build upon the work of the economist, such as Marconi, the inventor, built upon the discoveries of Hertz.'[9]

Economics, *pace* Professor Schumpeter, who was clever and cynical enough frankly to extol the virtue of useless theorizing,[10] was not created to delight the aesthetic sense of failed mathematicians. It was fashioned and aimed at resolving, or helping to resolve, real problems.

No one makes this clearer than the principal founder of the Austrian neoclassical school, which underlies much of the dominant orthodoxy of the present day, Professor Menger. In his famous essay on the methodology of economics he 'proves', in a rather obscure passage, the existence of a 'theory of economy' distinct from the 'historical or practical sciences of the economy':

> The *theory* of economy must in no case be confused with the *historical* sciences of economy, or with the *practical* ones. Only the person who is completely in the dark about the formal nature and the problems of theoretical economics could perceive in it a historical science because the general (theoretical) knowledge which it embraces ostensibly, or really, shows less strictness than in the natural sciences; or else perhaps for the further reason that the development of economic phenomena, as we will see, is not without influence on the way and manner in which economics is able to solve its theoretical problems. Only a person who cannot keep apart the natures of theoretical and practical sciences could perceive in

economics a *practical science* – perhaps for the reason that it, like other theories, forms the basis of practical sciences.[11]

This shadowy mystical being, of course, would only be of use if the relationship of each of its parts were such as to give acceptable predictions in real life. Professor Menger or his followers, however, neither prove this nor do they accept the limitation of this method. On the contrary, and in stark contradistinction to the scientific 'modesty' of their 'model', they claim: 'The purpose of the *theoretical* sciences is understanding of the *real* world, knowledge of it extending beyond immediate experience, control of it. We understand phenomena by means of theories as we become aware of them in each concrete case merely as exemplifications of a general regularity.'[12] It is on the basis of this very high standard that they wish to be judged. It is to say the least astonishing that it was on the basis of this twaddle that the historical school was eliminated as a serious effort at elucidating concrete problems. The explanation probably lies in the lack of analytical power and the increasing diffusion of the latter's efforts.

3. Interwar landscape: imbalance and the Keynesian revolution

Thus Say's Law was generally believed, for more than a century. Indeed, so effectively did its influence frustrate common sense and dominate policy-making during the interwar period that it contributed to the transformation in 1931 of a severe economic setback into a social and political catastrophe. Economists, for the most part, steadfastly attacked and ridiculed spending programmes in the midst of an unprecedented collapse in confidence and demand.[13] We are presently suffering from the same fallacies.

Keynes
It was these follies which were, for a time at least, successfully attacked by Keynes. He pointed out that the market for labour was by no means like any other market. It is an appreciable part of the economic system itself, and changes in it, provided they are general, will affect the economic system as a whole, especially if (as is likely) the economy is dominated by oligopoly, by a few large-scale prod-

ucers in each branch, where a movement of wages is with a certain lag or perhaps even without a lag, followed by a change in prices and therefore in other incomes. Keynes, however, unlike his closest collaborator, Joan Robinson,[14] eschewed the discussion of this inflationary aspect of the problem: he was writing in a period of deep depression and wanted to concentrate on showing that involuntary unemployment could persist, but could be reduced by appropriate policies.

By the end of the war the Keynesian revolution had freed economics from the first of its neoclassical shackles. It was no coincidence that the intellectual upheaval started in Britain, where the domestic economy had not benefited from the postwar boom. It came too late to prevent political disintegration in Central Europe, let alone to permit the Western world to arm itself betimes, on the basis of its abundant superfluity of material resources, against the Nazi assault.[15] The commonsense view nevertheless made some progress, and finally prevailed during the war: that, in an economy based on individual profit and risk-taking, profit depended on demand, and that investment bore some relationship to production and the pressure on available capacity.[16] It was acknowledged that there existed no mechanism which would automatically restore full employment after a monetary disturbance; the modern capitalist system was liable to cyclical fluctuations generated even by random shocks.

The first and pathbreaking systematic analysis of the relationship between additional aggregate expenditure and the total increase in demand was made in 1931 by R. F. (now Professor Lord) Kahn in a paper on the 'employment multiplier'.[17] More important, it pointed to the impact of an increase in expenditure which he established and the consequential increment in aggregate (real) supply that effected the essential break with orthodoxy – this being the fundamental truth, the theoretical device of the multiplier being a convenient concept through which to give it formal and quantitative expression.[18]

The revolutionary insight of Kahn's argument lay in denying the classical principle that aggregate output was uniquely determined by the availability of real resources, whether of manpower, machines, or technical knowledge or managerial ability, because full employment of labour was assumed to be continuously maintained. By relating output to *demand* rather than to supply, Kahn was thus able to crack the tough carapace of classical economics (successful as it had been in withstanding so many prior attacks) before even Kalecki or Keynes.[19] He pioneered – as did Nicholas (now Professor Lord) Kaldor[20] subsequently – an open-ended system which could accommodate, and hence serve as an analytical framework for, any historically unique conjuncture of facts, influences, motivations and expectations. In other words, the business cycle was at last brought within the legitimate purview of economic theory, no longer banished to skulk around the periphery of the subject as what Lionel (now Lord) Robbins was pleased to call a 'residual problem'. Some residual! No longer could the elegant charade of formally determinate systems pass for economic analysis and yet claim relevance for the real world.[21] But, although common sense and intuition had long exposed the pretentiousness of these claims, not until its bitterest lesson had been learnt was the theoretical dogmatism of the past to be attacked intellectually on its own ground. The path was at last open towards a more flexible and empirical approach, based on sociological observation.

Micro-economic upheaval

The attack on the neoclassical dogma in the 1930s was double-pronged. It did not merely show up Say's muddle for what it was; it also struck at the very roots of the general and special equilibrium theory which, as we saw, rested on the assumption of the prevalence of perfect competition with all its implications for both demand and supply. Not only (in that view) was the market mechanism an automatically balanced system, it also provided an optimum use of resources for the satisfaction of the sovereign demands of consumers. That was supposed to maximize their satisfaction (or utility or welfare or whatever) from given resources.

In the forefront of the attack, Joan Robinson,[22] in association with Richard Kahn, smashed the hypothesis that, with a given scale of operations, 'just' or 'optimal' prices would be established and a distribution of income would be secured corresponding exactly to the contribution of each productive factor.

This thesis depended on the proposition – increasingly accepted against overwhelming evidence to the contrary – not only that perfect competition (or something sufficiently like it)[23] prevailed in the greater part of the economy, but also and totally inconsequentially that its rational, and hence optimal, functioning depended on the private ownership of capital. In turn, all this rested on a prior assumption that individual firms operated under conditions of increasing (or at best constant) costs of production. This constraint would then set an upper limit to their expansion, thereby assuring that competition remained 'perfect' – that is, characterized by a multitude of small firms each on its own unable to affect market prices. Any divergences between firms or industries in their externalities, uses of public goods or other relations to public revenue were belittled, as were the advantages of mass production; monopoly was treated as a rare exception, usually contrived by the State. The major inference to be drawn from such a schematization was that private and social costs would coincide: that the costs of output incurred by producers would correspond exactly to the costs that such production imposed on the community as a whole, and that, given the resources, their optimal use is guaranteed.

The origins of these new attacks on the neoclassical equilibrium system lay in two neglected papers of a few years earlier. Partly they sprang from Professor Alleyn Young's conclusive demonstration of the critical importance of the cumulative reduction in costs that could be reaped by increasing both the *scale* of production and also the resources committed to research and development, in accounting for the new dynamism that was infusing large areas of the world.[24] Partly it sprang at a fundamental level from Piero Sraffa's critique of the very concept of perfect competition.[25] As we shall see presently, the arguments that were used to defend 'perfect competition' as a coherent and plausible simplification of the economic system were fallacious: not only were they logically inconsistent or circular, they also rested on assumptions about human behaviour and modern technical development that robbed them of virtually all practical relevance.

As soon as the possibility of prolonged and widespread unemployment (and the reasons for it) had been demonstrated, conventional theory, and policy advice based on it, were thrown into disarray. One might have supposed, quite reasonably, that this twin revolution – which in any other discipline would have sounded a deathknell for the failing orthodoxy – would have marked the beginning of a completely new, case-by-case, approach to the analysis of economic questions. But such an approach clearly entailed the need for the closest interaction, if not fusion, of economic theory and policy-making with historical and sociological studies.

The proud self-sufficiency of the discipline would perish. This would have been too much. Economics, after all, aspired to the status of a true science, claiming to itself a decisive superiority over other so-called social subjects in its ability to support not only objective, i.e. 'positive', but also empirically quantifiable judgements. Thus, as Professor (now Sir John) Hicks put it, when confronted with the threat of the micro-economic imperfect-competition revolution:

It is, I believe, only possible to save anything from this wreck – and it must be remembered that the threatened wreckage is that of the greater part of economic theory – if we can assume that the markets confronting most of the firms with which we shall be dealing do not differ very greatly from perfectly competitive markets. It we can suppose that the percentages by which prices exceed marginal costs are neither very large nor very variable, and if we can suppose (what is largely a consequence of the first assumption) that *marginal* costs do generally increase with output at the point of equilibrium (diminishing marginal costs being rare), then the laws of an economic system working under perfect competition will not be appreciably varied in a system which contains widespread elements of monopoly. At least, this get-away seems well worth trying. We must be aware, however, that we are taking a dangerous step, and probably limiting to a serious extent the problems with which our subsequent analysis will be fitted to deal. Personally, however, I doubt if most of the problems we shall have to exclude for this reason are capable of much useful analysis by the methods of economic theory.[26]

So much for the vaunted scientific character of economics. Even Keynes, who was far from wedded to his own ideas (and much less to those of others), shrank from cutting this umbilical cord.

4. A return to the womb

Keynes' vision, which for several decades after the war seemed to usher in a new era, did not in the end succeed in leading the profession towards an interdisciplinary method by which changing trends and incidents can meaningfully be analysed. Contemporary economics present, instead, a depressing picture. Neoclassical theory is reasserting most of its pre-Keynesian follies, and helping to bring on and intensify prewar types of depression and deliberate inhumanity. Governments are advised to rely absurdly on monetary manipulation. They try to balance budgets at high levels of unemployment. They disguise and depersonalize these immoralities by speaking not of social values but of mechanical criteria such as the domestic credit expansion (DCE) and/or the money supply (M). Yet on all (even conventional) criteria the Keynesian epoch was an unparalleled success. Unemployment was a fraction of that of the prewar years, the growth of the real product a multiple. There was also some lessening of inequality in the advanced industrial countries. This was true even in those countries which, like Britain, had a relatively inferior record. Though economic fluctuations persisted, they were so much lighter as to be from a social viewpoint different in kind. Their basic mechanism however has not changed, as we know to our cost.

The unexpectedly sharp reversal from Keynes is the consequence as much of what I call 'classicization' or conventionalization of the Keynesian revolution, whose essential merit lay in creating an open-ended system, as of the obvious practical defects of the resulting 'liberal'[27] Keynesian' quasi-neoclassical dogma. The only difference between the liberal Keynesian and the pre-Keynesian orthodoxy was some disagreement about the governmental help the market might need in order to be self-stabilizing. The ignorance of the new problems caused by full employment and by the changes on both sides of industry was a further potent cause of the sudden débâcle. The drive to obtain determinacy proved irresistible. The tendency to accelerating inflation and its sociopolitical consequences has for the moment proved fatal to a sensible policy.

It was this 'classicized', formalized liberal Keynesian doctrine, sometimes in social democratic guise,[28] which failed some basic practical tests and opened the way for the monetarist revival. Just as the old orthodoxy had failed to deal with unemployment, so the new failed to deal with inflation. Underlying both practical failures was much the same critical scientific mistake: the obsessive desire to build a *determinate* science about an *indeterminate* world. The drive towards logical rigour and quantification thus robbed the original Keynesian revolt of much of its liberating power by trying to make the 'new' system determinate. This could be done only at the cost of assumptions which do as much violence to reality as those Keynes attacked. The 'woolliness'[29] of the open system of understanding – which knows that its theoretical expectations are potentially unstable, and vulnerable to their changing environment

- gave way to the falsehoods and irrelevance of the closed system. Bad forecasting followed – and ironically, prompted a reaction towards the classical (or neoclassical) doctrines – especially on the monetary plane. There was at the same time some crude social reaction against the interests of the weak and the less well endowed, and monetarist economics did much to encourage and justify it. So – once again with abundant academic and professional encouragement – we turn back the clock towards the conditions, and the crisis, which prompted the Keynesian revolution half a century ago.

There is thus a bitter irony. It was the original conservatization of Keynesian doctrine that weakened its practical power, and so exposed what remained of it to a more decisive rejection a generation later. Hardly had the *General Theory* been published before the process of formalization and systematization had begun to emasculate it. Keynes had given economists for the first time practically since Adam Smith a sensible, historically-based framework with which to analyse the many different possible reactions that might follow from a given policy decision; hence, probably, the rather frivolous accusation that the book itself was untidy and difficult to read. More damagingly for the development of economic analysis, it was contended that if the Keynesian approach was to provide an alternative 'system', its relationships would have to be made consistent; not only more rigorously specified, but made to yield 'determinate' answers.

As a result, within months of the appearance of the *General Theory*, Hicks had succeeded in freezing macro-economics back into its classical mould, as it was to be enshrined in the 'progressive' textbooks for the following thirty years.[30] No doubt the simple relationships, however defective they were proved to be as a guide for action, provided for the Keynesian economics that accolade as a 'system' needed to make the doctrine palatable to the ordinary professional economist. The so-called consumption function, the rigid relationship between income and savings which allows prediction, is an assumption, unless one defines income in so artificial a way as to make it operationally meaningless. The constants turn out to be more unstable than the variables they are to explain. Changes of stocks overwhelm flows. Consumer credit; the increase in importance of the mass of durables; the rapid psychological changes on the part of people in their roles as consumers, asset-

44

owners, taxpayers, and entrepreneurs – all this not only renders scientific prediction hazardous but also defeats practical attempts at stabilization by 'global' methods. Both stimulus and restraint, in order to be effective, tend to overshoot the need. The system, instead of settling down, swings from higher to lower levels of employment and activity. Yet the economists go on as if there were a determinate system, as if economic relationships were stable and firm enough to base firm policy recommendations upon them.

Small wonder that much of this new 'scientism' and 'consensus economics' has proved as mischievous and misleading as the neo-classical doctrine it displaced. On general economic policy, on taxation, on monetary manipulation, there has come a stream of contrary advice based, as we shall see, often on irrelevant and surprisingly simple assumptions about the delicate interrelations between various sectors and factors of economic life. These 'models', so-called, of the productive mechanism of diverse communities, with variegated social relationships and motivations, disregard those differences, and their historical rise and determination. They claim universality for what is an extremely restricted validity both geographical and temporal, applicable if at all, like the neoclassical orthodoxy, to a nineteenth-century environment in a strictly Protestant-North Atlantic area.

Thus did the aborting of the revolution begin: in making its content palatable to the profession, it was robbed of its essential usefulness. As Professor Samuelson once put it:

> The classical philosophy always had its ups and downs along with the great swings of business activity. Each time it had come back. But now for the first time, it was confronted by a competing system – a well-reasoned body of thought containing among other things as many equations as unknowns; in short, like itself, a synthesis; and one which could swallow the classical system as a special case. A new system, that is what requires emphasis.[31]

Or does it?

Later in the same piece, in hot pursuit of a 'general' General Theory – that monocausal explanation of economic reality which, like Maeterlinck's bluebird, continues to elude capture – Samuelson declares triumphantly:

> But behind lies the vitally important consumption function: giving the propensity to consume in terms of income; or looked at from the opposite

side, specifying the propensity to save. With investment given, as a constant or in the schedule sense, we are in a position to set up the simplest determinate system of underemployment equilibrium – by a 'Keynesian savings-investment-income cross' not formally different from the 'Marshallian supply-demand-price cross'. Immediately everything falls into place.[32]

The Keynesian revolution, thus disarmed, was reduced to the role of an alternative determinate 'system' and frozen into stable relationships. Thus was its potentially liberating impact on economic analysis defused.

Regaining respectability, losing relevance

Ideologically, and of course politically, there was much to be gained for the *beati possidentes* by this approach. It could serve to resuscitate the neoclassical moral claim that the distribution of income reflected the due rewards of all contributors to national output. If a (slightly) underemployed system were stable, the old theory of 'real' marginal contribution as determining incomes could be (indeed, has been) revived. A modern and reinforced defence of *laissez-faire* capitalism was at hand. The crucial snag in the new conventional wisdom, however, was that, no sooner had these neo-Keynesian claims been made, than they were rudely controverted by events. So long as this unavoidable truth is ignored, our escape from consequent general instability – not restricted to this country, nor even to the West – will be uncertain.

The current liberal neo-Keynesian argument, then, like its neoclassical predecessor, is conducted not in terms of the real world, with its massive polarization of economic power, but in terms of that same imaginary microsystem which Keynes so fiercely attacked, yet in which he at the end of his life believed.[33] The lessons of experience remained unlearnt: a suitably defined level of 'full' employment could be achieved and price stability and economic growth could be ensured by 'global' measures by the judicious management of the budget, aided by monetary policy, and, reluctantly, credit control. Thus what began as a revolution was in the end made acceptable to the old authorities: to politicians, by promising painless remedies for economic ills; and to economists, by promising once more the appearance of a formal and determinate science. There was only one flaw: those two promises were flatly incompatible.

5. The point of weakness: inflation

In all this theorizing the threat of inflation was dismissed, especially by the 'liberal' Keynesians; and, apart from Joan Robinson, there were few Keynesians who did not incline to liberalism and (save for the acknowledged need for some global management) did not subscribe basically to the neoclassical approach. It was liberal-neoclassical Keynesians who dismissed any fears that the 'new economics' would bring with it a new and critical problem of inflation. That mistake was fatal to them.

Of the importance of full employment there can be no dispute.[34] Full employment not only makes domestic help scarce but it generally removes the need for servility, and thus alters the way of life, the relationship between classes. It changes the balance of forces in the economy. This is its outstanding, indeed revolutionary, consequence. Yet it is precisely this very fundamental change in class relationship which tends to undermine progressive governments, because it is the main cause of the continuous rise in costs and prices which offends the majority who in fact benefit most from the new achievement. It is this conflict of everyone against all whose growing bitterness undermines the social basis of any full employment policy that is not buttressed by an incomes policy.

Full employment is, then, not merely a means to higher production and faster expansion. It is also an aim in itself, weakening the dominance of men over men, dissolving the master-servant relation. It is the greatest engine for the attainment by all of human dignity and greater equality, and not merely in respect of incomes and consumption, important as these may be. Most other social advances since 1940 were, if not a direct consequence, at least conditioned by it.

The achievement of full employment has, however, in my opinion, wrought fundamental changes in the functioning of the social and therefore the economic system,[35] which in its turn has seen an acceleration of change producing a difference in kind and not merely degree. The concentration of industry, the rise of oligopoly and managed price markets on the one hand, and the increase in the power of unions on the other, have created a critical new problem of reconciling full employment and stability. No fine-tuning of demand by broad fiscal means has resolved the problem

– or can ever resolve it. Governments nevertheless kept on trying those inadequate methods for a long time, undeterred by their continuous failure. There was no fundamental reconsideration of the causes of inflation. The cyclical 'stop-go' pattern, which characterized the economic management of most of the advanced countries in the West, persisted.

Clearly, the nature of inflation has altered: it is not a simple product of excess demand. And yet economists continue to believe steadfastly in the determinacy of economic systems, as if economic relationships (Keynesian now, rather than Marshallian or Fisherian) were sufficiently firm or stable for definite and quantified policy recommendations to be based upon them.[36] The dilemma – how to avoid coexisting unemployment and inflation – remained unsolved. Indeed in each 'stop' phase unemployment rose in comparison to the previous cycle. Yet inflation seemed to accelerate until the last boom and bust exhibited the characteristics of the pre-Second World War cycles. As we shall see, in a modern economy controlled by global policies the policy measures necessarily 'overshoot', for psychological reasons which in turn have led to a resuscitation of the most primitive type of quantity theory of money.

6. Counter-revolution and schism

The successful 'containment' of the revolutionary restatement of economics of the interwar years, begun by sympathizers, has at length left economics floundering in a state of multiple schism. Because the attenuated Keynesian system could not cope with reality, there has been a renaissance of pre-Keynesian fallacies.

There coexist at least some five different approaches to the study of economic problems: two micro-economic, two macro-economic, and the fifth, impossible to categorize, dealing with 'normative' problems under the name of welfare economics, claiming falsely to be able to provide an objective means of evaluating policy. The point which must be emphasized, however, is that not only has the study of economic phenomena been fractured; there is even disagreement about the nature of the fracture. On the one hand, we have complicated subterfuges reaffirming the old supply-oriented macro-economics of Say's Law and the refurbished

Quantity Theory, joining however incongruously with the pristine neoclassical microstatics of Walrasian general equilibrium. On the other hand, the demand-oriented macro-economics of Keynes joins forces in some authors (though not always consciously or consistently) with the imperfect competition revolution, while others combine a varying dose of the Master with a rather greater dose of neoclassicism, provided employment is maintained.

There are objections to most of these old and new mixtures. In the first place the study of large economic aggregates like national income, consumption, investment, savings, money supply and circulation and the various price indices is completely divorced from that of the determination and movement of individual prices, output and incomes. Indeed, it was this dichotomy between macro- and micro-economics, together with the demonstrable failure of the Quantity Theory of Money to provide a reliable basis for policy-making, that made the neoclassical edifice so vulnerable to Keynes' attack. Keynes displaced the old Quantity Theory, simultaneously bringing unemployment into the centre of economic analysis as a variable that could be – indeed has to be – explained. Of course, 'theories' of the business cycle (under one name or another) had been in existence for a very long time;[37] the scandal was that the inevitable concomitant of economic fluctuations, unemployment, was never reconciled with the strict neoclassical model of implied full employment and instantaneous adjustment.[38]

Now, in response to Keynes, there were desperate efforts to rationalize and rescue the old structures. Some tried to show that it was not the inherent defects in the price mechanism which were at the root of the trouble, but rather the rigidity of prices, and especially of wages; in the end monetary forces would therefore put an end to the slump. Some argued that if only prices would fall, the consequent appreciation of money and financial assets in real terms (the so-called Pigou effect) would induce an increase in expenditure. But in fact prices declined gradually throughout the 1920s, and sharply after 1929; conversely, in the recovery phase after 1933, prices started to rise again.[39] Ominously enough the prices of primary commodities repeated this pattern after 1970 under the pressure of the return to monetary policy as the main policy weapon. They had (apart from the Korean war boom) been under pressure relative to the prices of manufactures. It has once more been demonstrated that a valid analysis of what are nowadays

49

indeterminate macro-economic processes on the basis of a static 'real' system is impossible. Nevertheless, because of the liberal Keynesians' own failures, the Keynesian critique of the neoclassical mixture has once again been repudiated not only by a majority of economists, but by politicians and bankers too. We shall return to this main point of these essays.

7. The Keynesian failure

When some erstwhile Keynesian optimists finally accepted that inflation represented a problem - which by 1962 was difficult to deny - it was somehow hoped that, one way or another, a solution could be found without implying radical changes in the system. One such contribution (though later rejected on grounds of administrative impracticability) was Professor Meade's 'liberal socialist' solution,[40] based on the direct regulation of wages without offsetting price controls or a comprehensive social programme; not much liberalism here. To make matters worse, Professor Meade's prescription would entail the introduction of wage controls at the precise moment when a devaluation (a floating of the exchange rate) would tend to raise domestic prices and cut real wages. It is the persistence of such schemes, lacking both social awareness and political sense, which discredits income policies in the eyes of labour, and makes the adoption of a more balanced approach to economic problems (then as now) unlikely.

One of the most notorious tenets of the liberal Keynesian synthesis has been the belief in a stable inverse relationship between the rate of change in money wages and unemployment which, if it could be discovered empirically, would allow for stable prices at a slight, or at any rate reasonable, cost measured in terms of output and expansion foregone. Hence the extravagant enthusiasm with which this 'discovery' was greeted;[41] for if such a simple and stable relationship could have been proved, then the reinstatement of the neoclassical theory of social harmony in a slightly modified form would have been complete.

This mischievous and patently false doctrine owes its survival directly to the 'classicization' of what we called the open-ended proto-Keynesian approach to economics. With investment, consumption, savings, imports and exports neatly compressed into a system of equations, policy-making degenerates into a ritual of conditioned responses, totally dependent on the periodic computation of misleading, because too rigidly circumscribed, short-term economic forecasts. Thus, what was once celebrated by so intelligent a person as Professor Samuelson as the 'alternative to classical economics' perishes by the same defect as the old system, by supposing that (with the modern addition of a little demand management) the price mechanism would suffice to reconcile full employment with stability.

Almost as much suffering has been caused by the obstinacy of 'liberal' Keynesian mathematical economists and econometricians, in their desire to enclose the facts within a rigorous framework, as by their neoclassical forebears. Some of the mistakes in policy-making can certainly be attributed to consistently wrong (and usually far too optimistic) forecasts based mainly on Keynesian models.[42] The trend rate of growth of real output and international competitiveness are assumed to be independent of short-term policy, and the balance of payments to be extremely income-sensitive both downwards and upwards. The former is obviously nonsense; the latter, because of its neglect of the same, has also been shown to be fallacious.[43,44]

In an affluent society, the sort of indirect controls envisaged by Keynes, and particularly by his neoclassical followers, seem to work only imperfectly. Changes in interest rates, for instance, take time to work themselves through, thus inducing, indeed necessitating, successively more forcible applications. In fact interest rate policy has never functioned in accordance with neoclassical conceptions – that is, through its instantaneous impact on the cost of marginal investment projects – in which it was assumed, at least tacitly, that the impending crisis would leave the expected returns from such projects unaffected.

Further impediments to their successful operation include the development of the modern structure of taxation, the increased concentration of market power, and technological change. (The inducement to depreciate capital more quickly, the faster the rate of technological change, tends to reduce interest charges as a proportion of the total saving cost of an investment project.) Wide fluctuations in saving through the extension and redemption of consumer credit, the use of large reserves of idle money, and the accumulation of consumer durables, can offset (or more than offset) changes in taxation or monetary policy. Expansion policies, such as budget deficits or the pumping of purchasing power into the economy, can be offset by increased savings or by apprehensive increases in the flow of debt repayment. The parameters are more unstable than the variables.

After the Second World War the principal economic problem was not unemployment, it was inflation. This problem has proved difficult, if not impossible, to resolve by purely Keynesian methods. Demand in that period never actually fell; indeed it has run ahead of supply, and all fully industrialized countries have experienced a relentless increase in prices, which has continued even during periods of relatively slacker demand. Employment meanwhile was maintained at unprecedentedly high levels, and this undoubted social gain was attributed to the wisdom acquired at such cost during the 1930s, and to the great sophistication of modern economic analysis and policymaking.

It was doubtful, however, even when governments gave priority to the goal of full employment, whether its achievement was chiefly due to human wisdom. And whatever caused it, some powerful interests always found it uncomfortable. As we shall see in a subsequent chapter, full or even fullish employment - with unemployment anywhere below three or four per cent - entailed grave social and economic drawbacks for the propertied and managerial classes. It also proved less and less compatible with the maintenance of price stability. This in turn set classes, professions and occupations against one another.

A solution safeguarding employment while restraining inflation to tolerable levels might have been found. It would have had to include direct controls on key factors. Unfortunately the European Social Democrats - in the US the Democrats - who from time to time attained power did not quite realize the magnitude of the related problems of employment and stability, and failed with both. They supposed, or hoped, that the nature of inflation had not changed: that it was still induced by excessive demand, arising from misjudged budget deficits, and could be managed by easy adjustments of fiscal policy. Their failure gave a tremendous impetus politically to the new Conservatives who became champions of liberty, interpreted as economic *laissez-faire*. They were helped by economists returning all the way to the primitive, pre-Keynesian arguments for *laissez-faire*.

8. The revival of neoclassical macro-monetarism

The neoclassical-Keynesian failure made opportunity for the neoclassical-monetarist revival. What is the substance of the revived faith?[45]

There is of course no God-ordained rate at which money will be used.[46] Money can only act through *expenditure*; but there is only a tenuous relationship between money supply and expenditure: certainly it cannot be closely related to interest rates, either to the short-term rate, as for instance was thought by Sir Ralph Hawtrey, through the old *deus ex machina* of stock-holding merchants, or to the long-term rate, as was presumed by Keynes and his liberal followers. Increased interest charges, if sufficiently general, can be offset against taxes or shifted on to the consumer, although a general looseness in the money market might act as a direct stimulus to speculation, or investment or consumption outlays.[47] Traditionally, and rather inconsistently with the basic tenets of the dogma, it was assumed that, following a fall in money demand, losses would be incurred and the least efficient firms would go bankrupt. This would discourage investment, especially in stocks, which in turn would provoke a further decrease in demand. As unemployment increased, so consumption would fall. Before the Second World War, governments did nothing to counteract this cumulative process:[48] indeed, they aggravated the situation by their adherence to the dogma which insisted that budgets must be balanced. Further, the basic instability was increased in such circumstances by entrepreneurs anticipating violent alterations of psychology. The elasticity of the monetary and banking system enabled these changes to become effective. This was reflected in the booms and slumps of the century and a half before the Second World War.[49] We cannot assume on the basis of historical experience that the system would be stable in the absence of government or Central Bank intervention. All practical and historical knowledge points in the opposite direction.

Both of these approaches, neoclassical Keynesian and monetarist, have been equally deficient in their ability to predict the movement of economic variables. They lay absurd claim to unconditional generality and they continue to ignore the immense importance – indeed uniqueness – of historical conjuncture, whether present or past. Neo-Keynesians and monetarists alike blind themselves to the fact that the law of large numbers (a highly slippery concept in economics) does not apply to the historical turning-points of large countries with different pasts and, therefore, different aspirations and expectations. I shall discuss later in greater depth the reasons why the profession has stubbornly refused to accept what seems so self-evident – the need for an open-ended framework for analysis, and no more.

In this field of liberal (or liberalizing) economics *les extrêmes se touchent*. On the monetarist side we find Professor Friedman arguing that the market power of unions and employers cannot cause cost-inflation, but that it simply 'distorts' the optimal distribution of wage incomes. It is clear that Professor Friedman in this context (though not in others) must be assuming the existence of both full employment and constant money national income, for otherwise the 'leapfrog effect' would increase *all* money incomes, if not all in the same proportion. True enough that strong deflationary action causing unemployment on a scale approaching that of the 1930s would bring about bankruptcies and in the end stop the boom; but it would be the unemployment caused, and possibly a general financial collapse, which would have brought about the reversal.

This sequence is of course what caused the prewar type of cycles into which we now again seem to be sliding. No Walrasian equilibrium can be established that way. The monetarists of course tried to conceal the fact that their identity $(M) V = PT$ could not be regarded as a meaningful equation and used for policy-making because the definition of the volume of money (M_1 cash or M_3 cash + bank deposits) involved implicitly the definition of its velocity. If the narrower definition (M_1) is used, *its velocity* of circulation would influence the volume of the wider definition (M_3) which was its reflection. Moreover M contains money which is used in a broader field – assets – than the income, and it is illegitimate to take GNP as a proxy for total turnover because the non-income items might well cause imbalance which might cumulate. Nor was it legitimate to assume that T (or 'real' volume of turnover) would not be affected by movements of MV, as indeed they were in pre-Second World War cycles and with the victory of the monetarists once again since 1973. The claim of the monetarists to be able to keep a smooth expansion going merely by manipulating a parallel smooth expansion of the money supply has not been borne out by at least 150 years of economic history (unless the history is subjected to curious statistical manipulation).

This is evidenced by their efforts to minimize the level of the 'natural' rate of unemployment, that is the level below which unemployment cannot be pressed without necessitating accelerating inflation and collapse. Professor Paish[50] asserted that unemployment of $2\frac{1}{2}$ per cent would assure price stability. Hardly was the ink dry before that level of unemployment failed to prevent the acceleration of inflation to above 10 per cent p.a. As recently as 1975 Professor Parkin manipulated his statistical evidence (by omitting the awkward years 1971-2 from his equation) to show that the 'natural' rate which before 1967 was 1.78 per cent (two decimals at that!) had only risen to 3.7 per cent.

By massaging the (non-existent) 'Phillips curve' (the primitive, mostly linear relationship between unemployment and wages and prices) such reasoners can 'prove' that incomes policy exacerbated inflation.[51] Some people would believe anything, especially if it eliminates awkward social and political problems.

The monetarist theory is based on a (not-so-very-good) empirical correlation between the volume of money and prices. But this can by no means prove the causal connection.[52] Tuberculosis sanatoria were numerous when tuberculosis was rampant. Their number declined when tuberculosis as a general menace was eliminated. But it was not the suppression of sanatoria which caused the malady to disappear.

The monetarists are, curiously, paralleled at the other extreme; Messrs Godley and Cripps have argued that the problem of cost inflation can be solved (at least in Britain) by the introduction of wage subsidies in conjunction with an increase in Value Added Tax. But such a scheme assumes perfectly competitive behaviour on the part of entrepreneurs; if the case were otherwise, under inflationary conditions the increase in VAT would be shifted on to prices, rather than absorbed by profits, regardless of the wage subsidies to be recouped later (and, given the complexities involved, this could be much later). They also subscribe to the Friedmanite view that anti-cyclical intervention is necessarily counterproductive; an average budget surplus or deficit should be maintained. If our analysis of cycles based on the psychological school's finding is right, such a policy might intensify cycles. We shall return to this problem in a different context.

Equally fallacious is their second remedy.[53] This is based on an empirical observation that the private sector balance is a constant and that the foreign balance is self-adjusting. Thus it follows that a reduction of the budget deficit (shades of Keynes) would automatically reduce the deficit in the balance of payments. This surprising recommendation was based on identities masquerading as strategic equations, identities whose composition is by no means stable. Characteristically, they did not seem to realize that the rise in oil prices will – in the absence of an agreed incomes and prices policy – not necessarily act as a deflator: it might give a further push to cost inflation – as it did in Britain but not in Germany. It is for this reason that their method of analysis must be criticized; it obscures the essentially political nature of the problem. They do not seem to have considered that a different identity might have emerged through different changes in the subtotals; e.g., if important prices had risen less. The domestic causes of inflation were less important here than in many other countries.

It will be observed that in every attempt to bridge the gap between an extremely *elastic* and therefore potentially (and in fact effectively) unstable monetary system and the self-adjusting quasi-factor micro-economics, there has to be some major relationship which must be assumed to be fixed. The Keynesians had the multiplier and the liquidity preference; Professor Kaldor the absorption curve; Friedman, following Fisher, the velocity of circulation, and now the neo-Keynesians, the public sector deficit and the so-called Phillips curve (which lately bred a family, thereby conceding that there might be only points without 'curves'). In all these cases the empirical basis – if one was ever proved – vanished into nothingness. We shall return to this point.

9. The revival of neoclassical micro-economics

With the revival of the old and discredited Quantity Theory of Money there came also a revival of the neoclassical approach to relative prices. Both the Marshallian partial and the Walrasian general form reappeared. More and more refined models were produced. This was such an extraordinary development, at a time when real economic life was moving in an opposite direction, that it calls for comment.

In line with traditional neoclassical micro-economics, the argument (as noted earlier in this chapter) is carried on in 'real terms': the 'veil' of money has been removed. Analysis is then restricted to a system in which a specific number of goods are produced (at the simplest level, two) by two or perhaps four factors of production. Fundamental to the coherence of this stylized picture is the assumption that, as demand for one commodity increases, its price will rise and vice versa; in other words, production is assumed to be carried on under conditions of increasing costs. (This condition comprises not only diminishing returns to factors, normally depicted in the short-run U-shaped cost curve of the firm; it includes the essential rider that returns to scale in the 'long run' are also diminishing, or at best constant. In other words, the assumptions of the analysis preclude the possibility of individual firms expanding relative to the size of the market, so as to be able to influence the prices of their products. Perfect competition is thus guaranteed.)

The treatment of factors, moreover, is no different from that of commodities. The labour market is like other markets. The Walrasian model, as we have seen, is not only without money; it is also timeless. Thus the influence of the historical past and of expectations for the future play no part in the analysis. Indeed, in the context of such a model, it would be difficult to envisage a realistic role for money. Certainly its function as a 'link between the present and the future' would be precluded. Difficult to rationalize also would be its place in the utility function of individual consumers – for example, as a store of value – in a pure exchange economy characterized by the random allocation of bundles of goods at the start of each 'period' of exchange. Equally, its use as a medium of exchange would upset the equilibrating mechanism of the market, since the necessary correspondence between buying and selling intentions would be lacking; the possibility of speculative instability would then have to be acknowledged. There remains only money in its guise as a unit of account, that is, *numéraire*; but then one is no longer discussing something of analytical economic consequence.

The behaviour of employers and employees alike, then, is totally cocooned from the exigencies of the real world; all that remains to be studied is their reaction to impersonal forces in the context of 'perfect' markets which neither party can influence. Given all the assumptions, buyers and sellers (whether of factors or commodities) reach a position of unique and stable equilibrium in which individual utilities are maximized (within so-called budget constraints). The essence of this equilibrium is that all variables are determined *simultaneously* (that is, in the mathematical sense; since time is excluded by definition it could hardly be conceived otherwise). The composition of final output, along with relative commodity prices, is determined by the pattern of demand in the goods market which 'in turn', though also simultaneously, is determined by the supply of factor services (since in a barter economy supply 'is' demand). The relative amounts in which factor services are 'offered' determines their relative price and, given their respective marginal value products (derived from prices set in the commodity market), the relative demand for factor services. The pattern of final output which emerges is then produced at minimum cost (this is a condition of equilibrium as long as perfect competition is assumed) and at a set of product prices that corresponds to marginal utilities to all individuals. At the same time, unemployment is ruled out as impossible by definition in such a schema; if factor services of any kind are not being fully used, this can only reflect the fact that their supply is excessive relative to their marginal value product. The 'remedy' is to reduce supply by allowing the reward to the factor in question to fall; in other words it is only *involuntary* unemployment that is impossible, since, as the wage rate falls, labour merely curtails the offer of its services in favour of more 'leisure'.[54]

At the other end of the scale, micro-economics comprised the familiar Marshallian *partial* analysis of individual markets in isolation from the rest of the economy. Again, the same assumptions held - perfect competition, profit-maximization, increasing costs - but the object in this case was not to determine the conditions necessary for the existence of stable equilibrium, but to specify the conditions under which a certain industry (and, hence, the 'representative' firm within it) faced with given demand and cost schedules would be in equilibrium. But, by so confining its scope, the partial approach inevitably laid itself open to comparison with the 'mere facts' of observation. Those facts usually contradicted the theory, as had been shown by Piero Sraffa, Alleyn Young and Joan Robinson, to name the most remarkable among others. De-

spite increasing insistence, a reluctant profession refused to admit
that the very concept – let alone assumption – of perfect competition could no longer be defended, and that, henceforth, oligopolistic or monopolistic competition had to be accepted as the rule,[55]
so far as manufacturing (and increasingly finance) are concerned.

When under pressure, the neoclassicals (and in micro-economics
this embraces both the liberal Keynesians and the Friedmanites)
assert[56] that:

1. the modern criticism is old-hat;

2. it can be accommodated with what Solow would call 'consensus'
(and I, neoclassical) economics;

3. 'any recent Ph.D. from MIT would embed it [the existence of
a dichotomy of the economy between a planning (oligopolistic) and
market (competitive) sector] in a model which takes account of
trade and mobility between the two sectors'[57] – I wish some recent
Ph.D. would construct such a model which actually works and can
be used; unfortunately they are busy on other important matters;

4. the planning sector is smaller than, e.g., Galbraith pretends;

5. there is no evidence that the oligopolistic portion is sacrificing
profit for growth – though it is obvious that the sharpness of
competition has been blunted;

6. it is not true that risks push corporations to planning because of
the immensity of investment. Risks, according to Tobin, existed,
say, in railways and shipping in the old days. But railway building
is not exactly a free competitive market and the owners (especially
in the US) secured immense land grants to minimize risks. They
still had many of the losses and failures which modern corporate
planning seeks to avoid.

None of these objections seems valid. It is not true that oligopoly
in services (especially finance) is not increasing. Whoever the price
takers are, they take prices strongly influenced by the price leaders
of the oligopolist sector: a central part of Galbraith's argument
relates to the unequal terms of trade between what he terms the
planning sector and the market sector. Nor is it safe to neglect the
ever-increasing capital intensity of production, that is capital at
risk per unit of output.

Disregard of the problems posed by the growing importance of
single decision-making units with their own psychological bias is

another weakness of the conventional style of 'scientific' (apersonal) economics based on mechanical, determinate interrelationships. In that completely static and perfect system, in which all adaptation has been performed, nothing ever changes, the past runs into the future. Absurdly, comparative static analysis assumes that 'all other things are equal' and that in economics 'bygones are bygones'. These assumptions are as foolish and damaging as Say's were. In real economic life the relationship between an initiating disturbance and its consequent effects is complex, partly indeterminate, and quite likely to be different every time. It cannot be stressed too often that the immediate historical antecedents will have a most important influence in the world of concentrated economic power. Reactions between individual strong countries and individual strong firms can no longer be disregarded. Only a case-by-case analysis, done with flair and a profound awareness of history, can do much to improve understanding and policy. It is hopeless to try to build a cumulative structure of durable generalizations, each based on a limited set of observations at some past time.

Why does such sterile argument survive? There seem to be two basic reasons. To recognize that micro-economics must now deal with a world of pervasive oligopoly and chronic instability would threaten some basic ideological defences of the *laissez-faire* system, and (worse, perhaps) it would threaten the whole rosy dream of a pure, cumulative, objective, non-political science. In short the extraordinary *micro-economic counter-revolution* was stimulated by the fact that the *micro-economic revolution* represented an *even greater threat to the profession* than did the Keynesian attack on *macro-economics*. This could not have happened in an intellectual discipline with any pretensions to genuine scientific method. But despite a flood of empirical work establishing the compelling character of the new approach, the 'consensus economists' still refuse to incorporate these fundamental historical developments into their general body of economic theory. One of the many ill effects of that is the continuing failure to understand the nature of contemporary inflation.

10. The growing fissure

The fissure which opened with the neoclassical response to Marxian economics grew steadily deeper and more complex as the intellectual integrity and practical relevance of Walrasian general equilibrium theory and of the Quantity Theory of Money were shattered by the experience of the Depression, and as a consequence of the Sraffa-Robinson and Keynesian revolutions.

For the time being the cluster of neoclassical factions has won, in the sense that it commands many of the major journals and academic departments, and can fairly claim to represent 'majority', if not 'consensus', economics. Yet its real scientific power is as poor or counterproductive as ever. The clash between the explanations of economic phenomena at the micro- as against the macro-level is as glaring as ever.[58] This incapacity to achieve an integrated analysis of economic life is at the root of the most important of all problems confronting policy-makers recently, that of cost-inflation. The conventionally taught economic theory is still largely inadequate as a basis for short- or medium-term policy-making; and its protagonists still do not understand why a generally acceptable set of criteria for policy-making cannot possibly be evolved on the basis of the conventional type of deductive economics.

That is as true of the neoclassical Keynesians as of the neoclassical monetarists. Ironically, it is currently helping the monetarists to seize power from the Keynesians. For twenty-five years or so after the Second World War the 'neoclassical Keynesian synthesis' seemed to explain and also to assure full employment. Both claims may have been too sanguine; the high average levels of employment through those years may have owed at least as much to the postwar half-life of direct controls and their accompanying psychology, then to the increase of arms expenditure and the export of capital by the US. Whatever the causes, unemployment ceased to be regarded as a central problem of economics. That may have been a mistake: there is a sense in which what we now suffer from is a failure of prevailing theories and policies to explain or control 'full employment disequilibrium'. But it is more usually perceived as the problem of inflation; and just as the failure with unemployment discredited the neoclassical doctrines of the 1930s, so the undoubted failure with inflation has discredited the neoclassical Keynesian doctrines in the 1970s. But why should that failure turn the profession back to the worst follies of the 1920s? Some reactionary social and business and media pressures may help to explain it, but it also reflects the old, blinding yearning for a pure deductive science like physics rather than an open, uncertain, practical art like politics.

But however pure its aspirations, economics has massive political effects. The highly unsatisfactory state of economic theory is far from being a matter purely for academic shame and concern. The history of despair, revolution, hatred and war which marked the first half of this century reflects only too plainly the destructive potency of this objective, pseudo-scientific body of theory, which misled policy-makers over and over again.

Since the Second World War, policy-makers, more wary perhaps than before, have been deluged beneath a flood of confusing and contradictory advice on matters of general economic, fiscal and monetary policy. Yet the so-called general models on which this advice is usually based have important features in common: their underlying assumptions about the delicate relationships obtaining between the various sectors and phenomena of economic life are mostly irrelevant or unconscionably naïve. Moreover, with complete disregard for the importance of historical and sociological diversity, it is claimed to be within the competence of these models to analyse and predict correctly the economic parameters and variables at work within a variety of countries characterized by widely different social relationships and motivations. But in practice they cannot even keep up with changes of system within the North Atlantic societies for which they were designed.

Admittedly the dynamism of this limited area has permeated a large portion of the globe. But, as we now know, the complacency with which *laissez-faire* capitalism was expounded, especially by its economist-flag bearers, was not vindicated. The system as such has not been stable; it has not produced equality, whether nationally or internationally; it has done little or nothing to mitigate the privileged position of the richer areas by a more equitable international distribution of wealth. There has been no automatic tendency for countries (nor regions within countries) of unequal economic strength to become more equal merely through the mechanism of trade or growth. Only through political pressure and struggle - following the historical example of the domestic social development of the advanced countries of today - have the economically less developed countries been able to achieve any material progress. But such advances as have been made are very recent; their stability and endurance have yet to be tested; they have costs in internal inequality and political instability; above all they owe very little to orthodox professional teaching about the means to national growth or international equality.

CHAPTER FOUR

Evaluating Policy

1. Welfare and economic welfare

In the previous chapter we discussed, in a general historical context, the failure of conventional economics to assist in policy-making, and some of the general reasons for it. In the following chapters we shall look in more detail at some of the fundamental, often implicit, assumptions that underlie current economic analysis, and at their effects on the practical advice which economists offer.

The problem of evaluating the effects on social welfare, or utility or whatever you term it, of changes – either spontaneous or induced by policy measures – has a long history in Anglo–Saxon countries. It dates back at least to the utilitarian philosophy, with its optimism about the harmony of economic interests. Marx then disputed the harmony. Reacting against Marx, the marginalist theorists of the market economy created an awkward problem for themselves: if the utility of consuming a given commodity decreases as its availability increases it would be plausible to believe the same of income. But if income was subject to diminishing marginal utility, would it not follow that total social utility could be increased by redistributing purchasing power more equally than it was distributed by market forces with land and capital in private ownership?

The profession did not respond in the obvious way by referring to historical and sociological experience, to argue (for example) that confiscation or heavy redistributive taxation would endanger political stability or economic dynamism. Instead they declared that the absolute utility which people derived from their incomes was not measurable. Some admitted some weaker (ordinal) comparability of utility ('greater or less than') but most of the profession eventually concluded that interpersonal comparisons were quite unscientific – 'Economists *qua* economists must not give advice involving a redistribution of income.' Such questions should be excluded from the science of objective or positive economics.

Only personal choice between baskets of goods could be explained. This convenient discrimination is open to a number of fundamental objections, and from the 1930s they were expressed with suitable force in Myrdal's famous analysis, Professor Kaldor's *jeu d'esprit* and Professor Lerner's more ponderous work.[1]

Astonishingly, Myrdal's work was not translated until after the war, but it was then followed and developed by Paul Streeten, Graaf and Kenneth Arrow.[2] By then one would have thought that an honourable burial of the neo-Marshallian approach to welfare had been performed – it certainly would have been in any real science. Yet much of the current output of 'positive economics' seems to be based on the uncritical acceptance of that neoclassical position and on the construction of the 'empirical' relationships thought to buttress it. This is especially clear in respect of micro-problems – those concerned with 'single' markets. Even the basic critique of the welfare-economic implications of imperfections, of divergences between social and private costs (external economies and diseconomies), tends to be disregarded or at best 'absorbed' by acceptance in principle and neglect in practice.[3] This neglect sometimes takes the form of arbitrarily modifying, in planning exercises, the quantitative relationships which result from existing market forces, through the introduction of so-called shadow prices or artificial weights, thus giving the impression that it is possible to produce morally acceptable, yet *precise*, answers to social questions.

Even less notice is taken of the secondary repercussions of changes, repercussions which either because of their nature, or because of the importance of the sectors of the economy that they affect, such as for example the labour market, should never be disregarded.[4] Thus the economist increasingly slips back into the language and approach antedating not merely Keynes, but even Alleyn Young and Piero Sraffa. Any qualms are settled by the substitution of an irredeemably woolly general equilibrium system, which could only be applicable to primitive non-industrial societies, for the Marshallian partial market analysis which, under certain restricted circumstances, might yield valid answers.[5] In view of the treatment accorded to Professor Galbraith's published work,[6] it seems that it is still necessary to go through these traditional rigmaroles. The tenacity and pervasiveness of neoclassical theory is a curious and insidious phenomenon in the history of economic analysis: by understanding its implications, both political and sociological, it will perhaps be possible to explain its current undiminished influence.

2. The criterion of excellence

For economists to be able to give not only unequivocal and determinate, but also quantitative advice, it is essential that two sets of conditions be fulfilled:

1. a universally valid and acceptable measuring-rod must exist, by means of which the aims of economic activity and policy – that is, complex psychological phenomena such as satisfaction, happiness or pleasure or avoidance of pain and effort and their gradations – can be transformed into 'objective' magnitudes, and which at the same time takes into account the side-effects of change in terms of costs – pollution, exhaustion of resources – and benefits; and

2. the economic system must automatically ensure the maximization of certain of these magnitudes and the minimization of others – that is, in responding to the current and future wishes of the community (as expressed in the pattern of demand and the rate of saving) market forces must be shown to be able to establish the dominance of least-cost techniques of production and the most economic allocation and use of resources, not the least among (and by) different members of the family, tribe, nation or indeed the world – whichever group we are investigating.

Such 'objectivization' and aggregation are the province of Welfare Economics. Yet only if both sets of conditions are met can any objective significance be attached to the sort of popular shorthand expressions – thought to be scientific – propagated by the Austro-Chicago school among the more articulate classes, such as that a commodity has 'stood the test of the market', that is, that its production – including, by implication, its method of production – is in some acceptable sense 'optimal' or 'a good thing'.[7]

As we shall see, the theory of consumers' sovereignty is not meaningful in any realistic sense: this view, together with the notion of a decentralized system in which production is optimally, yet impersonally, organized through the interplay of market forces, can no longer be sustained as a plausible reflection of the real world. This is not to say that the analysis on which advice is based does not require a command of applied economics and skilled techniques. It is to say that technical knowledge alone does not sanction the advice. Political judgements have to value and rank the importance of the various economic, social or political factors at issue.[8] A further complication arises from the fact that values are not immutable; although values influence policies, these in turn will influence values.[9]

In the present context it should again be stressed that the justification for employing these techniques depends upon the implications of such advice lying on the same political plane; on the possibility of distinguishing and measuring *all*, and not merely some, of the relevant influences and their relationships, and on the stability and reversibility of these relationships; on the adequacy of the methods adopted to establish them; and finally on the reliability of the observations. On all these grounds, as we have seen, grave doubts arise. In practical terms the requirements are impossible. Important policy decisions will inevitably have repercussions beyond their immediate aims and will therefore raise questions about offsetting policies. Thus, the problem of choosing a point on the trade-off between (say) unemployment and inflation cannot be viewed in a purely economic perspective, without regard to its implications for income distribution, or for the unquantifiable loss resulting from the suffering caused by unemployment and (for an even larger number) by the fear of unemployment (see e.g. the very sensitive exploration of the experience and social effects of unemployment published in *The Times* during September 1976). Any such trade-off will be influenced by the given historical situation and its antecedents; but that in turn will be unstable through time, because the very act of choice will influence the political views and values determining the problem, and probably the anticipation systems of the various classes which make up the community. For example, witness the increasingly impatient insistence on employing orthodox methods which have proven ineffectual if not worse. The impact of monetarism has been astonishing.

3. Welfare and economics

Let us turn to the first of the problems of measuring economic success.

Until recently, economists – and for that matter politicians – did not question the nature of the relationship between production and the 'welfare' or 'satisfaction' towards which socio-economic organization and policy are allegedly directed. Explicitly or implicitly, increased national output – valued in terms of the prices ruling in some base period – was taken as certain evidence of increasing welfare: it seemed only common sense.[10] With a few plausible assumptions, then, an imposing analytical structure could be erected, purporting to provide mutually consistent theories of demand and production on the basis of which the economist could give determinate answers on questions of policy.

It was recognized, of course, that in the sphere of material human affairs the relationship between ends and means is far from precise or simple: a fundamental decision about values is needed. Hence, in the 'Western' world certainly, the ultimate dignity and happiness of the individual has been acclaimed as a basic principle. But men do not live on their ultimate dignity; they are members of society and as such they are also the means of keeping themselves alive. The individual as consumer, receiving aesthetic and material pleasures, must at the same time participate – directly or indirectly – in their production. It is in the integration of these opposing aspects of material existence in conformity with social sanctions that the possibility for contradiction and disharmony arises.

Here the 'scientific method' came to the rescue of the ambitions of the profession. The many-sidedness of social life makes it impossible – it was claimed – to analyse, let alone solve, all its problems at once. If the economist, *qua* economist, is to be able to discover some order in the chaos he observes, drastic simplification is necessary and therefore justified. The multiplicity of human motives and relationships must be stripped of any 'non-economic' connotations; complications noticed by specialists in other fields of social research, such as sociology or psychology, must be disregarded. It is easy to argue that modesty is the touchstone of the true scientist: let him tackle the problems for which he is qualified, that is, those in his own field.

The peculiar character of 'economic' problems (as defined) has, of course, been an important, if not decisive, influence on the method by which this process of simplification (or abstraction) has been effected in the theory of consumers' choice and welfare. By comparison with other areas of social inquiry, economics appeared to enjoy a particular advantage, in that the relationships between the variables with which it was concerned seemed at least super-ficially to lend themselves to quantitative expression; as such it could claim kinship with the natural sciences. The monetary medium and the price system, for instance, are singular institutions; with their help – so it was held – it is possible to state positively not merely whether X is greater or less than Y, but by how much. The pure logic of choice between different goods and services, and between different techniques of production, lends itself admirably to formal and rigorous treatment. Moreover, it has been claimed that certain branches of higher mathematics, such as the theory of games, can be used to explain, or at least simulate, the strategy of bargaining between powerful interest groups.[11]

Economics, then, it was confidently hoped, would be able to rise above the 'lower' social studies on to a strictly scientific level. For this to be done, however, and for economists then to be able to provide definite answers to problems of choice between different social and political policies, it is necessary to assume that *general* welfare is somehow uniquely related to something called *economic* welfare. The latter is, itself, susceptible of measurement, that measure being the value of production at the market prices of a base year.[12] In other words, the enjoyment or satisfaction thus defined which individuals obtain from consumption of goods and services and supplies for their maintenance and expansion is taken as the final criterion of the general welfare of the group, the country and, in international trade theory, the world. This procedure im-plicitly and illicitly assumes that the consumers' tastes and potential demands are given and not manipulated.

The drastic nature of these simplifying assumptions – which determines the character of economics as applied to the real world – is, of course, usually admitted in the introductory chapters of economic treatises. The momentous importance of the abstractions is fully acknowledged, and the qualifications and severe limita-tions of any policy conclusions are then duly discussed. We are informed in later chapters that these will gradually be removed in order to restore relevance and applicability to any subsequent recommendations. This has not yet happened. Indeed it is the qualifications which rob the refined manipulations of much of their applicability.[13] As we shall see, they involve the nature of individual consumers' choice itself and its relationship with other aspects of social life – that is, the position of the individual within the community and the stage of development and character of that community. In all these respects the conventional approach to welfare is open to serious objection.[14] Welfare, like liberty, must be – indeed, it is – indivisible.[15]

The late Professor Pigou himself, the founder of modern welfare economics, provides a typical example of this approach. He begins, modestly enough, by confessing that: 'a general investigation of all the groups by which welfare thus conceived [that is, general welfare] may be affected would constitute a task so enormous and complicated as to be quite impracticable....'[16] The course to be followed, however, is quickly mapped out:

The one obvious instrument of measurement in social life is money. Hence the range of our enquiry becomes restricted to that part of social welfare that can be brought directly, or indirectly, into relation with the measuring-rod of money. This part of welfare may be called economic welfare ... Though no precise boundary between economic and non-economic welfare exists, yet the test of accessibility to a money measure serves well enough to set up a rough distinction. Economic welfare, as loosely defined by this test, is the subject-matter of economic science. The purpose of this volume is to study certain important groups of causes that affect economic welfare in actual modern societies.[17]

Pigou admits and enumerates some grounds why 'economics will not serve for a barometer or index of total welfare',[18] but rejects these objections with the engaging reflection that, after all, 'full guidance for practice requires ... capacity to carry out quantitative and not merely qualitative analysis.'[19] In other words, in order to make use of his own formal conclusions he asserts, without more ado, that 'the burden of proof lies upon those who hold that the presumption [that qualitative conclusions about the effect of an economic cause upon economic welfare will hold good also of the effect on total welfare] should be overruled.'[20]

Nor did the intellectually seductive appeal of the market mechanism diminish. A generation later, one of its staunchest advocates, Professor Scitovsky, could still write: 'The usefulness of the theory lies not so much in the new light that it sheds on the consumer's behaviour as in the fact that it *proves* market prices to be an *expression of consumers' marginal* preferences.'[21] A clearer plea for the formulation of policy on the basis of current prices could hardly be asked for – that is, if we disregard all the issues raised by its impact on the distribution of income and its possible side-effects. Yet Professor Scitovsky himself specifically disclaimed any such ambitions by modestly averring: 'The theory of consumer's behaviour ... is *purely descriptive* and describes the behaviour of the rational consumer ... This means that the conformity of the consumer's market behaviour to his preference is the *assumption* we start out with and *not something that can be proved or disproved by our analysis.*'[22] The daring leap from economic welfare to total welfare, so hazardous but so necessary if practical advice is to be tendered on a seemingly scientific basis, has scarcely been questioned. Yet the whole edifice of neoclassical value- or welfare-theory appears on closer inspection to rest on surprisingly flimsy foundations.[23, 24]

Objections to this procedure occur on three interrelated levels.

1. *Consumption.* There are in effect two interdependent considerations here. First, the conventional assumptions upon which the theory of *individual* consumer demand is based are increasingly at variance with observation, and implausible. Secondly, individuals do not exist in isolation, but live in communities in which the distribution of economic power, and the social formation of collective and individual wants and tastes, may be far from desirable.

2. *Production.* An individual, as we have already stressed, is not merely a consumer, nor does he live in isolation. He is also a producer, in which capacity he is even more closely connected with other members of society. In particular, his interests as a producer will increasingly predominate with growing prosperity, increasing unionization and (latterly) with the possibility of extending the role of labour participation in managerial decision-making.

Dependence on the price mechanism alone, however, will lead to the neglect of certain moral, social and political values connected with the productive activity of the individual, and which are essential from the point of view of the 'good life' of the community.

3. *The price system and communal demand.* The price mechanism is severely limited in the sense that prices, as they appear in the market and form the basis for measuring national output, may not

correctly reflect the desirability of certain goods, services or amenities which it is only possible to articulate at the communal level and in the very long run.[25]

These problems and complications – to which economists make passing obeisance, only to ignore them at later crucial stages – arise, first of all, from the fact that the modern consumer is a very different sort of person from what he is taken to be in formal economics. This, in turn, stems from a tendency among economists, in common with other conservative academics, to disavow the existence of modern psychology. Further, there is the unavoidable fact that an increase in economic welfare – that is in consumption – has to be procured by additional effort. Short introductory allusions – such as to Marshall's noble servant girl – do not exhaust this problem. Identical expenditures might yield different results which in some cases debase, and in other cases elevate, the quality of life and the 'quality of people'.

Increases in economic welfare, as measured in the conventional way, may well be offset or more than offset by a deterioration of the conditions – in the widest sense, including the character of the social system, security of employment, etc. – in which man in his capacity as producer has to supply the goods and services that he consumes.[27] For example if an increase in income is dependent on a continuous increase in consciously felt 'needs' – that is, if the feeling of sufficiency or surplus can never be created – this alone severely qualifies the psychological value of the increase.[28] Conventional measurement moreover conceals the fact that different modes of production have different, and often permanently damaging, effects on the environment in which man in his role as consumer lives. Traditional economics, in its facile celebration of consumers' sovereignty, has actually subordinated consumers' interests to those of producers in this area. Whatever ills attend economic pursuits, whether pollution, dereliction of land or the deterioration of urban and rural amenity, should be disregarded as the producers merely acted in obedience to the sovereign wishes of consumers as the consumers 'voted' with their dollars in the marketplace.[29]

The existence of this problem – despite Professor Galbraith's persistent campaign – was not until recently very generally acknowledged. Similarly the political pressure on governments to provide employment, even at some cost in slowing down 'progress', has only lately and suddenly made any headway – and will in all probability manage to cause net harm by its appeal to monolithic solutions. While short-term solutions argue for the maintenance of existing workplaces, longer-term solutions demand so rapid an expansion of employment as to more than offset the loss of work-places due to the rationalization of techniques.[30]

This fundamental difficulty is quite distinct from that which arises from the fact that changes in income distribution may well vitiate any 'advance', in the sense that some consumers often contribute little or nothing to production, whereas workers may receive little or nothing of the increase in output. (We shall deal in the next section with the conventional escape through the so-called compensation principle.) In the modern world it is also increasingly difficult to accept, without qualification, that the pattern of output is determined by consumer demand which is not only sovereign, but autonomous, that is, that tastes are not susceptible to persuasion or demonstration.

4. The conflict of criteria

We have to accept the existence of a number of aims or criteria as a basis for the performance of the economic system; yet it is essential to recognize that these may, and in certain cases will, conflict, and so will the social interests which they represent. The choice of these criteria, therefore, is itself a political value judge-ment. That, it must be emphasized, includes any decision to measure welfare by a single criterion, or by a measurable criterion, or by an 'objective' criterion – because any of these includes a political decision to neglect other criteria. Nevertheless there is no end to the orthodox ways of denying or ignoring or misrepresenting this fundamental political fact.

In certain restricted situations we can measure satisfaction pretty well in terms of money: but on a larger canvas our measuring-rod breaks down, and we have to be content to treat the stream of aggregate real income as an 'objective counterpart' or indicator of the positive elements of eco-nomic welfare. This, too, there are difficulties about measuring, but they are by no means fatal to the usefulness of the concept. *Other things being unchanged*, net economic welfare will be greater (a) the larger this stream of aggregate real income, (b) the more equally (to speak roughly) it is distributed among persons, (c) the more steadily it flows, (d) the less the aggregate dissatisfactions at the cost of which it is set in motion. About all these factors there is a great deal to be said, and not until it has been said do we reach the frontiers of economic science.[31]

Sir Dennis Robertson eventually recognized, however, that somewhere along the line his criteria may conflict. Appearing to become impatient with these shackles, self-imposed in the attempt to be scientifically comprehensive and politically realistic, he freed himself by a short cut so abrupt that he seems not altogether to have understood its implications:

> But I should say too that in their [Samuelson's and Little's] preoccupation with distributional considerations they might on occasion, if we followed their advice, be causing us to let the best be the enemy of the good; while the defenders, Hicks and Co., in their dichotomy between the size of the real social income and its distribution and their primacy of emphasis on the former, have got hold of something solid and sensible which they may find it difficult to tidy up but which it would be regrettable if they were to abandon. For it enshrines a basic truth which any group, and especially a national group in an acutely competitive world, will neglect at its peril.[32]

It remained only for him to conclude, having finally subscribed to the primacy of the single criterion of national income (output):

> ... that it is the primary business of the economist to move on the economic plane as thus conceived, and that there is plenty for him to do there. But of course if we want to be statesmen, at however humble a level, then in the end we must send for the prophet and the priest, or conjure them up out of our own insides.[33]

That most economists, including men of the genius of Marshall, appear to have found this a satisfactory state of affairs is not perhaps as astonishing as it may seem. The 'purer' the theory the more captivated were they by it. Not only did it provide them with the necessary grounds for holding that they could give unequivocal and determinate answers to problems of policy, without at the same time abandoning their Olympian level of mathematical abstraction; it was also instrumental in establishing the principle that to 'do nothing' constituted the 'optimal' policy, thereby reassuring the élite that their privileged position in society, far from being simply economically desirable, was also morally justified.[34] Needless to say, this neoclassical Cambridge tradition was (and still is) strongly accepted by Conservative and Liberal economists, and, more surprisingly, by those economic thinkers who in the 1950s largely succeeded in revising the policy of the Labour Party in Britain, the so-called Gaitskellites or 'moderates'. They did not understand that, in so doing, they were opting, in all essentials, for a basically liberal solution to the problems of economic and social advancement.[35] In the early 1980s this led to a split in the Party.

The flimsiness of the theoretical structure was not questioned: to do so would have been to question the traditional basis of economic science. Few economists care to do that. The same hostility which first greeted Veblen is now encountered by Galbraith and Myrdal; and in professional circles their achievements still meet with silence, although this is testimony enough to the profound uneasiness that the raising of such awkward and fundamental issues has produced. At least one eminent representative of neoclassical orthodoxy, Sir John Hicks, has conceded that the 'economic welfarism' to which he himself had been so noted a contributor must be abandoned.[36]

5. Kinds of criteria

The kinds of criteria that might be relevant in deciding on policies intended to increase welfare, beyond the narrow confines of consumption measured in conventional terms, may be grouped into two categories: those which pertain to some measure of the ability of goods and services to provide satisfaction, and those which relate to the conditions associated with the supply of those goods and services. Under the first would be listed, for instance, (a) a high level of output and, more particularly, of consumption; and (b) a high rate of growth. The second category would comprise (c) a more egalitarian – that is, more socially just – distribution of income; (d) security – as found in the maintenance of full employment, and social services to deal with cases of individual or family hardship; (e) wider social considerations, such as increasing leisure – including a gradual decline in the need for disagreeable, and an increase in self-fulfilling, work – although this might require some sacrifice in consumption or of its potential increase; a sense of individual participation in the productive process, and an awareness of the impact of present economic activity on the environment in the broadest sense, and its consequences for the future; and freedom and decentralization of power.

On any reasonable definition there are obvious conflicts between these criteria – although many writers in their more polemical works introduce definitions of some of them which are tailored to suit certain preconceived notions about other equally political criteria. Thus, a number of economists would define full employment as a state in which prices are just stable, no matter what the rate of unemployment happened to be: in such circumstances less unemployment would simply mean 'over-full' employment. This seems a good dialectical or political device, but it cannot claim any scientific merit.[37] It also ignores the vital social role of full employment in ending the master-servant relationship: full employment is desirable *per se*. Thus when economists talk of running the economy at *less* pressure, this entails the subjection of the majority of the working population to the *greater* social and economic pressures implicit in the restoration of the old command position. This means a decisive but quite unquantifiable subtraction from the welfare of a great many.

There is no doubt, however, that in the 1970s the problem of price stability – the problem of inflation – had assumed by far the greatest political importance among all contemporary economic issues. It is often considered as a factor important because liable to interfere with social justice and to militate against greater equality in income distribution. This is no longer its only significance. It is its political implications and its interference with the operation of the economic system that are increasingly at the heart of the matter. It sets classes and occupations against each other, and as each wishes to protect itself against the effects of rising prices, the spiral accelerates. The substance of the inflation problem is not the concern of this chapter. But it has elevated price stability, in itself, as another criterion of welfare: one which both conflicts with other criteria and is itself the subject of substantial conflicts of interest.

Nor does that exhaust the list of criteria. To be a member of a dynamically expanding community is in itself a factor making for confidence and satisfaction. The individual knows that he is wanted and, as he grows older, is likely to be given increasing scope – if only he is capable of fulfilling the requirements. This feeling of optimism, this conviction that the trend is upwards, would make up for much current hardship and sacrifice. Much of the discussion of the problem of development ignores this point.

It is equally necessary to include the desire not to be too economical – that is, the desire to be able to afford waste as an alternative to the effort needed in being economical. This, as against the more obvious manifestation of leisure, has often been disregarded because it conflicts with the traditional definition of economics.

Last, but perhaps most important, it is essential to consider freedom in some sense, and decentralization of power, as separate criteria. Both might be legitimate ends of a social system and it is by no means certain that they will not conflict.

The list does not end there. But it is already long enough to reinforce the point that the criteria can readily conflict, and that *any* choice, or use of *any* of them, is irreducibly a political act.

CHAPTER FIVE

The Individual and the Group

In this chapter we shall discuss those criteria conventionally applied in the analysis of individual consumer behaviour and welfare. The position of the individual will then be discussed in the context of his membership of a group, in terms both of his capacity as a consumer and of his function in the productive process. The question of the excellence of the market mechanism in impersonally guiding the economy in a modern industrial world will be treated in the following chapter.

1. The individual as consumer

The theory of consumers' sovereignty in its present form was originally formulated more than a hundred years ago in rebuttal of what was considered to be Marx's destructive use of classical analysis. It accorded to the consumer the supreme function of ensuring that, under conditions of perfect competition and the guiding impetus of the profit motive, the flow of goods and services coming on to the market would be produced by the most efficient (least-cost) means. Professors Menger in Austria, Walras in Switzerland, Jevons in Britain and Clark in the United States arrived independently at much the same solution to the problem.

The venerable classical theory, which explained the exchange values or prices of commodities by the labour necessary to produce them, served in the hands of Marx to prove that the owning classes robbed the workers of the fruits of their labour: while the proletariat got only enough for subsistence, the difference between this pittance and the full value of its work was pocketed by the capitalist. No better defence could have been devised against these charges than the theory now called 'neoclassical', which explains how demand is determined by the urgency of consumers' wants and how land, labour, capital and entrepreneurship receive, with perfect impartiality, neither more nor less than what they have contributed to the productive process. Harmony of interests and complete social justice were thus assured. 'Equilibrium' – the balance between supply and demand, both in the market for commodities and in the market for the factors of production required for their creation – became the supreme goal. Happily its achievement was automatic – unless the beneficent interaction of these natural forces were interfered with. But in reality, the view of man as an individual consumer affords the economist far less scope for objective judgement and advice than the profession has been ready to admit.

We have already seen that the ability to give definite policy advice from this viewpoint depends on the acceptability of the weighted market valuation of the sum total of goods and services sold as an index of welfare for the individual and for the community. But this could be the case. only if the consumption of such goods and services were the only source of satisfaction and happiness – that is, if man could be said to exhaust his being in his role as consumer of the commodities he buys; if his desire at the margin could be held somehow to equal his satisfaction; and if his income were judged to be correct by some general consensus of political opinion.

Nor is this all. A consumer's behaviour must not be impulsive; he must be assumed to have considered all the possible choices open to him and to have fully understood their implication. The consumer must not only be rational, but his tastes must be constant; any change in tastes would make the kind of comparisons discussed here impossible in principle. Hence, this 'ideal' consumer does not explore new possibilities; nor can he be influenced by persuasive advertising. In particular, he must not be influenced in his own choice by the consumption, conspicuous or otherwise, of others. In other words, in sociological parlance, the consumer must be entirely 'inner-directed' – an 'island of utility'.

The assumptions underlying such an absurdly restricted view of human behaviour have only to be stated for its potentially misleading and damaging consequences, through its influence on policy decisions, to be appreciated. The conventional theory of consumers' behaviour was developed specifically for the analysis of marginal adjustments in consumption; since actual behaviour is most unlikely to be of this kind, but of the nature of *grosso modo* choices, its practical applications will be severely limited, if not trivial.

If the 'consistent consumer' turns out to be a very rare bird indeed, the objects of his desires are, if anything, still rarer. Not only must all those goods and services which he may want to consume be available in infinitely divisible quantities, but there must be no strong complementarity or linkage between ranges of goods; only then will it be feasible to purchase the goods in any combination. Each item within any combination must represent a competitive alternative, such that the consumer should be able to choose between them on the basis of marginal considerations – that is, he must always be free to buy more of one good, say carrots, and less of another, say turnips.[1] The range of effective choice open to the consumer should constitute 'equivalences', and not alternative, mutually exclusive, *ways of life*.[2]

Of course it would be ludicrous to imagine that any actual consumer conforms to this pattern. Such assumptions about consumers' behaviour can no longer be defended as plausible – indeed, with an increasing proportion of consumption expenditure being devoted to durable goods, they are no longer even meaningful. Material abundance, technical progress and fashion: all these are an undeniable part of the real world. Yet as soon as they are acknowledged, how much of the conventional picture of consumers' behaviour remains? The artificiality of the theoretical concept is beset with doubts. How long is it permissible to take tastes as unchanged by time and experience and to recall past pleasures as the basis upon which to choose consistently between present possibilities? Can any significance be attached to the assumption that people's tastes in cars or refrigerators are unchanged as between successive moments of choice that may be years apart? Over how long a period indeed can we regard memory as providing an immediate basis of choice? Clearly, any belief in a simple relationship between the individual and his satisfaction on the one hand, and his income in the shape of a collection of goods and services in growing abundance and variety on the other, must be drastically revised.[3]

If it is true that consumption, within narrow limits, is determined by one's environment, but at the same time influenced by the consumption of others and varied according to the dictates of fashion, then patently the market mechanism cannot be regarded as effectively regulating the satisfaction of wants. Needs, *per se*, are recurrent. When incomes are low they comprise food, clothing and shelter, but little else. Such wants are comprehensive and clearly felt. As one's income increases, however, they become less regularly felt and less distinct; their recurrence, moreover, is less 'natural', in the sense of their being independent of one's mode of life or of fashion. The obsolescence of a 'toilet', the change from crinoline to bustle in the nineteenth century, or the continuously changing lines of the modern car: none of these reflects wear and tear or mechanical defect, but rather the dynamic of fashion – the desire to cut a figure.

Changing tastes, however, are themselves in part a reflection of changing 'needs', but the nature of these changes renders quite unrealistic the received concept of the sovereign consumer who, surveying with detachment the whole field of his consciously, genuinely and spontaneously felt wants, adjusts his demand accordingly. As incomes increase, needs – desires rather – become increasingly directed at goods which are not merely indivisible, but are strongly complementary to each other; the rational allocation of expenditure at the margin between a variety of *competing* goods represents a steadily decreasing proportion of the total. In other words, the importance or urgency of *choice* itself diminishes, while individual acts of expenditure have far-reaching implications. A large car does not fit into a small garage, yet a large garage would not be compatible with a certain type of house.

The legend springs to mind of the Voivode of Walachia, who received from his Muslim overlord a diamond button. In consequence the Voivode had to buy successively a coat, new suits, new horses and stable, new carriages, and a new house, surrounded by a large park with a lake, and was ultimately constrained to grant pensions to his courtiers to do likewise. So impoverished was the Voivode by the button that in the end he betrayed his Sultan for money from Vienna and, being discovered, was sewn into a cowhide sack and thrown into the Bosphorus. And, even if his story does end on a less spectacular note, is Mr Marquand's anti-hero in *Point of No Return* any better off? Having won his promotion to Assistant-Deputy-Vice-President of a bank, he finds more than the entire increase in his salary mortgaged in advance by social pressures demanding new expenditures – by no means all of which are satisfying. After weeks of excitement and frustration about the outcome of the struggle, ruefully he contemplates his victory in terms of his new suburb, new house, new club and new car – all more expensive than the last. The organization-man (and his wife), engaged in a rat-race against other organization-men, has little objective freedom of choice. Anything odd about his behaviour or tastes would brand him as eccentric, or something equally damaging to his career. Even his choice of car is only marginally free: discretion as to style (possibly) and as to colour (certainly) are permissible – but not as to make. He can as little buy a Cadillac or a Rolls-Royce for fear of offending against his President's status symbol as he would wish to be seen driving a Chevrolet or a Vauxhall. The choice that remains, in effect, becomes increasingly as between *ways of life*.

A further point might well be emphasized here. The consumer, far from being omniscient (as he would have to be in order to measure up to his traditional image of rationality and consistency) is largely ignorant of a wide range of relevant technical knowledge and market information. (This is not necessarily a reflection of the increasing technological sophistication of consumer goods, to say nothing of durables; it pertains even to such mundane items as washing powders.) In many cases people do not use the price of an item as an indication of the competitiveness of the seller, to be weighed against other considerations, but rather as a measure of quality. This sort of behaviour makes nonsense of the conventional theory of demand which is still rooted in the myth of perfect (that is, price) competition.[4] Worse, uncertainty about prices – as, for example, in the case of active price-competition between rival supermarkets, with continuous switches in 'bargain offers' – is as likely to be met with irritation and resentment, as greeted as an opportunity for economical shopping. A fixed price rather, promising fixed quality, may exercise a powerful attraction for a growing number of consumers, whose improving standard of life would permit a certain amount of waste. As we shall see, this fact may well explain the sort of policies adopted by some of today's large and sophisticated corporations.

If anything still remains of our traditional concept of the sovereign, rational and consistent consumer, its plausibility is undermined by the fact that, over an increasing range of goods and services, demand is largely created or manipulated by the producer. Save in exceptional circumstances, we must abandon the notion that firms adjust their output in response to the wishes of consumers. Rather it is the reverse. Enormous profits are to be made in assuaging the restlessness, the feeling of dissatisfaction, even un-happiness, which producers themselves create and implant in the mind of consumers through the skilful application of the adver-tiser's 'art'. Thus vast sums are spent on the promotion of a host of, if not intrinsically worthless, at least unnecessary, articles to-wards which the majority of consumers would perhaps otherwise be indifferent. The producer's advantage extends even to items which serve basic needs, such as bread and soap. Here the consu-mer's fancy is channelled towards a particular brand of the good in question. Whether or not a new product – or a specific (or possibly new) model of an age-old product – is the 'best' means of meeting a certain need, when one takes its price into account, appears to be a matter of decreasing significance. It is rather its connotation, its 'image', its impact on other people, the suggestion that mere possession brings with it the promise of social, economic or physical enhancement, which have come to constitute the basic ingredients of the typical advertising campaign. We may perhaps quote a particularly vivid and important example of this phenom-enon:

The modern technique of developing new desires and demands is illustrated by the recent triumphal march of television in the United States. The aim of the new industry was to attract commercial sponsors who would buy time on the programs to advertise their products. To attract them, manufacturers of television sets had to induce people to equip their homes with these sets. Since little could be said about the merits of television programs, the industry has made a supreme effort to win the support of the least experienced, the least critical, consumers – the children. It has succeeded in creating a psychological climate in which the absence of a television set in a home is a humiliating stigma, not only among middle-class families but also among some manual workers.[5]

If some systems create more wants than others, or even than they are able to satisfy, how are they to be judged? As Professor Galbraith has pointed out: 'it can no longer be assumed that welfare is greater at an all-round higher level of production than at a lower one. It may be the same. The higher level of production has, merely, a higher level of want creation necessitating a higher level of want satisfaction.'[6] Should those wants that the system cannot satisfy somehow or other be counted as a negative quantity in the measurement of social wellbeing? Is a system that creates these excessive wants to be judged as inferior to other and differently organized systems, even though productive capacity might be increasing at a 'faster' rate in the former?[7] Or, alternatively, should the creation of wants, the fostering of 'divine discontent' and the continuous 'enlargement of the field of choice', be looked upon as the *camino real* to the superior lifestyle? These are awkward questions, yet these latter interpretations have all at one time or another been offered in solution. Even so, the mere maintenance of an ever-present margin of excessive, but eventually satisfied, wants is by itself not sufficient to sustain this materialistic vision; for how is one to judge whether these newly-created wants are superior or inferior to those already 'within the margin'?

The solution to such an insoluble problem, of course, lies in avoiding it or in demonstrating its irrelevance. In fact this is precisely what has happened. As we have mentioned, the trend is increasingly in the direction of the creation of needs, the fulfilment of which is no longer an independent source of satisfaction. At best their indulgence enhances the pleasure derived from wants already satisfied; at worst, it becomes a necessity if an actual decrease in (psychic) wellbeing is to be avoided (as in the sales technique for TV sets, just quoted). At all events, such purchases have very little to do with rational, autonomous, economic behaviour; rather they are a manifestation of a way of life, and all that that implies in terms of self-esteem and personality. In the world of our fictional anti-hero the question of inferiority or superiority does not arise: free will has been replaced by determinism.

Marshall, of course, had pointed the way out of this difficulty. 'New activities' give rise to 'new wants'.[8] Something spontaneous is involved here, something inherent in economic activity, in 'progress', which it is not the function of the economist to question. Indeed, to hold otherwise would be tantamount to allowing the possibility that the 'man from Whitehall' (or Harvard or Oxbridge for that matter) might know better than other people what is good for them. Hence the intolerable arrogance of which critics of high-powered advertising, such as Veblen and Galbraith, are accused.

At this point one could also invoke the support of Professor F. H. Knight's view that such changes in desires stem from the improvement and education of tastes, which is a basic human social objective. Thus, new tastes, new desires, it is said with perfect justification, need not be inferior to existing ones. After all, education is aimed precisely at such conscious transformation of needs and tastes, at modifying man's innate and antisocial impulses. And some progress is better than none, even if associated with admittedly less desirable elements. In any case, it is very difficult clearly to identify a want in order to distinguish it.[9] But we must distinguish it to be able to say that it is a new want 'created' and not an old want recurring or a latent one which has become conscious. Moreover, even if a want has changed, it may have done so 'legitimately' as the result of individual, uninfluenced, experience with a product, or as the result of legitimate education, of which we are bound to approve as broadening people's horizons. Only if we could exclude all these cases could we condemn those changes in tastes, etc., which result from the use of persuasive advertising and its exploitation of modern psychological insights to foster active discontent or to play on the painful, hidden weaknesses of the consumer's psyche.

Having created a diversion by raising all these legitimate difficulties, the next step is to assert what is obviously true, that there must be genuine improvements in commercial products and that there must be some criteria by which people can distinguish those from the merely meretricious. Anyway, if the abuse becomes too obnoxious, there are well-tried ways in which government regulation can limit the mischief. If there were no such criteria, all changes would have to be condemned, including those which the critics of advertising would be the first to regard as genuine and legitimate in the higher sphere of human endeavour generally.

The confusion then having been made complete, the defendants of the status quo can go on to suggest some interesting refinements in the theory of demand, which obviously fail to come to grips with the basic problem of consumer conditioning, and to conclude happily that all that can be legitimately proposed is a modern, active, form of the Spencerian negative *caveat emptor*. A better education, possibly some government-financed counselling or counter-propaganda, and, for the rest, reliance on the solid common sense of the general public are all that is required. Anything further on this sensitive point would, obviously, open the way for dictators, and we should find ourselves pushed down the road to serfdom just as the *laissez-faire* economists predicted, were the market mechanism tampered with in any way. The plea, therefore, is for a plurality of cultures or systems of wants which might coexist

THE IRRELEVANCE OF CONVENTIONAL ECONOMICS

peacefully side by side, and which, after all, *need* not express any hierarchical social distinctions.

By contrast, the opponents of advertising and *laissez-faire* are accused of wishing to impose a common culture on society, which, by the fact of being imposed, cannot possibly satisfy. Only a freely accepted way of life and system of wants can be really satisfying, according to modern psychological wisdoms.

> The liberalized society is one where men fulfil themselves according to their own view or conception of life – provided, of course, that in doing so they do not interfere with, or upon, the self-fulfilment of others. To achieve this they must be free both of the dictates of established authority and of the subtler but no less effective power of social pressure. Furthermore, they must have free access to the principal ideas evolved in the course of human history concerning the conduct of life...[10]

All this sounds wonderful and noble. But what sense does it really make to say that 'men [should] fulfil themselves according to their own view or conception of life', when the question is that of the mass conditioning of consumers by powerful vested interests? The problem in the modern non-Soviet State is no longer one of dragooning by the State; it is the contrast between the unorganized, unskilled, unadvised mass of consumers existing in small family units, and the vast array of corporate power unaccountable in any direct way to anyone. How can one say that men should be free of the 'dictates of established authority', that is, the State, and of the 'subtler but no less effective power of social pressure', unless one can envisage the imposition of far-reaching controls over the economic power wielded by the advertising interests through the private ownership of the means of communication?

The problem of education, of enabling people to have 'free access to the principal ideas evolved in the course of human history', also poses a serious dilemma for the libertarian. It is easy to talk about 'free access', but are we to understand that this is feasible without a radical transformation of the system of education? Professor Wollheim rightly stresses the need for a large increase in the educational effort to give some substance to the claims of 'equality of opportunity'. Yet in practice, and even under the most progressive conditions, education will involve some degree of persuasion and compulsion. It is therefore interesting to observe that it is the most libertarian authors who are among those to have been sub-

86

jected to the most thorough process of intellectual conditioning (which in other institutions they would describe as brainwashing) which it is possible to encounter outside the most stringent Communist élite schools of propaganda or the Roman Catholic Church – the English preparatory and public schools, followed by Oxbridge.[11]

It is odd, therefore, that there should be any objections to the 'imposition' of a more comprehensive form of education along less totalitarian lines. Yet, while protesting their advanced thinking, libertarians seem to have fallen victim to rather simple eighteenth-century rationalist notions of human nature.

We learn from the psychologists that the process of conditioning begins at birth.[12] To presume, therefore, that men might fulfil themselves according to their *own* view or conception of life in a modern community, or that they might obtain 'free access to the principal ideas evolved in the course of human history' without education, is rather misleading. The collective word – 'men' – simply obscures the problem of the plurality of cultures with which the non-Soviet world is faced. Without education 'men' cannot absorb ideas and form them into their own conception; they are provided with a conception. Education itself makes possible the inculcation of a set of moral and aesthetic values determined by contemporary society. And here is the rub: the eternal dilemma of the liberal reformer. Since education implies compulsion, the reform of the traditional cultural climate must entail counter-compulsion.[13] The reformer who does not face the dilemma but averts his eyes, pleading non-intervention in the interests of preserving liberty, implicitly displays his preference for the compulsion inherent in the status quo.

2. The discontinuity of economic progress

While the achievement of full employment brings with it the need for a radical adjustment in social attitudes and responsibilities, the increases in production and productivity to which it so largely contributes may be attended by unforeseen political developments. In helping to reduce the incidence of grievous poverty, it appears to have the effect of lessening interest in social justice and equality at the same time as their achievement becomes more practicable.

This may well be due to the basically discontinuous nature of the process by which living standards rise.

A major change, such as occurred in the US in the 1920s and in the UK in the 1950s, with the widening of the accessibility of durable consumer goods through hire-purchase, and the sharp increase in real income, may give rise to corresponding changes in attitude. In periods of exceptional transition, people conceive hopes – of further prosperity and of 'classlessness' – which project into the longer future the rate of progress currently experienced. Once this material progress has, so to say, been digested, with yesterday's luxuries transformed into today's necessities, social and political problems are likely to reappear in a sharper form. It is not a matter of coincidence that class-consciousness and bitterness have re-appeared in the United States with an increasing sense of the emptiness of the progress that has been achieved, however impressive its material trappings. In Britain, new levels of expectation bring more violent responses to unemployment in the 1980s than in the 1930s.

But it would be an oversimplification to say that these phenomena have a regular or predictable pattern. Satiety with new 'models' may induce violent shifts in attitude in favour of greater security, more improved education or health services, more leisure, or towards a better physical social framework, as might come from town-planning. There is, perhaps, a cyclical pattern in community tastes, with the desire for material advance followed by a swing in favour of security and equality, in turn to be followed by a renewed thirst for material goods. Such shifts will not be regular, nor stable in any functional sense. They will not represent fine adjustments at the margin of the sort that the traditional tools of economics have been designed to analyse; nor will they be independent of the quality of leadership. Mere acquiescence in the popular mood implies the abandonment of the majority to persuasive propaganda and the consequent disillusionment that this ultimately brings. Such lack of political courage, moreover, entails a waste both of time and of opportunity. It is this aspect of historical development which makes mechanical predictions of long-run trends in social and electoral behaviour so rash – and which after the event makes their results look so inept.

3. The bias against collective needs

The foregoing may also go some way to explaining the distortion which characterizes and lately threatens to dominate the typical Western economy as seen in the growing discrepancy between the capacity to produce material goods, and the dearth of general educational facilities aimed at their sensible choice and disposition. So long as the wartime and immediate postwar pattern of anticipation held, and the progress in the economy accelerated, this lacuna did not lead to extreme imbalance. The governments of both US and UK promised to maintain employment and income and the promise itself contributed substantially to the success of the policy. But since the even growth was disturbed and the relatively mild rise in prices assumed a more menacing rhythm, accelerated inflation has wrought destructive changes of attitude. Rising affluence had increased the demand for public as well as private goods. For a long time 'fiscal decay' or 'fiscal creep' - the automatic increase in tax revenue from the combination of growth and mild inflation - had served to finance the growing production of public goods and services, especially education, health services and social security. But when inflation came to be seen as the overriding economic problem, that comfortable process turned sour. There were tax revolts, and other lurches to the right. Despite increases of taxation huge deficits arose and further escalation of imports threatened. Under these circumstances there was a growing audience for the monetarist explanation of inflation, especially because it proposed a ruthless slashing of public expenditure. But public employment, and also public fixed capital, have considerable rigidity. Such job reductions as can be contrived tend to increase unemployment and social security payments while simultaneously reducing the tax base and the public revenue. So the budget savings are minimal, and the only way to save more is to cut not public employment but social security transfers. The real intent of these policies is a general attack on trade unions and the welfare state.

The quality of these attacks on the public sector, and their increasing stridency, suggests that the prime cause of the imbalance in the pattern of final demand lies in the organization of production. The private sector produces for profit, advertises its wares directly, and manipulates demand in diffuse and indirect ways through the profit-seeking ownership and use of many of the media. As productivity expands beyond the 'primitive' needs, and multiplies the ways in which the primitive needs themselves can be met, more and more expenditure is discretionary. Choice becomes technically more difficult, and manipulating wants and tastes becomes more possible, and more profitable.

There is – to adapt a phrase – both micro and macro manipulation. Firms create demands for particular products. But also, the private sector as a whole, ably assisted by the media and a great many orthodox economists, works hard to direct demand toward profitably supplied goods and services, and away from public and non-profit goods and services. That bias of demand is directly profitable. If it incidentally reduces public expenditure on education and shifts the balance of persuasion further towards the profit-seeking media and the advertisers, so much the better. So campaigns against taxation and public expenditure serve several profitable purposes at once. They also put progressive parties on the defensive,[14] while the satisfaction of various wants which may have harmful effects on other people is not sufficiently discouraged.[15] In a democracy, however, such imbalances are often difficult to redress without a degree of agreement and cooperation between the major political parties. That may require some sinking of major political differences; yet unless it is achieved, any programme set in train to restore balance (most importantly, a programme of social education) is likely to be threatened as often as power changes hands.

Vigorous opposition to a policy of 'counter-persuasion' would not be lacking, particularly from those powerful large-scale organizations (including the trade unions affected) whose markets are most likely to suffer. Moreover, with their vast resources and accumulated experience, these corporations would constitute a menacing force for arousing public opinion against any attempt on the part of government to influence public tastes and consumption habits. They have had to accept public campaigns against one or two proven and specific dangers to health: cigarettes and drunken driving. Beyond that they will not easily tolerate State encroachment on what has been a traditional preserve of private enterprise. It would not be long before the spectre of Communist brainwashing would be invoked, as it has been by Sir K. Joseph and Mrs Thatcher. Greater outrage still: the State, in persuading people of the need for more public expenditure – and hence for increased taxation – would be using 'taxpayers' money' to do so.

The danger of neglecting collective wants is the greater as in many instances its effects – for example in education, health, nutrition and housing – are not felt in the shorter run. Yet in the end, such neglect may produce a downward spiral of (relative) backwardness, as an undereducated public, taught to look to its money income and its retail shopping to satisfy more and more of its needs, has its opinions shaped increasingly by and for the private sector, and grows less and less willing to pay taxes for better public services, including 'countervailing' social education. It was, at least in part, a 'vicious spiral' of that sort which in America, after 1921 and again after 1953, resulted in the weakening of the drive for equality, and in the social complacency which characterized first the era of Coolidge, Mellon and Hoover, later of Eisenhower and more recently of Nixon and his crowd. Similar social forces were unquestionably at work in Erhard's Germany and accounted also for the strong Conservative trend in Britain during the 1950s. Yet as material prosperity advanced, social dissension grew; the violent outbursts of the 1960s in the United States, Germany, Italy and France reflected a growing, almost anarchistic, repudiation of those social ties and values which, while fostering the amassing of economic wealth at an unprecedented rate, could at the same time tolerate continued maldistribution of income, against a background of growing social injustice and cultural impoverishment.

Some advances in living standards go far beyond what might be attributed to them in the conventional measurements of real income. Even a marginal increase in national output can represent a veritable revolution in people's lives, and so long as these changes remain fresh in their minds, the impact will be extremely vivid. This constitutes yet a further important reason why an index of economic welfare which relies solely on the value of goods and services supplied in terms of prices ruling in some base period is likely to mislead. It is unable to take account of qualitative changes in living standards, and this for two reasons: (a) improvements in design and efficiency are very often not reflected in prices, a frequent attribute of technical progress in affluent societies characterized by oligopolistic industrial structures, and (b) this in turn makes it difficult if not impossible to attribute an adequate quantitative weight to such changes in the measurement of price changes, and hence changes in the pattern of consumption. As we shall see later, this is a serious obstacle to the maintenance of price stability in democratic countries.

The point to emphasize here, however, is that improvements in design and efficiency (not to speak of the introduction of new products) render it difficult to make significant comparisons as to differences in living standards between periods that are separated too greatly in time, or where really important changes in consumption habits have occurred. By extension, it is equally hazardous to attempt quantitative comparisons between different economies (even with similar social systems) at the same moment in time; while comparisons between economies with radically different social systems will be even more arbitrary, or rough-and-ready.

In order to be at all representative, welfare estimates of the same economy at different moments in time ought to comprise two further constituents of the economic or material basis of social and private satisfaction. First they should take account of the enjoyment that comes with the accumulation of social and private consumption capital. In housing, home-furnishings and other durable and semi-durable goods, the bequest from the past contributes to current consumption; the same is true of roads, town-planning, and public buildings and amenities. Secondly it is important to consider the attraction or otherwise of the place of work or habitation, including the difficulties of getting to and from work. Beyond these two points stretches an unlimited range of imponderable elements, including climate and social values; to these aspects we now turn.

4. The change in the urgency of needs

With rising consumption per head, the urgency of consumer needs 'ought' to diminish; this implies that, in principle, the importance of further increases should also decline. Yet we have seen that this need not be so if the growth of the productive system feeds on the creation of new wants. Moreover, economists have traditionally argued that it was not their business to look beyond demand as it manifested itself in the market. Had not Marshall himself pointed the way? To inquire into non-market phenomena would comprom-ise their objectivity, and this they were not prepared to risk.

However, these very increases in real income, and the way in which they are brought about, have mischievous consequences – first, the increasing incidence of the indirect effects of production and consumption and, secondly, a strengthening in the tendency to discriminate against collective needs (itself aggravated by the inability of the price system to express them appropriately). Discrimination, as we have seen, is especially fierce in the case of those collective needs which can only be met by taxation and produced by collective effort, especially where this takes the form of public services or enterprise and not in the issuing of government contracts to private firms. It is also clear that the further along the path of unplanned material advancement the community has progressed, the more will these two problems (indirect effects and discrimination) be connected. Discrimination against the provision of collective goods and services seemed to have little adverse repercussion on living standards and security as long as consumption was something that went on mainly in the privacy of the home. Older textbooks on economics, rather tortuously perhaps, usually referred to such now-classic examples as 'smoke nuisance' or river pollution, and, as such, considered them to be (rightly so in their day) rather unimportant.

In modern life, however, the interrelation and interaction of external production and consumption effects on individual welfare assume an importance which can no longer be ignored.

The impact of the motorcar on privacy, on casualties, on national investment programmes, on hospital expenditure, has been discussed,[16] as have chemical poisoning, pollution and industrial waste, which are all spoiling the human environment, especially the countryside. The concentration of office building in urban centres, stimulated partly by huge development profits, not only kills the individuality of cities by its drab and repetitious architecture, but increases the irksomeness of travel to and from work.[17]

It is not to be denied that what are derisively termed the 'anti-growth' brigade neglect (and are for this reason under attack) the interests of the less prosperous in the advanced countries, and, even more vital, the interests of the poverty-stricken areas of the world.[18] No doubt Dr Mishan has erred in neglecting the danger of 'élitism' in his strictures. Who should be able to enjoy solitude, and where? If we are to reduce traffic congestion in towns, who should be allowed the use of cars? The counterattack against the opponents of growth, conducted for example with characteristic robustness by Mr Crosland[19] and with greater balance by Professor Beckerman,[20] tends to neglect the fact that much of the 'necessity' now felt for certain goods and services has been created deliberately so that their supply should yield profits, and for no other purpose. Even if it is undeniable that some of this need arises through the spread of education, much of the increase in resources is devoted to pursuits which are no more than a response to appeals to greed, envy and ostentation.

There is, in short, a large field of consumption in which the consumer, as an individual, can do little to secure a balance of satisfaction in his needs. This applies not only to those needs catered to by the market, but also to those which can be satisfied only through collective action. The preservation of beautiful surroundings, of the country's historic architectural heritage, seems, more often than not, to be incompatible with unrestricted individual freedom in the use of land. Yet it is difficult to regulate the use, and at the same time ensure equity for the owners, of various assets, especially land, unless public ownership is extended to those fields where such regulation is essential.

Finally, as incomes rise, there will inevitably be a concomitant increase in the importance of non-material social or political requirements. In this sense, the boundless nature of human desires seems apposite, although it has been wrongly used as an argument to support the ethical neutrality of economics in judging the quality of consumption which increased wealth makes possible. If social amenities and increasing individual leisure are included among the goals of economic activity, as they should be, the need for a continued expansion in the capacity for fulfilling material ends with less effort will persist, although the uses to which it is put will be modified. What the anti-anti-growth propagandists forget is that the modification of the socio-economic system and its motive mechanism, through which growth could be accelerated and sustained at a high rate, might itself be (as in our view it definitely is) self-defeating. If a higher rate of output is to be gained by a greater 'abrasiveness' in the quality of life, this cannot be greeted as a great social achievement.

5. The individual and the group

The neoclassical theory of the consumer, as we have seen, is based on an obsolete psychology. The consumer fit for economics as a deductive science is not a living being such as one might encounter: he is a fiction, and the growing refinement of mathematical economics based upon that fiction can be no more in practical terms than a fiction.

Beyond the nebulous nonsense of the perfect consumer and the conflict of welfare criteria there looms a further and even more serious threat to conventional economics as a basis for policy-making. This stems from the fact that, in the 'West', the individual lives in a society based on property rights; and the rewards which he receives in return for his part in the productive process, or indeed his wealth and income in the absence of any contribution, are powerfully influenced by this. Moreover, the possibility of converting changes in income into capital gains and vice versa, to escape taxes, exaggerates the claim of the property-owning class on current output. Fluctuations in capital values can (and do) affect demand (and hence the composition of output), even when these fluctuations are only the result of psychological (for instance, anticipatory) factors.[21] It is quite probable, therefore, that the distribution of consuming power in society (as well as the status and security attaching to it among the various members of the community) will not meet with general approval, or even acceptance;[22] for in Western society the ethics of the Reformation and of the Enlightenment alike demand that the income or welfare of large groups should be measured exclusively in terms of the income and welfare of their individual members: practically speaking this amounts to no more than the simple sum of all incomes, with which welfare is defined as coinciding.

Economists have been especially taxed by the possibility that the total income of a group might increase, though its distribution 'worsens'. We have discussed the possible, indeed likely, conflict of welfare criteria and indices. Yet an obvious solution seemed to offer itself. In principle, at least, the distribution of income was measurable; it seemed reasonable, therefore, to include it in the main body of economic theory. Other factors of economic life, such as instability of income or the anxiety created by certain conditions of work, were amenable to quantitative expression: the former was

95

usually dismissed as being the result of frictional elements 'in the broad sweep of progress'; the latter problem was simply assumed away, or 'explained' by the payment of differential (that is, higher) incomes to those whose work involved particular mental or physical hardship.

The concept of distribution is by no means straightforward and, as we have already seen, constitutes of itself a crucial obstacle to the objectivity of economic analysis and advice. This threat was met at first by an illicit simplification. Thus Professor von Wieser, for instance, one of the leading lights of the Austrian school: 'The theory of the "simple economy" ... begins with the idealizing assumption that the subject is a single person. However, we do not have in mind here the meagre economy of an isolated Crusoe ... [but] the activities of an entire nation. At the same time millions of persons are regarded as a massed unit.'[23] Yet it is, of course, quite illicit to attribute personality and the capacity for feelings and satisfaction to 'millions of people' *as if* they were 'a massed unit'. The incidence of economic development or economic policy affects different individuals in different ways. Von Wieser's reasoning offers a good example of the fallacy of misplaced concreteness – quite apart from the difficulties already discussed that any individual, 'composite' or otherwise, would have in trying to measure his enjoyment.[24]

An alternative course (of some long standing in economic and political thought) has been to assume harmony of interests. A favourite device, in effect it means that the problem of distribution can be ignored – at least by the economist. 'Concentrate on real income,' we are exhorted, 'and distribution will take care of itself.'[25] But can such harmony of interests be legitimately or safely assumed, when neither tastes nor distribution remain constant?[26] It is virtually meaningless to speak of real (as opposed to money) income without reference to distribution; and this in turn cannot be separated from the question of relative prices and the market effects of the different tastes of people with different incomes. Similar considerations apply to the effect of policy measures; indeed, it is difficult to conceive of a policy that has no distributive implications, or which, consequentially, will leave tastes unchanged.[28]

At the beginning of the present century, marking the ascendancy of the theory of general equilibrium and its concentration on the problems of production and markets, this question was thrust from the centre of theoretical interest. Nonetheless it remained as a nagging reminder that all was not well with the system of free enterprise, of which the unequal distribution of income was its most obtrusive manifestation. The implications of the doctrine of measurable (or, as the economic jargon has it, 'cardinal') utility were clear; if it was accepted that each increment in a person's income brought with it a diminishing quantum of utility, and if it was the agreed aim of society to maximize total utility, then the logic of the argument pointed to furthering the equality of distribution. That this condition was so far from being fulfilled, and even clashed with their private convictions, would be sufficient explanation of the intensity with which a considerable number of professional economists campaigned for the overthrow of 'cardinalism'.[29]

The classical case for equality of distribution rested not so much on the measurability or cardinality of utility, however, as on the assumption that all individuals were endowed with an identical capacity for enjoyment or satisfaction. If this was accepted, then the case for equality followed; cardinality itself was not of the essence.

The rejection of the Marshallian theory of marginal utility – and with it the remnants of classical Utilitarianism – concentrated, not surprisingly, on the 'endowment' postulate. Enjoyment, it was argued, is strictly a private sensation, not amenable to objective measurement. Equality of capacity for enjoyment can be no more than an idealistic or metaphysical shibboleth, a quite unfitting precept in practical affairs (that is, in the sphere of distribution policy) which the facts of observation refuted daily. It followed then that equality of distribution was not the logical path whereby to maximize total utility. Yet if endowments between individuals differed, any policy of maximization would clearly entail, *horribile dictu*, 'interpersonal comparisons of utility'; but it is precisely such comparisons which, it is contended, must be ruled out as unscientific. What we are left with is an 'ordinal', that is unquantifiable, concept of *revealed preference*. We can order these preferences into a scale; but even that procedure produces equivocal conclusions.

The distinguishing feature of this 'New Welfare Economics', as it has been styled, is that it says nothing very interesting about social welfare as a whole. Indeed this is intentional; to do otherwise would be unscientific. All that can be said is that society is at an *optimum* welfare position if it is impossible to increase one person's welfare without it entailing a reduction in another's. But there will be an infinity of such positions, and the actual optimum point reached will depend on the initial distribution of income. We have no objective means of choosing one distribution rather than another, or one optimum rather than another. Hence, by abandoning the assumption of cardinality and the 'identical endowment' assumption, indeed by demonstrating that they were unnecessary and that weaker assumptions would work just as well in the analysis of consumers' behaviour and its implications for general welfare, it could be claimed that the ordinalist approach, far from diminishing, rather enhanced the explanatory and predictive power of 'positive' economics. In fact it soon became apparent that utility, even as an ordinal concept, was unnecessary.[30] Thus, as long as rationality is assumed, it can be postulated that the consumer, in buying one from a given feasible range of commodity 'bundles', will be in a *preferred* position as against all feasible others. The *imputation* of welfare-giving properties to such positions is unnecessary; that the consumer's behaviour has *revealed* his preference for a given bundle is enough. Needless to say, this rules out any meaningful comparisons between different individuals' preferences.

Equally, so it is said, it follows that the economist, if he is to be 'scientific', is not permitted to make recommendations about distribution; the only assumption that he can make is that if 'real income' increases (whatever that may mean and in whatever manner its increase is established) all will be well. Given certain initial conditions, the economy will attain to *some* 'optimum' equilibrium as a result of the interaction of the impersonal forces of the market. Why the equilibrium will be 'optimum' has never actually been explained. One leading neoclassical theorist of Walrasian equilibrium, Professor Frank Hahn, has pointed out that there is in fact nothing whatever in general equilibrium theory to justify the claim of social optimality, and he condemns writers who make the claim.

The textbooks do make the claim, almost universally. They commonly note but then neglect the fact, already stressed, that 'real income' is measured in terms of a certain set of prices ruling in a given period and that these prices will reflect the prevailing distribution of income. (With no Texan oil millionaires there would be little chance of selling a baby blue Rolls-Royce, or a functionally ordinary watch, at a price ten times the yearly income of a small farmer or sharecropper.) If 'equilibrium is just equilibrium'[31] we are, in effect, accepting what *is* for what *should be*; we are implicitly accepting the *existing* distribution of income as *desirable*. It is tantamount to assuming that the *capacity for enjoyment is strictly proportional to income* – a daring, if wholly implausible, hypothesis indeed. Yet it must be so: otherwise the alternative would have to be accepted, that an increase in social wellbeing could be achieved by redistributing income. It was against this basically 'progressive' or 'leftish' conclusion that Professor Robbins had revolted by claiming the impossibility of making interpersonal comparisons of utility.[32] The fact escaped him, however, that this way of excluding interpersonal comparisons is altogether inconsistent with his acceptance of 'equilibrium' as a desirable aim on the basis of the existing distribution of income and wealth, because it implied interpersonal comparisons, although in a conservative sense.

However, in a bid for scientific respectability, the New Welfare Economics imposed complete restraint on the giving of policy advice solely on the basis of economic analysis. It was this turn which led Professor Kaldor, in a witty paper written just before the Second World War,[33] not so much, perhaps, to attempt a rescue operation, as to show up the weakness of the 'value-free' science. (This approach was to be extended by Professor Scitovsky[34] and ponderously amplified by Professor Hicks.[35]) Kaldor suggested that it was wrong and illogical to try to support the status quo by denying the competence of economic analysis to pronounce on the matter of income distribution; the status quo is a particular pattern of income distribution which can hardly be *supported* by a body of theory that is incompetent to pronounce on that very subject.

In Kaldor's view a way out of the impasse could be found, which would permit the 'soundness' of a policy to be tested even if that policy entailed a change in the distribution of income. All that one needed to know was whether or not those who benefited from a given measure would be able to compensate or 'bribe' those who lost as a result of the changes brought about by the latter's acquiescence in the policy, and yet still derive a net gain thereby; in other words, gainers must be able to *overcompensate* losers. If this

99

were the case, then surely the changes brought about by the proposed measure would be favourable.

This brilliant idea was adopted by the scientific Establishment with uncritical enthusiasm, not to say a sort of teutonic thoroughness. It was earnestly amended to take account of those queer cases where, after the change had taken place, losers in turn could 'bribe' erstwhile gainers to give up the new policy. The possibility was also explored that consumers might gain more than was indicated by the relative change in prices and incomes. Oddly enough, however, for years it was not recognized that even this method could not provide an 'objective' guide to policy; and this for two reasons. First, the principle of compensation rested on the implicit and completely illicit assumption that the pre-existing distribution of income (and, following Scitovsky, the distribution resulting from the change) *should* serve as the basis of comparison. And second, it was held that the mere *possibility* of compensation was sufficient recommendation for a policy; *actual* compensation – in practice often improbable or even impossible – was apparently thought to be unnecessary.

The economists who propagated this view were, for political reasons, desperately anxious to maintain the notion that economic policy had to be judged exclusively in relation to individuals *per se*, and not, say, as members of a (national) group. Hence, the internal contradiction in their argument ought to have been – but was not – all too plain. The actual losses that some individuals would suffer ought not to be disregarded (by such people especially) merely because of the *hypothetical* possibility of compensation. Some losers, on the other hand, might not deserve compensation for their loss, since their initial position might have been too favourable. Only if all those among the losers who deserved compensation (including compensation for the uncertainty arising out of the disturbance of the initial situation) were *in fact* compensated would this sort of analysis yield any meaningful answers. But it could then be argued that the very fact that such discrimination had to take place, that value judgements had to be made, ruled this method out of court as a means of furnishing policy recommendations on the basis of 'pure' or 'objective' economic analysis.

Nothing shows better how complete is the conquest of this odd attitude of regarding consumers' current real spending power as the sole criterion of welfare than the fact that even socialist writers sometimes feel impelled to state dogmatically that: 'The underlying principle, for any Labour Government, must, of course, be that *consumer interests* and national interest are *identical* and *paramount*: in a Socialist society (although one fears some trade unions would not admit it) there should exist no such thing as producer interest.'[36] In a socialist society the disutility of work, the nature of the hierarchic arrangements and relations with management, and many other problems connected with changes of demand, remain important criteria of welfare arising out of man's role as a producer. It might well be that a 'smaller' income, better distributed, gained at the cost of less distress, less effort, or less social tension, would be preferable to a 'larger' one. Lenin laboured under a similar (mis)conception when he argued that, with the expropriation of the capitalist class, all problems of relations between producers would be solved; charwomen would be able to take over the State administrative machine, and all could concentrate on the interests of the consumer.

Even if the 'economic test' of a policy is reduced to a combination of two criteria, such that the definition of a 'better' position is taken as one in which 'real income has increased' and its 'distribution has not worsened',[37] we shall not have progressed far. In the first place, there remain all the other problems as to how national 'income' is to be measured, even if, given changes in distribution which bring about changes in prices, the same answer is obtained when income is valued on the basis of all possible relevant price levels. In the second place, it will still not be certain whether a *large* increase in real 'income' should not be preferred (at least temporarily) even if its distribution has worsened (or vice versa). The choice of policy cannot be made on the basis of these two 'economic' criteria alone. It may well be that in some instances a fall in the conventional measure of national income might be welcome (as in some cases of decolonization); in others, a large increase in income might be favoured, despite a deterioration in its distribution, if it is accompanied by such a prospective acceleration in the growth of total income that those who have been harmed by the initial change will soon be more than compensated (a contemporary example of this being postwar Germany).[38]

It would be possible, of course, to redistribute the increase in income so as to accord more closely with prevalent political views. But this has not happened even in the 'socialist' countries where, quite apart from reasons of incentive[39] or the need to provide for the disagreeable nature of certain jobs,[40] startling inequalities remain - whether of historical origin or as a result of the creation of new opportunities by those in power to gratify their desires, albeit limited by the abolition of private property. The problem of redistribution, however, is generally couched with reference to the costs which the raising of taxes, whether direct or indirect, impose on the system in terms of allocative and productive efficiency. The sensitivity of individuals to price or tax changes leaves ample scope for scepticism and we would not attribute too much weight to this argument. But clearly the reverse is the case for those who believe in the perfect operation of the unfettered price mechanism. Thus, the distributional effects of proposed measures must not be brushed aside on the plea that these can be taken care of by taxation if the need arises. At that level, the only theoretically valid course would be the imposition of lump-sum taxes at random intervals, so as to forestall anticipations. This alone, however, is sufficient to preclude it as a practicable policy measure.

The unsatisfactory character of the traditional academic approach to welfare problems (at least in the context of a developed capitalist economy) was nonetheless recognized at an early stage. If economists were to be able to make objective statements on economic matters, some means had to be found whereby to escape the impasse into which they had driven themselves by the New Welfare Economics. Such a device - the Social Welfare Function - was proposed by Professor Abram Bergson.[41] With apparent rigour, and evident formal elegance, Bergson's *deus ex machina* had immediate attraction for a stymied profession. All the crucial problems with which the policy-maker would be confronted could now be supposedly resolved by investing the Social Welfare Function with all the preferences and values that characterized the members of the community: in effect, it becomes the notional embodiment of the General Will. On this point we may profit by again quoting Professor Arrow:

The operational and epistemological basis of the social welfare function is never analysed. Individual preferences refer, however shakily, to conceivably observable behaviour. Whose behaviour or whose judgement is referred to in the social welfare function is never clarified. Presumably, the function is an expression of the ethical attitudes of any particular observer, but this attitude leaves open all the problems which centre about the concept of political or social obligations; why should any individual accept policies inconsistent with his own social welfare function?

Even apart from this profoundly difficult problem of political ethics, the development of the social welfare function as a tool for policy formation seems curiously stunted. Certainly no attempt is made to show how specific policies follow from specific choices of social welfare functions, not even by way of example.[42]

Typically, Professor Tinbergen reveals the meaninglessness of the concept as a guide to policy when he says that 'our value system finds its expression in the social welfare function', which we should think of 'as the sum total of all individual welfare or utility functions'.[43] Yet we have seen that it is impossible to derive even individual, let alone social (group), welfare functions in any meaningful sense. Criteria and values, often mutually inconsistent, forever subject to persuasion and manipulation, far from being constant, are in a perpetual state of change.

Even on the narrowest 'economic' plan, that of measuring real income, quantitative criteria for formulating policy or weighing up alternatives are seen, on closer inspection, to be quite elusive, if not illusory. One does not need the tastes of an ascetic to question whether the growth of a changing collection of goods and services at the disposal of the individual, valued at a certain set of prices ruling in some period, necessarily reflects an equivalent increase in 'welfare' in any meaningful sense. In the modern world, the conditions under which this correspondence could reasonably be said to hold do not obtain. In particular, it depends on the validity of the assumption that men's wants are inborn and cannot be changed, that their urgency can be taken as given, and that acts of choice (between certain substitutable commodities) will have no perceptible repercussions in other spheres of choice; in short, choice must not be between different ways of life. The growing impact of advertising and persuasion over an expanding field of our consumption habits, the close dependence of these habits on those of other people and the interdependence of consumption of a wide range of goods – all these fundamental features of modern life render such assumptions obsolete.

These considerations, then, rule out so-called pure economic analysis or theory as an arbiter of policy in respect of the two vital problems of our age. It cannot as such decide the issue between the two opposing social systems – private enterprise based on 'free' markets or mixed economies vis-à-vis total or modified planning. Nor can it chart a way for the development of poor, primitive peasant communities. It is completely illicit, for instance, to compare situations 'before and after trade' on the basis of geometrical models illustrating 'real world income' in order to prove the superiority of free trade; and equally false to assume that such theories – except in rare historical circumstances – provide a sound basis for economic policy.[44] The impact of such changes on the distribution of incomes, tastes, and so on, would be so great as to fracture the static *ceteris paribus* framework upon which the analysis and consequent policy had been based – a particularly acute danger if this entails the destruction of tribal or peasant societies and the enforced change in incentive mechanisms.[45] In such circumstances the economist *qua* economist – and quasi-economist – should be very modest indeed in recommending or opposing policies.

What this amounts to, then, is that we must chiefly make *grosso modo* political choices and that we must make up our own minds on the economic, political and other implications of a proposed change. Such decisions cannot be 'scientifically', but only politically, defended; and the economist cannot provide objective guidance on policies relating to matters which may have far-reaching consequences for the way of life of whole communities. This applies especially to those communities of a divided character, as exist in the less developed countries, or even in developed countries riven between a more prosperous, usually exploitative, urban sector and a primitive, mainly rural, sector. Only in the case of marginal or small issues, in politically settled and economically and socially integrated communities with established social institutions, will the economist's particular viewpoint take on some authority.[46] But then any guidance that he can give on such matters will be of quite minor significance in practice.

CHAPTER SIX

Production: Freedom and Efficiency?

In the previous sections we have tried to discuss critically the traditional approach of orthodox economic theory to the problem of 'welfare', more specifically consumption, in relation to people both as individuals and as members of larger social groups. In so doing, it became necessary to touch on certain aspects of the theory of production and the market mechanism; indeed, in stating the necessary conditions in whose absence conventional welfare criteria would be inoperable, we were, in a sense, anticipating the present chapter. However, as will have been appreciated by the numerous references to the sphere of production in the foregoing discussion, where matters of 'welfare' are concerned, the consumption and production aspects of economic relations are for practical purposes, if not analytically, inseparable. The roles of individuals (or households) as consumers cannot legitimately be distinguished from their roles as producers in contemplating their general, or even their economic, welfare.

It is now time to turn more fully to an analysis of the problems of production in the context of the industrialized Western world. We shall try to assess whether there is any justification in the conventional claim that our system of decentralized decision-making (i.e., through the medium of prices set in the market) not only ensures the freedom and dignity of the individual, but is also superior to a planned system in its sheer productive performance. In what follows, however, we shall not be able to confine ourselves to the limited *economic* aspects of production, these being inseparable from their social implications.

The question of the efficiency of an economic system is not simple. Efficiency itself cannot be measured without an agreed standard of comparison; moreover, the system whose efficiency is to be assessed can only be fairly judged in terms of its own criteria or goals. We shall first try, therefore, to restate the traditional Western view of the individualist free market system and its *modus operandi.* We shall then try to assess to what extent the system does in fact conform to the analytical model on which its protagonists base their claims.

1. The mirage of optimum production

The traditional theory of production as it had evolved by the end of the 1920s was comforting. It was able to prove, or at any rate was said to be able to prove, at one and the same time a number of admirable claims for the existing order of things, each mutually supporting the other, and together providing a warrant of optimal arrangement. It reconciled the Judeo-Christian repugnance to inequality and domination of man over man with the evidently hierarchical structure of society, as being essential to the capacity to sustain life and satisfy wants by means which were in essence harmonious and self-adjusting. It showed that private property and private enterprise, controlled and impelled by 'free' markets, afforded not merely the most efficient possible, but also the *only* efficient way of organizing production, of utilizing scarce resources for the good of all. Without free markets no rational behaviour, no satisfactory economic planning, were possible.

The system, decentralized yet guided as it were by the invisible hand of destiny, provided also an impersonal, systematic guarantee of everyone's individual freedom within prescribed limits, an essential constituent of the 'obvious and simple system of natural liberty'. This balance of social forces was not accomplished by conscious planning or physical controls; not by trusting a menacing degree of power to human and fallible central agencies, such as the State, the oppression and exactions of which, once admitted, are impossible to keep in bounds; it was assured, automatically, by the myriads of entrepreneurs and workers trying to secure the greatest gain for themselves. The entrepreneur dominated over his enterprise and staff only seemingly. In fact he was under complete compulsion of the market. His actions merely transmitted higher commands ultimately stemming from millions of ordinary consumers – commands which were assembled, and their fulfilment enforced, by impersonal forces of the price mechanism, without the intervention of anyone. The consumers' desires, and not those of the owners of the means of production, governed the system; it was therefore profoundly democratic in character.

This sovereign dominance of the consumer, on his part striving as we have seen for the greatest possible contentment, was assured by free and unhindered competition for his custom: in the end all benefited. Employers were induced to produce what was wanted by the prospect of profit. If they miscalculated, or refused to obey the dictates of demand playing on vast markets – which no single enterprise was able to influence, much less to control – they were instantly eliminated by the invisible hand. With an abundance of capital, technical knowledge, and entrepreneurial ability, there were always enough potential competitors to spring into the fray. Thus small movements of price subtly influenced large numbers, and brought elastic response.

The economy was based on free competition. This ensured that land, labour and materials were used for the most urgent purposes and in the most economical way. Just those things were produced which were most wanted, and at the lowest possible price: exactly the sort of technique of production was used which was appropriate to the current state of knowledge and wealth. All waste was eliminated by the price-system and its fateful sanctions.

Some hardship and injustice did, no doubt, occur. They were, really, inevitable; and the system automatically tended to reduce them. Perfect competition provided a guarantee that all productive factors, including the workmen who had freely cooperated in the creation of goods and services, received remuneration impartially and with perfect justice exactly in accordance with the contribution they had made. Exploitation was impossible, for the entrepreneur who tried such abuse would be sure to lose his men. As the community grew richer, the accumulation of capital would depress its own reward and increase the remuneration of labour. Better social balance would automatically be brought about through greater equality.

The pessimism of the great classical writers was exorcized. They had argued (as the contemporary scene in Asia eloquently shows, not altogether without justification) that human fecundity would for ever keep wages down to subsistence level. The young Marx had taken up their thesis just when the tide seems to have turned. The rapid growth of population of the early nineteenth century was slowed; wealth seemed to catch up with humanity. There was new hope: the neoclassical case was optimistic, for all its austere damnation of would-be do-gooders.

This harmonious evolution could, of course, be disturbed, by interference by the State trying to flout the 'law' of supply and demand, or by the efforts of workers' combinations, the trade unions, to secure wages higher than those the market ordained, would be fruitless. The economy irresistibly and inevitably would revenge itself on its violators. Britain's tribulations after the return to the Gold Standard in 1925 were held up as a warning of what would happen to a State which shortsightedly wanted to aid the weak, and in the process 'deprives its successful citizens of their product, and gives it to the less successful; thus it penalizes industry, thrift, competence, and efficiency, and subsidizes the idle, spendthrift, incompetent and inefficient. By despoiling the thrifty it dries up the source of capital, reduces investment and the creation of jobs, slows down industrial progress ...'[1] Unemployment and stagnation were the penalty.

Harmony of interests and justice were thus assured – at any rate in the long run, and within the limits of the practicable. It was all for the best in the best of all *possible* worlds. 'Equilibrium', the automatic balance between supply and demand, both of goods and services and of the factors of production needed for their creation, became the test of the enduring perfection of the system. Without markets and perfect competition alternative systems such as physical planning and direct allocation could not establish a rational test of what was needed, or how it should be produced to make the best use of everything available.[2]

Admittedly the mathematical model representing the modern economic system on which this optimistic theory could consistently be based was, if elegant and intellectually captivating, also extremely simple. It had to be, first of all, completely unchanging, static, or more euphemistically, 'evenly rotating'. And it had to be assumed not only that perfect competition prevailed, that each buyer or seller was unable to mould the market (for otherwise he would have had discretion in his reactions and the 'natural law' would have been suspended), but also that the problems could be analysed under the overall postulate of 'other things being equal', i.e. that secondary reactions would not alter the end-result. Otherwise the solutions offered would not be determinate. The first assumption of the absence of any substantial changes was needed because only if it could be assumed that nothing ever altered, and all would recur, could perfect foresight be postulated; and the assumption of perfect foresight was needed to give determinate solutions, because if uncertainty and risk had to be considered, the entrepreneur could rationally react to the same sort of situation in different ways, according to his judgement of the degree of uncertainty based on his past experiences.

In that case historical sequences became unique and each had to be analysed individually. In the second place it had to be assumed that the relative urgency of needs was given, and correctly expressed by the demand which became effective on the market. Otherwise relative profit opportunities could not express social urgencies and the 'best' or most efficient production would become uncertain if not meaningless: goods are only valuable because they satisfy demand, and the efficiency of production can be ascertained only in relation to the ultimate destiny of what is produced.

We have already seen that the concept of optimal demand bristles with difficulties due to problems connected with the distribution of income and the changeability of tastes. But even if we disregard these difficulties the assumption of unchanging resources presents unresolved and almost insuperable problems. What do 'unchanged or given resources' mean in a changing world? Would an attempt to treat the problem 'other things being equal' not necessarily change essential elements in the very nature of the system which vitally affect its reactions and working? Would analysis not be reduced to implicit theorizing, to spelling out in difficult jargon the assumptions with which one had started?

Next, some role had to be given to capital, and one which was consistent with general harmony. Nor could change altogether be ignored. An ingenious contrivance was evolved to cope with this complication. It was to compare two states of affairs in each of which balance had been achieved, i.e. all adjustments to past changes were assumed to have been accomplished. The difference between the two would then be ascribed to the change of a single factor. Thus the problem could be isolated and rendered manageable by algebra or higher calculus. With that modesty which characterizes the true scientist, economists refused to deal with 'all problems simultaneously'. By isolating the issues one escaped being unsystematic and immature. Thus inseparably interconnected problems were dealt with independently under separate headings. Incidentally this permitted scholars to choose those problems which plastically demonstrated the needs of efficiency under perfect conditions, leaving to other sciences or to other branches of economics any 'complicating' effects on distribution of income and general social conditions.

The method of static analysis still had to be reconciled with the dynamics of growth and capital accumulation. To achieve that, there was developed a theory of thrift in a strictly monetary context, which left the 'real' system based on 'real' transactions, on barter, in a pristine static state. The rationality of the system was extended to the future by individual saving. Capitalists refrained from consumption impelled by an instinct of prevision. 'It gave the saver the most desirable level of consumption over the span of his existence.' Providing for their own old age or rainy days, the thrifty stimulated the use of capital. This promoted physical productivity. The profitability of investment on the one hand, and on the other hand the individual's preference for immediate rather than deferred consumption, determined, through the rate of interest, the optimum amount of saving. Savings were then allocated to the entrepreneurs capable of making the most productive use of them by subtle gradations of the reward of abstinence, in the shape of a host of varying rates of interest. Waste of resources was thus avoided; the best only, of an unlimited potential number of entrepreneurs, inventions and uses of capital would be selected.

Finally, as the 'technical arts' improved, profitability should increase. This should increase saving, permitting higher investment. At the same time accumulation meant a gradual decline of income from property. It was thus in spite of their own immediate interest that the savers promoted the general progress. In the end, the system would bring about equality, the euthanasia of the rentier, and social equality would at last be established.

Unfortunately this theory of accumulation could hardly be grafted on to the neoclassical general equilibrium theory, or even Marshall's more restricted system, which demanded a static model to give determinate and optimistic answers. Its connection with the main body of economic dogma explaining the formation of prices and allocation of resources was never made explicit. The abyss between the picture of firm immobility needed for demonstrating harmony in production, and the stormy process of expansion, was not easy to bridge, and was never bridged. The accumulation of capital and the transformation of productive techniques were treated separately from the analysis of the productive system; they were integrated with the analysis of the monetary system. The two parts of the analysis had little if any connection. We shall presently discuss the implications of this fissure for understanding reality, and for policy.

Even in the relevant field of 'micro-economics', dealing with the relationships between firms and individuals as producers, drastic simplification was needed. Here, too, uncertainty and discretion had to be excluded, otherwise it could no longer be maintained that the employer had no option in his treatment of his employees – and this was needed to sustain the moral case for the atomistic system. It was thus assumed that no single individual or firm would be able to affect the market by his purchases or sales. From this it followed that he had no option but to follow the iron law of price and minimize his costs. He had to produce a standard product known in quality to all the buyers, who in their turn knew the market with all its ancillaries, and had unobstructed access.[3]

In default of these assumptions, clear-cut answers would be impossible. The claim for exclusive rationality in economic behaviour on behalf of the existing productive system would also disappear. This could not be tolerated. In order to sustain this claim, however, a further postulate was needed: costs had to be thought of as increasing with expanding scale of production. The picture follows easily from primitive agriculture: as demand for a product increases, less and less suitable land is brought into production, and more and more effort has to be expended to obtain the same additional crop. If this condition is satisfied, no single competitor can snatch an advantage by producing more, and thus more cheaply, and gradually ruin his unfortunate fellows who are less and less able to keep up with him. Only thus could it be demonstrated that profits would be competed away as they arose: only a bare minimum would remain, just sufficient to keep a minimum number (of the most efficient) units in production. Without that condition, i.e. if instead there were *falling* costs and *increasing* returns to scale, the number of competitors would shrink away, and with them would vanish the state of perfection on which both the moral and the mathematical appeal of the system rested.

Alfred Marshall, who initiated this, as many other, ingenious rationalizations of the existing order of things, never quite explained whether these 'minimum' profits needed for the 'representative firms' – that elusively abstract collective image of a whole industry – could not be exceedingly high. Social or economic or technical circumstances might make people unwilling or unable to enter the industry without the expectation of monster gains. Thus even within the original framework a tolerable resemblance of the model to reality would have depended on a certain (and rather exceptional) Judeo-Protestant, competitive and individualist, austere and imaginatively creative social structure, based at the same time on the coexistence of myriads of roughly equal competitors. This was obviously not prevalent in the greater part of the world. Thus even if the survival of the small firm were not made difficult or impossible by the conditions of production, by the possibility of reaping high rewards through mass production and mass advertising, it would not necessarily follow that production would be, in the jargon of economists, 'optimal'. The argument that the large profit exacted needs to be regarded as a minimum cost from the viewpoint of the community is at best circular, or a description couched in approving words of the existing order of affairs.

Monopoly – the dominance of a single firm over an industry, or over the production of an important commodity or service – was treated as an anomaly, likely to occur only if created by the State. When the rise of private industrial or merchanting giants could no longer be disputed, the destructive effect of this regrettable fact on the structure of economic theory was simply circumvented or (as in the theory of international trade) ignored.[4] It was argued that even if competition was not perfect or pure, it had served society well. It had created affluence out of hopeless poverty, in a matter of sixty – at the most a hundred – years, a moment in the history of man.

Theories of 'workable' competition grew up,[5] arguing that 'it remains true that the imperfectly competitive mixed economy we have is better than the impossible abstraction of "perfect competition", largely because of its dynamic quality; and because, while competitive processes change their forms, competitive pressures continue to be forceful'. Or it was suggested that 'the general assumption of monopoly' or of a monopolistic administration of prices would not, after all, alter the 'laws' obtained by assuming free competition, because it would lead to 'similar' results, and that was all that mattered.

Thus by dividing the subject matter into arbitrary compartments, and concentrating on the parts which could be reduced to simple mathematical models, an imposing structure was built up. Objections to this procedure were brushed aside by two academically potent arguments. It was contended that it was always necessary to simplify, if science was to elucidate difficult interrelations. If everything was regarded as variable in so complex an organism as a fully developed economy, all would suffer continuous change and nothing could be analysed. The principle of selection, of varying only one factor and seeing the consequence of this change, was a scientific device which had produced unparalleled progress in many fields since Copernicus and Galileo. When the investigator has gained all he can from the simplified model, he can begin to relax its assumptions step by step, and move towards more complicated hypotheses. What he cannot do is to study everything at once. He must limit his science to what can be done with rigour, objectivity and internal consistency.

2. The quality of decision

The most forceful argument in favour of individual enterprise and decentralized decision-making is ultimately political. This is an argument which dates back to Adam Smith and, as do most of his views, still retains its relevance and persuasiveness: 'The statesman who should attempt to direct private people in what manner they ought to employ their capital ... would ... assume an authority ... which would nowhere be so dangerous as in the hands of a man who had folly and presumption enough to fancy himself fit to exercise it.'[6] The implications are clear. Whatever the shortcomings of the market mechanism, however inefficient or undesirable the allocation of resources as determined by the price system, there is a good chance that the alternatives will be even worse. Centralization and State control mean delay, bureaucratic routine, inflexibility and a lack of imagination. On the other hand, the individual, actuated by his own interest, will try to exploit his opportunities to the full. The competition of his rivals will be a constant spur to innovation. Thus, even if the volume of investment should lag behind, its quality alone will render it superior to the best efforts of a centrally planned system.

Marshall was even more explicit about the dead hand of collective enterprise: 'government intrusion into businesses which require ceaseless invention and fertility of resources is a danger to social progress the more to be feared because it is insidious ... A government could print a good edition of Shakespeare's works, but it would not get them written ...'[7] Every new extension of governmental work in branches of production which thrive on ceaseless creative initiative is to be regarded as *prima facie* antisocial, since it retards the growth of that knowledge and those ideas which comprise incomparably the most important form of collective wealth. This is the doctrine which captured Mrs Thatcher.

Even if the consumer's choice could be, and is, manipulated, the system nonetheless retains some flexibility; and it is even this modicum of flexibility which might be of considerable importance, indeed decisive. Moreover in the narrower sphere of producer goods, that is, capital goods and intermediate products which do not enter into final demand, professional faces professional. Here persuasion and the subtle manipulation of demand are largely excluded. The unrelenting competitive pressure to improve on existing models must be a powerful influence in favour of progress. Self-interest, if it could be harnessed for the good of the community, might be a far more efficient means of bringing out the best in man than direction from the 'centre'. To this end the price mechanism provides the non-violent incentive while at the same time it is claimed to be a signalling system which secures the optimal use of resources.

More recently, moreover, the neoclassical ideal of individualistic *laissez-faire* has become identified with the notion of political as well as economic freedom. The identification was understandable: in Eastern Europe the end of private capitalism was linked with political dictatorship, and in Western Europe economic planning was associated with wartime and postwar austerities, and with controls which necessarily restricted both private income and consumption, and business freedom of action. In reality the controls directed scarce resources to the overriding purposes of war, or rationed consumption more fairly and productively than 'the market' would have done. That is to say, the controls did not create the scarcities – but nevertheless got blamed for them, by many people, with plenty of liberal and conservative encouragement. Thus the fact that all socio-economic systems, so long as there is not absolute abundance, have to enforce control and 'regimentation' over individuals, e.g. by curtailing purchasing power, was successfully obscured. So was the fact that the economic freedom of the majority can often be widened, and so can the scope of their choices, if some benevolent control can be exercised over powerful economic minorities, including for example monopolists, foreign investors, financial speculators, deceptive advertisers, etc.

To sum up: as the economic history of the twentieth century unfolded, there was less and less relation between its main problems and the main concerns of orthodox economic theory.

The static approach of theory led to the neglect of whole areas of political economy, especially the fascinating and crucial problem, which had dominated the writings of the earlier classical school, of what determined the expansion of the productive system. If the problems of capital accumulation and technical progress were treated at all, it was more in the manner of an afterthought, and rather surreptitiously, under the guise of monetary or capital theory. For what can 'given resources' mean in a changing world? Does not the attempt to analyse economic problems *ceteris paribus* necessarily transform the essential features of the system with which one is concerned?

In reality the capitalist world was growing and changing apace. Individual firms were expanding at times spectacularly, both absolutely and in relation to the market as a whole. The formation of trusts in the United States at the turn of the century and the spate of mergers and takeovers in Germany and Britain in more recent times stimulated ambitious corporate legislation. But because it was based on the conventional wisdom, it could not forestall the relentless growth of corporate size, power and comparative autonomy. That growth was built on legal monopoly (State franchises, patents) and even more on the many advantages of large-scale production.[8] Experience all over the world has shown that in a modern industrial system, which relies for its effectiveness on mass production, the needs of productive efficiency will reduce the number of firms in most industries. These efficiencies arise partly from the advantages of specialization which accrue with the increasing scale of operation and partly from the greater opportunities for technical progress as larger and larger firms command increasing resources for research and development. Certain new science-based technical innovations may fall outside the scope of this general pattern, of which computer software is an important example. Broadly speaking, however, the wastefulness of large-scale organization (particularly from the point of view of the individual) has unfortunately not yet reached the stage at which it outweighs the massive advantages to the producer in terms of mass production, standardization and persuasive power.

Since the Second World War the reaction of the economics profession to these changes has been twofold. On the one hand they produced a number of 'growth models' which on being closely looked at are even more restrictive in their assumptions than the 'static' theory which they wish to transcend and supplement. (In fact no better and more analytically convincing explanation of differences in economic activity of a single country in different periods and of a number of countries in a single period has as yet been vouchsafed than the famous observation of Keynes on the animal spirits of entrepreneurs.) On the other hand a number of attempts have been made to demonstrate that there is no tendency under capitalism for the degree of concentration of economic power to increase. In most cases there has been no difficulty, as Professor Sargant Florence has shown,[9] in exposing the statistical mistakes or tricks upon which these demonstrations were based. It is beside the point to refer to the vast number of firms that survive, or to discuss the competitive conditions in certain industries as if they typified the rest, for instance bakeries in the United States.[10] The problem is not how many survive, but why and how they survive. Thus, large-scale enterprises may find it neither profitable nor politic to eliminate small firms, however ineffectual or inefficient they may be. On the contrary, they will preserve them sedulously as a sort of protective layer against charges of monopoly, and often also as exploitable suppliers.

In most industries the process of concentration among the large firms usually halts before the point is reached where a *single* firm is dominant. The final struggle between the last few would be too risky, too costly, and too likely to provoke government intervention.

Rather the normal pattern is that there evolves an uneasy balance among the remaining few giants, in which each is forced to take into account the likely competitive and political reactions to its policies, which in turn may have to be appropriately adjusted. In an environment of precarious coexistence it is more than likely that firms will eschew active economic warfare, or will confine it to competition in design and advertising. It is significant that periods of unrestrained price competition, which are remembered as price wars, have occurred rather less frequently than actual military clashes, whether before the Second World War or since.

In its pricing policy the large-scale enterprise can charge high profit margins because its costs are substantially below those of its smaller competitors. In that and other respects there is more to be learned of the determinants of price from the reports of the National Board for Prices and Incomes than from the mass of conventional textbooks, though some of those reports were unduly influenced by price mechanism enthusiasts who read into delicate and complicated situations shot through with monopolistic problems – e.g. the pricing of North Sea gas – the simplicities of the Marshallian 'cross' and marginal cost considerations in situations in which they were wholly inapplicable. As Professor Maurice Clark has pointed out, while small firms become increasingly specialized under the pressure of technical innovation, large diversified multi-product groups may proliferate, with the result that one firm may achieve effective dominance over a self-contained industrial sector without actually appearing to do so, because it happens to be an important supplier of components for that sector.[11]

In most industries, as we said, the process of concentration usually halts short of monopoly. An uneasy balance is evolved between a few giants, a balance in which each has to take into account the probable and possible moves of everyone else. That element of oligopoly is quite enough to destroy determinacy in the formation of prices. This is very far from implying that the consequential changes in industrial organization and in the qualitative and quantitative functioning of the productive system have necessarily redounded to the detriment of the consumer. Any possible harmful effects which may have been associated with the decline in competitive pressures, such as the emergence of excessive profit margins or an abatement in the innovatory urge, may well have been more than offset by increased investment and faster technical progress because of large-scale research expenditure. In any case, as manufacturing production becomes increasingly dominated by large-scale organizations, it is difficult, as we have seen, to regard demand as independent of the management of supply.

3. Oligopoly

The case for a signalling system based on the price mechanism (which at the same time is a system of absolute yet impersonal compulsion) in the context of decentralized, individualistic decision-making, whether argued in economic or in political or moral terms, depends as we have seen on the *inability* of the individual entrepreneur to take into account the reactions of his competitors or customers. The asserted superiority of a system of decentralized management lies in the energy, knowledge and skill with which decisions are handled. Provided that the signals operate well, self-interest will ensure determined action. As we have seen, the theory of the price mechanism on the production side relies on certain assumptions which are the obverse of those postulated in the relationship between price and consumer satisfaction: i.e., that movements in prices and costs provide enough information for efficient decision-making; and that the entrepreneur is so constrained by the competitive framework that he is effectively inhibited from doing anything inconsistent with the optimum use of resources. In other words, he must be faced with 'perfect' markets. An instance of this ideal might be found in a community of small farmers, supplying a large (foreign) market, as exemplified, perhaps, by the American settlers at the time of the Revolution.

A number of historical changes have for a long time now been robbing that theory of much of whatever realism it ever had.

The first of these is the impact on the signalling system of the concentration of economic power not merely in the sense of the rise of giant firms often very much larger than the governments of many independent countries, but also in the more insidious sense of entrepreneurs having to look over their shoulders in their decision-making to watch the reaction of their competitors. In more and more industries they are also few enough to conspire against the public, if that seems expedient, in the manner denounced by Adam Smith. The second basic change is in the problem of risk and its influence on investment. The third is the increasing importance of indirect gains and losses which ought to, but cannot be, taken into account by private enterprise in its decisions. Finally there are the related problems of collective consumption.

The concentration of economic power in the hands of fewer and fewer people tends to limit competition, to make for many market imperfections, and to alter basic attitudes to costs. This as we shall see is of the utmost consequence when analysing the probable consequences of full employment. Furthermore its implications for international trade and the distribution of income and wealth have rarely been considered, except in so far as these might serve the purpose of condemning mercantilism. The possibility or desirability of suitably controlled monopolies, whether for technical or social reasons, has been similarly neglected.[12]

It is not really surprising that the force of these changes has been neglected or underrated by the neoclassical profession. To admit them is to remove the lynchpin from the political and economic case for trusting to the price mechanism and a policy of *laissez-faire*.[13] As soon as it has to be conceded that entrepreneurs, acting as a group or class, exercise a wide discretion over the policies that they pursue, whether in terms of what and how much is produced, or in regard to the level of prices, it can no longer be contended that the free market mechanism will ensure automatically the fairest possible solution as between workers and the propertied and managerial classes.[14]

This has momentous consequences, particularly when it is demonstrated that the successful working of the system depends upon economic – in effect human – inequality. We have already noted that the theory of harmony and its automatic achievement are essential to the moral defence of the present socio-economic system. To argue against intervention must then entail arguing for the protection of acquired privilege. One of the shrewdest and strategically most important victories of the economic élite since the war, however, has been its success in identifying freedom with freedom of private economic enterprise, that is with the lack of accountability of the economically privileged.

Beyond these all-important social and moral implications of the spread of monopolistic elements in the economic structure, there are important politico-economic consequences, which are no less destructive of the simplistic neoclassical vision. In the first place, the concept of consumers' sovereignty, at least in its traditional facile formulation in terms of rationality and independence, has to be abandoned. This we have already discussed in an earlier section. Secondly, protagonists of the decentralized system of individualistic decision-making can no longer claim that it is necessarily more rational or efficient than other modes of decision-making.

Professor Clark was certainly correct in his contention that a dynamic economy, even though shot through with monopolistic elements, is to be preferred to a perfectly competitive, though stagnant, economy. To anticipate one of our most important conclusions, economic growth -- albeit correctly planned growth – must, so far as the maximization of 'economic welfare' over time is concerned, be accorded pride of place as an object of policy. But the superiority of a dynamic monopolistic economy over a stagnating perfectly competitive economy is not sufficient for the former to claim absolute superiority over all other feasible forms of socio-economic organization.

We are not here claiming superiority for a wholly or partially collectivized system, nor denying the possibility that the price mechanism might be adapted as an instrument of control. The point to be made is simply that as soon as we abandon the determinateness of the traditional order, it is no longer evident that alternative social arrangements will not have a superior claim, since the efficiency of the decentralized system itself will then depend on the discretion, quality and energy of the economic élite and the success with which the chasm between social and private costs can be bridged. Bridging that chasm can often - though perhaps not always or necessarily - be more difficult in a private enterprise economy, where bitter resistance will be encountered from injured private interests.

Each economically advanced democratic society is likely to need a *unique* and *changing* set of solutions to these problems. The particular mixture of decentralized, market-priced decision-making, indirect controls, direct controls and public productive and distributional activities must fit the technological facts of the time and place, must fit the historically-developed institutions of the country, and should express the ruling values and democratic conflicts and compromises of the society. All those conditions are in principle subject to continuing historical change, some of it rapid, much of it unpredictable. In these circumstances it is absurd to hold a doctrinaire preference for 'least control' or for indirect as against direct control – *or* a doctrinaire preference for their opposites. The question is whether, how far and how quickly improvements can be brought about, by whichever methods can be made to work best in all the circumstances.

These conclusions follow from the changing size and influence of firms, and their changing relations with each other and with workers and consumers. But that is not the only basis of the argument. The conclusions are further reinforced by the internal changes which the firms suffer from their own growth. To these we now turn.

4. Short run and long run

The increasing size of the business firm, along with other restraints on free competition inherent in modern manufacturing, means that prices and price movements do not and cannot provide a uniquely appropriate framework for decentralized decision-making even if the series of structural considerations did not negate this claim. Not only are costs not independent of demand; in many cases the entrepreneur may have no unambiguous idea of his costs, particularly his marginal costs.

This problem arises especially in the case of the modern multiproduct firm, where it is difficult or impossible to allocate costs accurately. In principle the relevant information about marginal costs and revenue may be experimentally ascertainable. The cost of any one product then becomes a matter of accounting practice, as is the case in nationally-owned industries. But costs are not independent of output, and output is not independent of sales policy. We are thus confronted with a degree of indeterminacy worse than that experienced in a planned system, where at least the total costs including selling costs can be regulated from the point of view of the community as a whole.

There are similar uncertainties between the short and the long run, which make it hard for firms to decide their policies, or for others to predict them. It may not be in the interest of firms to maximize short-run profits if doing so may prejudice their positions in the longer run. No doubt short-run demand conditions can be fairly accurately gauged, and these will tend to respond only sluggishly to changes in price. Hence there are opportunities for short-term profits. But the firm has to stay in business, and the typical case is not that of the speculator who can exact his profit and live off it happily ever after. Nor is it like a small farmer, selling in such a large impersonal market that his actions cannot influence his future. The firm must take into account the ramifying effects of its policies and, as we have seen, this entails the abandonment of the simple concept of the interaction of independently given supply and demand conditions, whose net result was to impel a 'representative firm' with unerring force to take the right decisions.

There is a further difficulty. When considered in a dynamic context the difference between short-run costs (reflecting the degree of utilization of existing capacity) and long-run costs (reflecting changes in plant size and composition) is not so much that in the former case adjustment takes place relatively quickly and that in the latter adjustment may take some time; it lies rather in difference of response (and, hence, costs incurred) to what is expected to be a temporary and what is expected to be a permanent change in demand. The problem of stating the distinction in these terms, however, is that, whereas expectations about the degree of permanence of any change in market conditions may be clearly formed, the implications of those changes may be far from clearcut. Thus, even the most temporary of changes in demand may have some bearing on longer-run business decisions, and even a 'permanent' change in demand must be interpreted in the context of some kind of decision-making time horizon.

Moreover, the U-shaped short-run cost curve of the firm, as traditionally depicted in conventional neoclassical theory, hardly gives a faithful picture of modern business conditions. Empirical investigations have long shown that manufacturing costs tend to be constant over the relevant operational range of the firm, and then rise steeply, indeed vertically, when full capacity is reached.[15] Two related consequences flow from this. First, it is necessary to abandon, or at the very least seriously reconsider, the notion that there exists some objectively ascertainable level of output conforming to optimum utilization of capacity. Under conditions of constant costs the existence of unused capacity can no longer be rationalized in terms of profit maximization subject to independent and objective demand and cost functions.[16]

Some allowance must also be made for subjective uncertainty with regard to the market. Whereas in the traditional schema production is limited by rising costs, here production may be limited as a deliberate matter of policy, so that any sudden increase in demand can be met quickly from existing capacity, customers need not go unsatisfied and goodwill need not be lost. Further, in the context of an oligopolistic market, the existence of reserve capacity may simply reflect each entrepreneur's tacit (or even explicit) contentedness with his share of the market. But this ties up with the second related point. If operating costs are constant in the short term, the familiar 'technical' relationship between short-run and long-run average costs no longer holds.[17] The long-run position of the firm is not an objective fact, external to the firm, but is a function of current policy decisions, expectations and judgements about its own situation in the market. Thus, investment decisions affecting the scale of operations are lengthy; there is no returning to the *status quo ante*. Whether policy decisions are correct or mistaken, they are a permanent feature of the firm's history and will accordingly influence future developments.

Yet further complications arise. In a world of continual technical change, the possibility arises that, although the technology exists, a given product may not be produced at least cost. This would happen, for instance, if the market for the product were too small for the full economies of the technique to be exploited, in which case existing small-scale techniques still hold the advantage. Even then, a market of sufficient size may never actually develop, either because of a change in the nature of the product or because of further changes in technique. Or, for unforeseen reasons, the product may not prove popular and not catch on. For such reasons, it may be prudent to allocate capacity to produce a number of different varieties of the same basic product, even though unit costs for each variety may then be higher than for a single standard article. Some equipment may be less 'productive' but more flexible. There will then be a choice between two or more techniques, in which the decision will depend on the firm's judgement of the future, and especially on the stability of demand for a given product. After all these qualifications, there remains little scope for the pristine signalling mechanism of market-determined prices.

Under these conditions competition between firms, whether large or small, is no longer a matter of who can produce a given homogeneous commodity most cheaply. Each firm seeks to provide a service along with the differentially specific goods it sells; it will try to persuade its potential customers of the superiority of its particular brand of the commodity, which it will attempt increasingly to differentiate from that of its rivals. When he purchases the product, the consumer pays, in addition, for all the attendant costs that have gone inseparably into its marketing – the consumer surveys, promotion, including display and advertising, transport, research and development, etc.

Professor Chamberlin, who first called attention to the potentially unfavourable consequences for welfare of this type of monopolistic competition, subsequently qualified the destructiveness of his argument with the plea that the variety and colour that it introduced into everyday life was a source of pleasure to all, and not only those fortunate enough to possess the products concerned. But it is not possible to prove the superiority of the price mechanism on the basis of such an argument: since there are no standardized alternatives, the consumer has no objective criteria (i.e. homogeneous all-embracing standard price) upon which to base his choice. Moreover, as the degree of product sophistication and differentiation increases, not only does the act of choice become more confusing and frustrating but the consumer's technical competence and command of relevant information in judging the merits of competing product types will tend to become increasingly inadequate. Despite the help of consumer guidance agencies, State intervention, in the form of the establishment and enforcement of strict standards, would be an essential requirement; but this destroys any remaining claims to superiority that a decentralized decision-making system may have had over a more centrally-planned approach, from the point of view of production as well as from the point of view of consumption discussed earlier.

5. Excess capacity

Some systematic creation of excess capacity follows not only from the changed nature of the competitive process, in which the price-cutting, market-clearing type of competition would be disastrous for most of the parties, but also because technical considerations may be more important than the extent of a firm's estimated potential market in determining plant capacity. In addition, firms will want to carry reserve capacity so as to be able to adjust output quickly to any sudden increase in demand. (At least, they often ought to do so. In the postwar decades a lack of such capacity, leading to long order-books – with delivery delays of months and sometimes years – has had a good deal to do with the decline of British competitiveness.) A vigorously growing firm, therefore, must expand its capacity ahead of its expected increase in orders. Thus an individualist economy will tend to carry more excess capacity than would be required in a centrally-planned economy, quite apart from underemployment arising from cyclical or balance of payment depressions. Even the amount of consciously carried reserve capacity will normally be larger, since each firm must cater individually to its own possible future needs (as Professor Kornai has shown).[18] A special aspect of this problem is constituted by the recurrent waves of optimism and pessimism which we shall notice later.

All these drawbacks have parallels in a fully planned economy, which have been underlined by western writers: bureaucratic rigidities; production delays as a result of shortages; the possibility that managers will hold back a part of their output with which to bargain for other scarce supplies. Those bureaucratic imperfections might become critical, but they deserve to be compared not with the flawless excellence of a theoretical system of perfect competition, but with the actual waste and overcapacity which follow from the rough-and-ready compromises which managers in non-planned economics must make when confronted with the problems of everyday life and the colossal waste of involuntary unemployment.

Even so, a good deal of the excess capacity represents only a once-for-all loss (and its abolition a once-for-all gain) for an economy. Thus this particular blemish on the decentralized system is unlikely to prove decisive in judging its relative merits. Only if increased competition (and, hence, a fall in the degree of excess capacity) were to result in a faster rate of growth could much significance be attached to this solution. As Professors Schumpeter and Galbraith have shown, however, it is more likely that the increase in uncertainty and risk entailed in that kind of competition, and the consequent weakening of the desire to invest, far from accelerating growth would slow it down. Another influence working in this direction is that firms would no longer have the means to undertake large-scale research. We shall be discussing this latter question again in another context.

6. Profiteering

Less than perfect competition; a rate of growth of output which exploits less than fully the dynamic potential of the economy (although faster than is likely to obtain under a system of atomistic competition); far higher overhead costs, as a result of advertising and comparatively short production runs: even in the absence of collusion, these are the characteristic outcome of the competitive process under modern conditions. Of these, perhaps the most important is advertising, not so much because of the resources which it absorbs (although this is an increasingly important matter), but because of the consequent distortion of consumers' tastes, with its unfortunate social implications. Otherwise, the waste of resources implies only a once-for-all loss of potential satisfaction. The fuss made by economists about monopoly and the laws against overt collusion and restrictive practices is usually a wild exaggeration of the importance of the problem.[19] The loss of a few years' national income growth would be vastly more important. In this respect Professor J. M. Clark's plea, already mentioned, for a commonsense approach is entirely convincing.[20]

Nonetheless, it is obvious that the private ownership of certain natural resources, including land, or the provision of certain services, if not subject to some form of public control, permits the exaction of a revenue from their users altogether out of proportion to the costs or risks incurred. This is well understood. The regulation or nationalization of such resources and public utilities (apart from oil products) are now an accepted feature of economic life. What has been much less well understood is the severely limited extent to which it is possible to restrict the profits of private industry, in the absence of a standardized system of accounting and of price controls. Indirect trust-busting measures have proved singularly ineffectual. Despite the vast accumulation of capital there has been no corresponding decline in the share of profit in the national income, as ought to have happened in the neoclassical scheme of things; and this even in an era when the bargaining position of the trade unions was being considerably buttressed by conditions of full employment and government intervention. We shall return to this problem.

Obviously it is no longer possible to claim, as some have done, that the normal tendency of the competitive process is to reduce profits to the level of managerial salaries, and that the market forces which determine the supply of entrepreneurial ability work in such a way as to ensure the availability of managers at the lowest possible cost. This is nonsense. Managerial salaries are largely a matter of convention. And there is no doubt that the prevalence of certain notions as to the remuneration which is due to higher echelon executives in the private sector has had a harmful effect in terms of its implications for improving income distribution. The fact that steps could be taken to redress this position through the extension of national ownership is, of course, an important argument in its favour, although one that has been persistently disregarded in practice. What improvement there has been in Britain – and its extent is disputed – seems to have resulted from the more progressive structure of income taxation in the Anglo-Saxon and Scandinavian countries since the First World War.

A most important element in this problem, and one that has been persistently neglected until recently, are capital gains, by which asset holders can transform the appreciation in the value of their capital into spending power. The vast capital gains arising from the appreciation of land values and from the growth of the productive and profit-earning power of large corporations have to a large extent offset the redistributive impact of taxation and the improvement in the incomes of the non-propertied classes on the distribution of wealth. Even in the United States an astonishingly large proportion of capital assets is held by an astonishingly small proportion of the population. On the Continent, moreover, the inequality of distribution seems to have increased since the Second World War.

Together these developments do not encourage hopes of combining better, more progressive distribution with rapid economic progress; nor does the increasing tension between the actual distribution of income and the bargaining power of the stronger collectives representing salaries, professional earnings and some but by no means all wages. More direct controls are possible, but they would involve more direct and radical intervention than the old and ineffectual trust-busting campaigns. At present popular sentiment is swimming in the opposite direction.

7. Risk and corporate management

We have seen that uncertainty and the possibility of losses influence both the choice and range of product and the technique of production. The simplicity of the neoclassical signalling and allocative system derives entirely from the assumption of perfect competition, which in turn requires perfect knowledge and unchanging conditions, that is absence of risk as normally understood. (Even in that pure world, cyclical fluctuations would create risks – but they were excluded from the analysis.) Under such conditions – except for occasional adjustments to once-for-all changes – the problem of allocation inevitably assumes exclusive importance. The entrepreneur has no real role to play.

In reality it is behaviour in the face of uncertainty which, apart from the gains from mass production, explains the contemporary development of decentralized, individualist enterprise. It is under oligopolistic conditions (and the cyclical fluctuations that were excluded from neoclassical analysis) that the entrepreneur as manager comes into his own. Quite understandably, firms will not take extreme risks; business policy, especially among the giant corporations, will therefore tend to be characterized by a certain element of timidity or conservatism. Whereas the ideal of the enterprising young man, willing to take on any odds, is assiduously preached, a large majority of real industrialists shrink from staking their futures on rash decisions. Of course, since mistakes have to be paid for in one way or another, and by the community in terms of lost income, such reluctance happens often to be in the national interest. The unwillingness to extend productive capacity, to use machines which, though more productive, are more specific and cannot be easily adapted to alternative uses; the tendency towards multiple products, thus mitigating the consequences of failure: all these are characteristics of decentralized decision-making which have no parallel in the centrally-planned economy.

It becomes clear from these considerations that one of the principal conventional arguments against socialism or national ownership[21] – the argument that in an individualist system firms will tend to be of optimum size in the long run – is incorrect. As Professor Clark has pointed out, such an illusion is founded on the notion that productive units of only one specific size can exist (that is, be economically viable) in a given situation. This of course is belied by the facts brought to light by the Censuses of Production, which did not exist until comparatively recently. Not only is plant size determined by many historical as well as technical considerations, but costs are constant over a wide range of output, and in the oligopolistic world firms of widely different cost levels can coexist. Under these conditions the advantages of decentralized enterprise in 'optimizing' production are less, its potential drawbacks greater than has been conventionally supposed. Individual risk-bearing, moreover, limits the rate of expansion closely to the rate at which a firm's share capital and ploughed-back reserves are growing. Access to the capital market itself is limited by conventional ideas about the 'safe' rate of expansion. And to increase dividends reduces the amount of profit remaining for ploughing back. Although this need not adversely affect firms' ability to raise new capital, for expansion based on ploughed-back profits will usually raise the price of a firm's securities relative to newly-financed expansion, nevertheless private enterprise operates within tighter constraints than public enterprise.[22] In a full employment economy there may also be important differences between private and public firms' exposure to wage pressures.

The consequences of this aversion to risk – however prudent and justified it might appear from the point of view of the individual firm – aggravate the drawbacks of a purely individualist enterprise already mentioned. They are compounded first by the fact that the functioning of such a system itself creates an even greater degree of uncertainty than is already unavoidable in a world of continuous and, probably, accelerating change; and further still, by the inability of firms to take fully into account the benefits which accrue to them as a result of the activities and decisions of other firms. The handicap imposed on decentralized economies by these incapacities is vastly more important than a mere 'misallocation of resources'. It is not that national product is not being maximized at some given point in time: it is that the full potential for economic expansion is hamstrung. There is no more to be said. On this decisive score the apologists for decentralized decision-making must retreat and argue on the basis of a possible reconciliation with central planning.

It is to be emphasized that we have been referring here only to the productive and allocative inefficiencies involved in a decentralized decision-making system. But we have seen that these defects can be severely aggravated rather than mitigated when combined with a regime of demand management, designed to maintain full employment and minimize business uncertainty, which relies too exclusively on minimal and indirect controls. After the Second World War, the advanced countries expanded at unprecedented rates as long as they continued some necessary direct controls, and indicative planning to coordinate investment. Since the revival of *laissez-faire* belief, and of monetarist management relying on generally indirect and negative controls – i.e. through the last ten years or so – the riskiness of investment has once more increased and the rate of investment and of the rise of incomes has declined. The diversionary manoeuvres of the conservative and banking fraternity, so reminiscent of 1929–34, have obscured the intimate relationship between the earlier policies and prosperity, and between current monetarist policies and depression, unemployment and increasing social division and conflict.

8. Further limitations

A number of other qualities of the system of production have been discussed in earlier chapters on consumption and quality of life. Here it will suffice to remind the reader of them, by briefly listing them. A system of decentralized, profit-seeking decision-making, even in its most ideal form, cannot rationally include any of the following among its aims:

1. making proper allowance for the quality or intensity of work or the hardship or lack of amenity involved in it;

2. leisure, the absence of competitive pressure and aggression;

3. security through full employment, and through it the assurance of human dignity and social acceptance for the individual;

4. protection from transitional and locational hardships caused by sudden changes affecting prices and production;

5. social equity in the distribution of income;

6. the maintenance of an economic system compatible with political freedom and decentralization of economic power;

7. more particularly, the modification of the hierarchical structure towards accountability and reciprocity in relation to the productive process;

8. securing a sense of individual participation;

9. the prudent long-term use of exhaustible resources, including any desired concern for generational equity;

10. good environmental management, and fair and efficient distribution of its costs.

We perceive that some of these goals may conflict with one another, and some may well be alternatives to increases in production and productive capacity. An increase in output, for instance, brought about by an increased anguish or uncertainty which enables labour discipline to be established, and exerts sufficient pressure on wages to prevent inflation, must be considered in this light. Surely this must be taken as part of the economic problem, even though it cannot be brought under the measuring-rod of money. Others which can – after a fashion – be measured in money have virtues just as doubtful. More smoke, more smoke-abatement; more cars and roads, more accidents, hospitals and wheelchair industries all counting as positive goods; and so on. Neither 'consumer sovereignty' nor decentralized profit-seeking production decisions can do much about any of those items, without substantial amounts of public enterprise, planning and control.

9. The managerial revolution

We have already noted in passing the argument that a decentralized system of decision-making conduces to a higher quality of management. Alfred Marshall, following Adam Smith, stressed this imponderable aspect of the problem, and rightly so. The picture of new entrepreneurs forcing their way to the top, innovating, opening up new vistas, is an attractive one. It is hardly surprising that the most entrenched defenders of *laissez-faire* should try desperately to prove that individual initiative and genius are still responsible for the great innovations of the day.

But their efforts have failed. Since the war the growth of new competitive firms has been restricted in most fields to those cases where the government was willing to foster new organizations in competition with existing giant corporations (for instance, Kayser Aluminum in the United States, the State oil corporations in many parts of the world) either by selling productive facilities on very attractive terms or, as in the case of jet engines, electronics and communications, by offering research contracts, thus freeing the firm in question from risk (although often there was no compensating limitation on profits). The Defence Establishment has played a prominent role in this development.

The growth of specialization and the attendant need for exports has limited the scope of the one-man firm. Already the Webbs could point out that the decision-making process had become similar in large-scale industry to that in publicly-owned enterprise.[23] In both cases there is of necessity a chain of responsibility; decision-making becomes a matter for committees. The question is: who appoints the committees and how do the pressures to which they are exposed differ from those which individual entrepreneurs would experience under *similar* conditions? Professor Pigou, dutifully accepting Marshall's case, could still argue in 1937 that private firms retained a great deal of independence despite their corporate structure.[24] That may be so, but it was not the main defence. The main defence had always rested on the superior directive power of perfect competition. With that no longer plausible, libertarian defenders of *laissez-faire* have found themselves in an awkward position. Some of course have argued blandly that the assumption of perfect competition was not necessary to the conclusions about productive efficiency and social harmony, and that has somehow justified the survival of the discredited conventions of neoclassical thought as the staple of most university economics courses to this day. But the political arena was different. A new defence had to be established; it was not slow in coming.

The new philosophy asserted that the very changes which had undermined the old assumptions of perfect competition and consequent harmony of interests had themselves entirely altered the motivation and animating principle of the decentralized economic system. If the perfect market had gone, so had the ruthlessly individualistic entrepreneur. That archetypal figure had 'optimized' in what were often very short-term ways; he had built a personal or at most a family business, the former constrained by his own mortality and the latter subject to decay as human frailty succumbed to the social temptations of an aristocratic environment.

By contrast with that, the new capitalism (it was argued) saw large corporations operating under utterly different social compulsions. Unlike the old businesses the new ones were in principle perennial. Their policies were determined by an expert managerial hierarchy which was not subject, as individuals are, to the corrupting effects of time and success. The modern manager is positively motivated to look to the long term. No doubt he will receive large bonuses from time to time and participate handsomely in the profits of the firm, but these will certainly not comprise the major part of his income. Thus even his pecuniary interest is not directly related to profit maximization but depends rather on the size of the business itself. Moreover the very prominence of large corporations, and the loss of anonymity which this entails, make it essential to avoid trouble. Shareholders certainly have to be placated. Takeover bids have to be avoided, but increases in profits may not always be exactly matched by corresponding increases in dividends. Labour troubles as well as political attacks also have to be avoided as much as possible. But even shareholders may prefer a lower but steady income to sharp fluctuations and uncertainty. In any case the dispersal of ownership makes the individual shareholder a silent and only in case of exceptional events an active partner. Ownership is said to lose its importance.

Control has been transferred to managements which have been chosen not from among the owners, but increasingly on the basis of performance. The rise of conglomerates and the increase in size really allow the best possible utilization of the very scarce managerial ability available.

The concept of profit maximization has itself become blurred by the interaction of moral, political and economic influences. When a large corporation forgoes profit opportunities in the short run in order to maintain good public relations with its clients, or to secure industrial peace, or to avoid government interference, this could equally be regarded as intelligent profit maximization in the long run. In either case of course the determinateness of output and price policy vanishes; and with it also vanishes the certainty that the policies followed will be in the best interests of the community. As an increased portion of savings emerges through life insurance, pension funds, unit and flexible trusts their managers would in any case exert some (in UK still insufficient) supervision over the handling of corporate affairs.[25]

This was indeed a beguiling model of the new mixed and indirectly-controlled economy, still based on the price mechanism and a modified form of decentralized private decision-making. It does not really reflect reality, but it has acquired powerful defenders.

At first, as we have seen, even Galbraith argued in his *American Capitalism* that the new system, though far from the beautiful picture of neoclassical imagination, would have its merits because the abuse of corporate power would often stimulate defensive reactions of 'countervailing power'. Not only would this check abuses, but the balance of forces so developed in the economy would be favourable to research and growth. A comparison of the record of concentrated large-scale industry in the United States with the sectors in which competition between small units survives can leave no doubt as to which of the two has been more successful and, even from the community's point of view, satisfactory.

The second and more complacent line of defence has a longer history, running from the work of Professors Berle and Means in the 1920s through that of Professor Burnham in the 1930s and (among many others) Professor H. Jones and Peter Drucker in more recent times. The last-named have finally consecrated the role of the modern manager: he seeks *nothing* but the good of the community, and what is good for the United States is most happily good for General Motors. Twenty years ago this view found support in Britain among those who tried to persuade the Labour Party to renounce 'Clause 4', which included among the Party's objectives the public ownership of the means of production, distribution and exchange. If ownership has become powerless, why try to liquidate it, especially if that would enrage a vast array of powerful vested interests which, through their ownership (and undoubted control) of the channels of mass communication, could influence public opinion powerfully, at election time, against any party proposing nationalization?

The argument formulated by Professor Burnham regarding the unimportance of ownership has met with rather rough treatment, quite apart from the strenuous efforts of owners to defend their apparently worthless rights. No sooner had this argument been revived in Britain than there followed a new vigorous wave of mergers both in this country and subsequently in the United States and Europe. In all of these the ultimate control by shareholders was made clear. If managers were ever under the illusion, fostered by Professor Burnham, that they could disregard the interests of their shareholders in high profits, they were soon sharply reminded by the successful takeover bids which were made possible through their failure to utilize reserves to the full or through not sufficiently maintaining profits. Thus one way or the other managers cannot seriously flout the interests of owners without incurring the risk of displacement. The rising importance of special institutions – pension funds and insurance companies – controlling vast savings funds may further extend the scope of management, but it also strengthens and enforces the interests of owners.

No doubt shareholders, so long as they feel themselves satisfied, will not be impelled to exercise their rights; indeed it would be foolish, because costly and with little chance of success, to attempt to mobilize them in this direction. It follows therefore that the managerial oligarchy will have considerable freedom of action, although constrained within strictly prescribed limits, and will be actuated by motives other than short-term profit maximization. But the same would be the case of any owner in similar circumstances – more so probably, since marginal profit would appear less urgent to him than to the average shareholder on whose satisfaction the manager has to rely. Thus the manager will be careful to conform to the long-run interests of shareholders, for in the ultimate analysis it is ownership and the profits derived therefrom which determine his fate, as takeover bids and struggles for control have abundantly shown.

This aspect of managerial dependence on ownership, interestingly enough, is brought out by some of those who wish to defend the new capitalism from a purely economic point of view. For instance, it has been pointed out (thus developing the case made by Professor Galbraith) that the large corporations depend for their expansion on the capital market to a greater rather than a lesser degree than the self-contained entrepreneur of the textbooks. It follows from this argument that, unlike the self-reliant entrepreneur, the corporate manager will be under corresponding pressure to produce results in terms of growth and technical innovation. The lassitude of accomplishment is less of a threat in a hierarchy in which the most energetic have yet to win recognition. On the other hand, any success will be immediately reflected in increases in stock exchange valuations, and these can of course be consumed. Such stock exchange quotations form in effect a kind of league table by which groups of owners can measure managerial success and on this basis take remedial action.

It is important, however, not to exaggerate the conflict between the interests of ownership and control, certainly not at least in terms of the social classes represented. Indeed the relationship between the managerial oligarchy and the owning classes is far closer (in the United States they are becoming increasingly identical) and their interests coincide far more nearly than Professor Burnham and his successors would have us believe. The degree of social mobility experienced in Britain since 1931 and in the United States in the postwar period is rather less marked than one would have expected to result from the acceleration in economic growth, the concentration of business and the increasing need for managerial personnel. In England this tendency has been slightly accentuated by a somewhat greater egalitarianism in the education system and by the increasing infiltration (resembling the French experience) of big business from the ranks of the higher Civil Service.

It became clear, however, to the protagonists of the managerial revolution that the harmful consequences for social wellbeing resulting from the increasing concentration of economic power (as discussed in earlier parts of this section) could not be ignored; certainly it was not possible to revive the myth of consumers' sovereignty. Thus, as an alternative to the managerial revolution two further lines of defence were prepared. In the first place it was contended that the State had already gained a substantial degree of control over the economy through its control over public current and investment expenditure. However, this has not been borne out by experience in the non-Soviet orbit and more particularly in the UK and US. The 'informal' relationship between private industry and the Civil Service has resulted in a massive migration of personnel from the latter to the former, impelled by the prospects of continued active service and correspondingly increased remuneration. This does nothing to encourage objective public control and cannot be termed democratic. In practice many civil servants in the higher echelons have tended to behave so as not to prejudice this blessed prospect.

Nor has the relationship between government and the nationalized industries been satisfactorily resolved in Britain. The refusal to review and control the policies of the nationalized industries by democratic means has brought the basic moral aim of nationalization, that is accountability, to naught. The establishment of a parliamentary organ, adequately staffed, has come late. These parliamentary organs, the specialized Select Committees, hold regular hearings and issue reports. The executive find them a time-consuming nuisance. But the British public, which before was not informed about specific scandals, has acquired a powerful weapon. Its influence was demonstrated in the inquiry on North Sea gas and oil, which forced the government to change its policy and thus saved billions of pounds for the Exchequer. The staffing of this as of other parliamentary committees remains indifferent. It is usual to argue that more effective parliamentary control would stifle 'risk-bearing'. On the contrary there is no reason to suppose that expert pressure brought to bear on the management of the nationalized industries would discourage venturesomeness. In the United States in a number of cases it has certainly led to the extension and intensification of government initiative.

The second alternative line of defence consists in the proposal that the problem of excessive managerial influence might be resolved by the appointment of one or more directors – up to half the total – to the boards of private companies either by the workers or by government (this possibly in conjunction with a scheme to purchase or otherwise obtain shares in the companies concerned). Some experience along these lines has already been gained in Germany, although it has not been at all favourable. Rather than enhancing the interests of workers, the result has been that the trade unions have lost a number of their potential leaders, who as worker-appointed directors have developed a greater loyalty to the company whose interests they became intent on promoting. Certainly as a curb on the excesses of private enterprise they were singularly ineffective. On the other hand, the appointment of government representatives in the absence of a far-reaching reorganization of the Civil Service and the establishment of democratic control would simply strengthen the symbiotic relationship of the two bureaucracies already referred to, and intensify to an intolerable degree their oligarchic control over the community. Thus as an alternative to – rather than as a method of – democratic economic control these courses should generally be rejected.

From the purely economic point of view two clear consequences emerge. First, the new capitalism, as opposed to the old, has lost its orderly organizing principle brought into operation by the interplay of given consumer demand and a determined structure of costs. While it gained in dynamism it lost its claim to exclusive economic rationality. Certainly from the social point of view its superiority could no longer be established a priori; this would now depend on a sociological comparison between the quality of decision-making in decentrally organized (but increasingly concentrated) economies and in centrally planned economies. The rise of a socially responsible managerial élite and its growing emancipation from the profit motive were shown to be a myth, very convenient no doubt to the managers but inaccurate as an analysis of social reality.

The problem of the dominant position of highly trained and skilled management (what Professor Galbraith calls the technostructure, including the Civil Service) has been much complicated by the enormous change in the structure of savings. This consisted in a large increase in the volume of cooperative relative to personal savings, which meant that savings, particularly in the US and UK, became increasingly institutionalized, and hence concentrated, as they were increasingly channelled through the life assurance companies and pension funds. The gilt-edged market and the trustee savings banks became correspondingly less representative of the main thrust of personal savings, apart from the increasing personal wealth of entrepreneurs. The increase in land values was a powerful force in this respect.

Before the Great Depression, the so-called merchant banks in the UK specialized in foreign fixed-interest issues. After 1933, and especially since the Second World War, they provided long-term capital indirectly through the stock market and the institutional investors. In sharp contrast, the banks on the Continent have played a far greater role in providing capital for industry and commerce; as a consequence the European stock markets have been of far less importance as a means of raising capital than their equivalent in the UK and US.

In Italy since the Great Depression and in France since the Second World War, the banks and the insurance companies have of course been brought increasingly under State control. In Germany the banking system, initially decentralized by the Americans after the Second World War, was later to be nationally unified, involving a large reduction in the number of independent banks. In all these countries of Europe (and to some extent also in the US before 1914), bankers traditionally had taken an active part in the supervision and rationalization of industry.[26] This process, which had the effect of concentrating shareholdings into fewer hands, was inevitably to the advantage of shareholders as a whole. Traditionally described as weak and hopeless in the face of the power of industrial management, the individual shareholder could now feel secure in the knowledge that his interests were being protected by institutions of immeasurably greater influence and bargaining strength than his own.

Now it could be argued that the aims of these groups - businessmen, bankers, investment financiers - were identical. Yet it would be equally plausible that whereas industrial management would show a preference for low dividends and a high rate of accumulation, the various sorts of institutional investors would exert their influence in the opposite direction, raising dividend rates above what they would otherwise be, and using their influence to moderate what they might estimate to be an excess of entrepreneurial zeal, not to say recklessness. It is quite possible, therefore, that a far less unequal balance of forces between 'ownership' and 'control' may have emerged than might have been expected on the basis of the literature that has accumulated since Berle and Means first raised this important issue. One might reasonably argue, indeed, that this was one of the points at which Galbraith's countervailing forces might result in a better balance.

At the same time, however, it is clear that private enterprise does not always produce more favourable results than public ownership; this is certainly the case when Britain's industrial performance is compared with that of France and Italy, where public control is considerably more comprehensive. The reason for this is partly to be sought in the extraordinary neglect on the part of the managements of insurance companies and investment trusts to recruit industrial experts, and in the fact that in Throgmorton and Threadneedle Street class still plays an important role in the selection of 'insiders' - who knows whom matters more than who knows what.[27] No large private German bank, for instance, nor indeed the Italian IRI, would tolerate the sort of amateurishness which, as a result of these practices, afflicts Britain's industrial financial scene.

Now, at a time when the threat to social and economic stability is particularly acute in Britain, the arguments against the extension of the public sector, especially in the sphere of finance, fade away. The only caveat to be taken seriously concerns the apparent inability of governments of whatever party to select the most appropriate managers; certainly there would seem to be little point in expanding the public sector until its present functions can be better managed, as for instance in the ineffectual handling of North Sea oil and gas, and the Bank of England's acquiescence in undermining the stability of the credit system. It should be said, of course, that large corporations in Britain and the United States have taken increasingly to recruiting civil servants into the highest executive offices, partly as a result of the growing influence of taxation and negotiations with government departments on the determination of profits.[28] The first and most urgent need therefore is the establishment of an acceptable system for selecting and promoting the best managerial talent available, for, without it, private industry in Britain will always have the advantage, and even the best conceived plans in the public sector will continue to go awry.

Full Employment and the Distribution of Income

The experience of a hundred and fifty years or so of economic history has discredited both classical and neoclassical pictures of the dynamics of income distribution. It is not true (as some classics argued) that wages can never rise above subsistence. But nor is it true (as most neoclassics argue) that market forces will automatically tend to reduce inequalities, and thereby justify the capitalist system in a moral way. The neoclassical revolution of the last quarter of the nineteenth century succeeded in dispelling the classical gloom of Malthus and Mill by predicting an automatic upward trend in the share of wages. If widely believed, that would actually have had regressive effects, because it would have dissuaded any attempts at deliberate redistribution. Classical economists at least admitted the existence of a problem, however sceptical they were as to the possibility of its solution by means of government intervention. In reality it was not the automatism of the system but mainly, if not entirely, the growing democratization of politics, and government intervention in the form of taxation and the provision of the social services, which brought most of whatever improvement there has been, and gave the lie to the pessimists.

1. Classical gloom

Political economy had been the 'dismal science', with its gloomy forecasts for the prospects of the 'labouring poor'. Except possibly for intermittent periods of relief, the working class could expect no more than subsistence; any increase would be eaten up by human reproduction; hence the iron law of wages. The destitution of the wage-earner, so far as the classical economists were concerned, was a sad but inevitable condition of economic life (or, rather, of its social organization). Unless the Malthusian devil were exorcized there would be little hope of improvement; efforts on the part of government (let alone private philanthropists) to alleviate poverty – whether by means of minimum-wage legislation or wage supplements – would be to little avail and transitory in effect. John Stuart Mill concluded ruefully:

No remedies for low wages have the smallest chance of being efficacious, which do not operate on and through the minds and habits of people. While these are unaffected, any contrivance, even if successful, for temporarily improving the conditions of the very poor, would but let slip the reins by which population was previously curbed.[1]

2. Neoclassical cheer

Yet by this time – 1860 or thereabouts – the tide of orthodox economic thought was able to move in a completely different direction, impelled not merely by rising standards of living, but also more decisively by the use that Marx had been making of classical political economy. As we have already mentioned, the 1870s saw the virtually simultaneous, though independent, development of a new approach in at least three separate centres of learning. We have seen some of the implications of this in our discussion of consumers' sovereignty. More germane to the present issue of distribution is the optimistic way in which it dealt with the wage share of output and income.

The neoclassical treatment of income distribution, while claiming to be completely pure of any social or value content, nonetheless sought to reinstate a certain notion of harmony or social justice, through which each class of income earner would receive a reward corresponding to its contribution to the total product. Based on the assumption of perfect competition, and all that this implies in the matter of certainty (there is no need of foresight when all is unchanging and unchangeable), the theory was eminently adapted to exposition in terms of simple calculus. Each factor would then be seen to earn a reward which was determined by the productivity of its marginal unit engaged in production.[2]

Thus, by the use of what amounted to no more than a tautology, the neoclassical writers claimed the rise in the level of wages above subsistence could be explained on the basis of a theory of markets. Hence, they asserted that a conclusive argument had been found, proving that the way to a better standard of life for the worker was to be sought not in 'social improvement' – and the government intervention which this implied – but in the steady increase in his productivity due mainly to an unfettered accumulation of capital. Hence, with the gradual increase in the supply of capital per worker employed, they asserted that the forces of supply and demand alone would mitigate the grossest inequalities in the distribution of income and wealth *both within and between nations.*

3. The Marxist vision and the orthodox defence

The importance of this new development cannot easily be exaggerated. For the previous century or so of its existence, economic science had earned its gloomy epithet. The great classical school had predicted perpetual misery for the working class, and for the greater part of the nineteenth century real life under the iron law of wages seemed proof enough. This classical doctrine Marx, with consummate legerdemain, adapted to his own political purposes: that is, to prove the transience of the capitalist stage of production, and the inevitable and necessarily catastrophic transition into the bliss of the Proletarian State.[3]

The first century or so of industrial history seemed to justify his analysis. The optimistic views of Smith seemed to be refuted. No automatic improvement took place in subsistence levels, or in the distribution of income and wealth. It is, however, characteristic of the relationship between economic history and the evolution of economic theory – as of the claim of economists of all schools, including Marxists, to be scientific – that Marx's bleak prognostication of unrelieved misery for the working masses should have coincided with the beginnings of a rise in real wages, and hence the palpable failure of the classical economics in which his theory had been founded. (Not until the 1930s, with the disintegration of the American boom – with its hopeless chaos of collapsing banks and holding companies, general agricultural bankruptcy induced by falling prices, lack of effective demand coupled with idle productive capacity, and increasing human misery and despair – did the alternative classical-Marxist view of the inevitable breakdown of capitalism seem to receive any evidential support.)

The increase in real wages during the latter half of the nineteenth century was restricted to the countries of Western Europe which, following Britain, had succeeded in developing deliberately their own manufacturing industries, or where sparsely populated territories such as the United States, Canada or Australasia had been settled by successive waves of European immigrants, themselves branching out increasingly along a pattern of urban industrialization. (The increase in real wages in the latter had, of course, little if anything to do with the sort of static balancing process described in neoclassical economics texts.) It was argued that an individualist economic system would, in the end, ensure increasing equality as real national income rose and capital was accumulated. In fact there has been no such large fall in the share of profits in total income. The share has fluctuated somewhat around a fairly constant level, rather than falling. It was the equality of income distribution *after* taxes that improved.[4] (The startling increase in the share of salaries – more akin to profits in a system of managerial oligopoly – was at the expense of rents rather than wages.)

The rise in the incomes of workers resulted rather from two quite separate forces, neither of which reflects the automatic tendencies alleged by neoclassical theory. The first of these forces was technical progress, which has never found a convincing place in that theory. The second factor – more important from the viewpoint of increasing equality – was the expanding scope of political suffrage, or at least upper-class fear of it. Political democracy, and not an automatic market mechanism, was the means by which the worst hardships were mitigated.[5] Trade unions began to gain acceptance and, even in countries where their judicial persecution continued, became increasingly effective. The one-sided power of the employers, based on their ample reserves, was met by the cohesion of the workers. Steadily, whether through direct negotiation or through political manoeuvre, and sometimes with the support of employers who were glad to have the State do what they would not do themselves, the material conditions of the labouring class were improved; more important, this period saw the first beginnings of the movement towards the setting up of the Welfare State. In this respect, then, Marx's predictions have surely been falsified by events, however likely they seemed when he first formulated them in 1846.

Marx was on surer ground with his other major prediction, of the increasing severity of economic crises. The severity of those crises did indeed increase, until the Great Depression threw tens of millions of ordinary people on to the scrapheap of unemployment, and opened the way to Hitler's destruction of the civilized Weimar Republic, and to the catastrophe of the Second World War.

The experience of a century or so before 1938 had been characterized by a cyclical procession of booms, giving rise to labour shortages and increasing prices, followed by slumps as a result of the efforts of the monetary authorities charged exclusively with the protection of the gold reserves and the maintenance of exchange parities. During periods of general optimism the orthodox pattern was to increase interest rates. This was supposed to dampen the demand for credit at the margin for investment, especially building. So long as optimism lasted this was hardly ever effective, and it would have been the greatest luck rather than good judgement for such a course ever to have resulted in the establishment of simultaneous and sustainable external and internal balance. The normal outcome was for the atmosphere of optimism to be dissipated by some speculative failure or violent monetary policy measure. At that moment, prevailing interest rates would be out of tune with expectations and the 'subtle' balancing mechanism of the economic system would overcompensate, resulting ultimately in a slump. On the other hand, once a slump had set in it was not enough merely to lower interest rates. New enterprise and investment could not be stimulated in such a way as long as existing capacity remained unemployed. Thus it was that the Central Banks found themselves in a position of always lagging behind events, of chasing after the cycle, and hence overshooting the mark alternately on the side of expansion and depression. The periodic unemployment and uncertainty that this caused were essential features of the orthodox economic balancing mechanism.

Because so many of the same mistakes are being repeated half a century later, there is point in emphasizing once again how much the orthodox expertise itself – in government, business and Academe – contributed to the instabilities, and therefore to their horrifying political consequences. Through the depths of the Great Depression most of the economics profession refused to accept Keynes' commonsense view in favour of a programme of deliberate demand-creation. Even in 1935 the most notable of American economists and bankers brayed in unison their condemnation of Roosevelt's efforts to stimulate expansion – the New Deal – timid and shamefaced as these were.[6] In most of Europe there was not even a New Deal, and business tended to be as blind as government. The imbecility of the international banking fraternity attained its apogee when a scion of the firm of Mendelsohn, the largest of the private German banking houses, not only supported and contributed to the enforcement of a deflationary policy under Luther and Bruning, thereby precipitating Hitler's rise to power, but opposed the reflation under von Papen when this came within an ace of success. Thus did Jewish bankers contribute to their own destruction. British Establishment opinion was no better. The 'Lloyd George Manifesto' and Keynes' and Henderson's essay ('Can Lloyd George Do It?') as well as 'Means to Prosperity' were countered by the so-called Treasury Doctrine and Professor T. Gregory's and Pigou's writings accepted by Churchill – who had previously been very sceptical of the advice he received.

Under that sort of advice and management, the *laissez-faire* system did not produce the real income and steady growth expected of it, and the violence of cycles did not decrease. In America from 1929 the chaos of collapsing banks and companies, falling prices and the threat of general agricultural bankruptcy, and lack of effective demand coupled with idle productive capacity, seemed indeed to presage the doom of capitalism. In the 1930s, Soviet Russia and Nazi Germany alone seemed able to solve these chronic problems. By contrast, endemic unemployment, the traumatic impact of which is still indelibly imprinted on the memory of those who lived through that period, persisted until 1941 in Britain and for a further year in the United States. It was the re-employment of the masses desperate in their idleness which furnished Hitler with the sinews of war and enabled a less populous and less well endowed Germany to obtain in 1940 a clear military supremacy over France and Britain.

But that long accumulation of disasters did at last shake people's faith in *laissez-faire*, and allow the Keynesian revolution to occur. The position after the war seemed for a time to be entirely changed. Excepting the less developed countries, whose intransigent problems are of a different order, the world was no longer plagued by enduring crises and slumping production. Year after year production increased – furiously so in some countries, like Japan; sluggishly in others – yet increase it did in *all* of them, and *more rapidly* than at any time previously, whether during the interwar period or even before the First World War. Growth with full employment was the great postwar achievement. In its wake however it brought inflation; the new nagging and relentless increase in prices: our greatest current political peril. Before long the accelerating inflation toppled governments. It induced exchange crises and undermined the international monetary system because it defied 'scientific' explanation and led to a desperate conservative return to the orthodoxies of the prewar era. Indeed the victory of monetarism seems to have ushered in a return to mass unemployment as the orthodox method of dealing with wage spirals.

This inability to reconcile stability with full employment once again threatens the very basis of the contemporary mixture of managerial and 'managed' capitalism. The profound structural changes that have taken place in the economic and social system have completely belied the gossamer model of finely adjustable market equilibrium which the economists have elaborated and over-elaborated. The satisfying determinacy of those theoretical solutions has been swept aside by the sheer brute force of bilateral bargaining. The problem appears in all countries, irrespective of their constitutions. It is not merely that the expectations of the workers have been sharpened by the long period of full employment; it is that the sanction of unemployment has lost its effectiveness because of its political implications. But since this new crisis – so unexpected by both 'scientific' socialism and 'scientific' *laissez-faire* – is *political* rather than economic, its outcome is uncertain. After a period of stable progress the non-communist world is once more in a crisis caused by the political consequences of full employment. It is as yet uncertain whether the lessons needed for recovery have been learnt.[7]

The classical attitude to this awkward problem was to deny it.[8] However, when something like full employment was achieved it became clear not only that the more articulate higher-income classes would suffer considerable discomfort by it, but that the stability of prices and money values would be endangered. Hence there was developed a new neoclassical approach with a superficial liberal Keynesian flavour.

As we shall see, economists with but few honourable exceptions became mesmerized by 'statistical proofs' with which they

persuaded themselves that the problem of indeterminacy and inflation could be solved automatically and painlessly by running the
economy at a 'reduced pressure', that is by permitting somewhat
higher levels of unemployment.[9] Moreover it was believed to be
possible simultaneously to eliminate an important and hitherto
obstinate source of conflict between welfare criteria: by a suitable adjustment in taxonomy, full employment was now to be designated
as that level of unemployment which was just compatible with price
stability (rising prices being evidence of overfull employment).

Meanwhile some genuine Keynesians adopted a rather surprising approach, in which the principle of the multiplier was used to
determine the distribution of income between wages and profits.
The method is to *assume* full employment – and, hence, a fixed
level of output – so that aggregate (planned) saving is determined
by the level of investment, rather than by the level of income, as
in the Keynesian underemployment scheme. Clearly such a system
breaks down unless one assumes further that trade unions suffer
from money illusion: but this is hardly realistic when judged against
contemporary experience. With full employment (or even less),
any increase in the level of real investment relative to real output
must elicit a corresponding increase in real savings. This, so the
theory goes, is effected by the inflationary impact on prices – and,
hence, increase in profits – as a result of the increase in total
monetary demand; the distributional effect of this, depending on
the relative propensities to save out of wages and profits, is to raise
profits and to decrease wages until the requisite increase in aggregate savings has been achieved.[10] The unreality of this picture is
evident. A profit inflation of the kind envisaged here would undoubtedly lead to compensatory wage demands (or more so) and
a consequent inflationary spiral: it would be impossible to achieve
a position of balance, whether in real or monetary terms. This neo-
Keynesian theory of income distribution accordingly breaks
down.[11]

4. The international distribution of income

Though it overlaps the subject of Chapter 9, it is worth noticing
at this point how the same orthodoxy has performed in trying to
explain and predict the dynamics of international inequality.

In contrast to the domestic sphere of the highly industrialized democracies, the Marxist prophecy of increasing inequality has been clearly vindicated, not only in international terms but also with regard to income distribution within the poorest areas. At the very moment when the European overseas empires – the political expression of capitalist imperialism – were being dissolved in most parts of the world, the industrialized countries under the leadership of the United States began to give government aid in undreamt-of quantities, not only to their remaining dependencies but also to the newly liberated countries and poor emergent nations of the world. Both for that reason and more powerfully for automatic market reasons, neoclassical economics predicted a reduction in inequality as between highly developed and poor countries.[12] In fact the very opposite happened.[13] The relative position of the poor areas of the world worsened, certainly since 1900 when imperialism was at its zenith, and probably even since 1938. A combination of modern medicine and social backwardness resulted in an explosive increase in population, and no doubt the reassertion of this intractable Malthusian problem has been a principal cause of the failure to mitigate inequalities. But it cannot explain the remorseless worsening in relative (and sometimes absolute) standards of life.

Throughout this period, academic economics in the field of international relations was based on a *choice of premises* whose logic *entailed* the universally beneficial effect of free trade and specialization; moreover, in the period since the Second World War, during which international income disparities have worsened, the theory not merely argued that *all* countries would benefit from international trade, but went so far as to predict that such trade would reduce inequality and, in fact, tend to equalize per capita income as between all trading nations.[14] The inability successfully to tackle dynamic problems, however, meant that the traditional theory was unable to deal with the influence of growth (and, implicitly, technological change) on the relative positions of different groups of countries. In the midst of growing inequality, 'rigorous' economic theory not only failed to explain this problem (let alone solve it); its existence was not even recognized.[15]

5. Stagnation and inflation

We have now arrived at the very centre of the present-day problems, the problem of inflation. The failure of democratic governments to control the rise in prices since the war has been responsible for the fall of more administrations than any other reason. The discovery of an economic policy technique which would permit democratic countries to combine monetary stability and full economic expansion and employment is undoubtedly the most important problem before the Western world. Further failure now threatens a return to the horrible experiences in the interwar period, a loss of steady full employment with all that would mean socially and economically. In view of the tremendous achievement of the first two postwar decades, this reversal seems astonishing.

The two postwar decades of Western economic history differ crucially and fundamentally from all previous experience. They are characterized by almost continuous full employment and correspondingly sustained economic progress. The great blemishes of the capitalist system, stagnation and lack of work, seemed for ever banished, and it is as a direct consequence primarily of this achievement that many, not to say most, of the advances in the social and economic fields have been made. The postwar period contrasts dramatically not only with the misery and indignity of the interwar years of chronic and sometimes massive unemployment, but also with the vulgar display and luxury of the Edwardian era. Those times, to which doctoral students nurtured on State grants at plateglass universities turn their nostalgic eyes, were in reality times of stagnant production and productivity, often with falling real wages. They also saw the long decline in Britain's relative industrial vigour. It is a sobering thought, then, that Britain's unsatisfactory economic record between 1945 and 1970 – which has been compensated for by many attractive features of life – was nevertheless by far her best performance for the last century or so. If the same comparison between the postwar and interwar periods is made for the United States, Germany and France, the results are even more startling.

The achievement of full employment owed a good deal to early postwar policies, including the (often reluctant) continuation of many wartime controls. It was also helped by the slowness with which attitudes and atmospheres adapted to the new realities.

Trade unions for example did not all, or immediately, use the additional clout which the guarantee of full employment offered them. So the promise of full employment was entrenched in popular expectations some years before its more unnerving effects began to show, or to make Conservative propaganda appear persuasive. By the time of the Conservative victory in the election of 1951 full employment had achieved Establishment status, and even the most complicated circumlocutions about personal liberty and freedom of choice, about the high pressure of demand, about excessive wage demands and inflation, could not at first succeed in making anything like prewar levels of unemployment politically acceptable.

Whatever problems it created, the achievement was profoundly valuable. We have argued earlier about its fundamental effects on class relations, reducing servility and opening to the working classes the virtues of independence and self-respect long prized by their betters. The psychological significance of full employment is that it is a condition in which people feel themselves to be wanted and needed members of a dynamically advancing community – a community in which material resources are accumulating for whatever purposes it may decide, be it for private or for public consumption, for housing, for amenities, or for other productive investment, promising a yet better and easier life in the future. Production thus has another aspect which has usually been disregarded. Human dignity and satisfaction are incompatible with unemployment, even if the fear of penury had been completely eliminated by the social services – as it has not. The knowledge that a man fulfils a role in the community, that he has a positive function to perform, has a value which no system of social security, however lavish, can provide.

Full employment, then, is not merely a means to higher production and faster expansion, it also has its own intrinsic value in its implications for social relations; unless it is consciously restored – with due accountability on both sides – economic progress, social peace and responsible democracy will all be increasingly threatened. But although I believe the measures necessary to reconcile full employment with stable prices are intellectually clear, they are politically extremely difficult. There is a sense in which they are bound to antagonize nearly everyone, at least until majorities come, by some mixture of better education and bitter experience, to accept the need to submit the distribution of income to what the Australians long ago named (though they also have yet to achieve it) 'a new province for law and order'.[16]

These particular implications of full employment are especially unpalatable to orthodox economists, to many traditional (and traditionalist) followers of the Labour Party, and to many affluent protagonists of free enterprise. None of the three will admit that the very mechanism of the mixed economy has been changed by full employment. They form an unfortunate alliance of enemies in their dislike of the new problems, and even distrust serious discussion of them. Thus, it is impossible for them (since it would contradict the initial purpose of the 'alliance') to combine in the mutual formulation of any constructive proposals with a view to resolving these problems.

Instead, all parties escalate their demands. Instead of a new province for law and order they initiate a new war of all against all. It is the setting of class against class, or profession against profession, in a desperate and mostly futile endeavour to reassert their status and protect their real incomes, that constitutes the real danger of the new inflation. Of course, it is possible to protect specific groups in the community, such as those dependent on fixed incomes, against the effect of continuous monetary instability – to make 'living with inflation' possible; what is far more difficult is to bring to an end the constant struggle to maintain relativities, which is persistently stimulated by the relentless increase in prices.

It is vital to understand that neither the Keynesian nor the monetarist schools have offered any valid analysis of the malaise or any viable approach to healing it. It cannot possibly be healed either by brutal levels of unemployment, or by the unaided use of indirect macro-economic measures, whether fiscal or monetary. The problem is deeper and more difficult than that. The achievement of full employment necessitates a complete reconsideration of our attitude to economic and social policy; a rethinking of social institutions, obligations and responsibilities, both for individuals and for groups. We need a new *contrat social* representing a deliberate agreement on economic and social policy.

It is right to acknowledge that 'free collective' bargaining was once a positive aid to equity and economic progress. The traditional union attachment to it is wholly understandable. So is union suspicion of modern incomes policies, which have too often functioned as one-sided 'wage freezes' with little enough resemblance to fair social contracts. Nevertheless, a free-for-all in the labour market, in which oligopolistically organized employers confront oligopolistically or monopolistically organized labour, is no longer compatible either with the maintenance of full employment or with the continuation of a satisfactory rate of increase in the material resources which society needs for the creation of a better, fuller, more civilized and humane way of life. Not only is free bargaining one of the principal elements in the spiral of wage-price inflation, hence posing a continual threat to the external position of the country;[17] it also militates against the attainment of greater equality in the distribution of non-profit income. Unions are not all equally well organized, nor are all occupations of equal national strategic importance, with the result that the lowest paid and the least aggressively organized classes fare progressively worse. This is evident, not only as between the various classes of wage-earners but increasingly as between the salaried and professional middle class on the one hand and the lower paid, unskilled workers on the other. It is the privileged middle-class minorities (e.g. doctors, airline pilots, petty managers, technicians) and the stronger labour unions who exploit the inflationary spiral to steal a march on their less advantaged fellow workers. No doubt a part of such unsociable gains is subject to tax, but the story does not end there, since pension arrangements are adjusted upwards with salaries, and hence become increasingly important. Partly, the strong improve their already unequal shares. Partly, their gains are temporary and as each round is completed the futility becomes apparent, and the leap-frogging begins over again. Meanwhile the lower-paid, the women, the defenceless and the handicapped have little or no protection, and no sure guarantee of their share in the national income, despite the declarations of the unions. The distribution of income before tax has deteriorated, and efforts to improve the position of the lower paid by the traditional device of free bargaining have merely made matters worse and the wage-price spiral more acute. Once, free collective bargaining reduced inequalities. In modern conditions it more often increases them.

What then must we do?

Joan Robinson in her seminal essay in 1938 foresaw the reasons why full employment would be incompatible with stability, but did not (at that time) propose any practical solution to the problem.

Professor Galbraith, in his early *American Capitalism*, suggested that it might be possible to achieve equilibrium by matching the strength of the great corporations with that of the trade unions – the concept of countervailing power. But this cannot be the solution: for either there is full or near-full employment, in which case neither employers nor unions have any incentive to prevent wages from increasing; or there is less than full employment, in which case progress is retarded and potential output wasted. Later, in *The Affluent Society* (1957), he gave up in despair and proposed higher unemployment as the only remedy, while advocating that the victims of such a policy should receive substantial compensation – although this, as we have argued, does not really deal with the social problem. In fact it was a policy much like this that was pursued in Britain after 1965, comprising high redundancy payments and wage-determined unemployment compensation, a policy, however, which proved futile in stemming the cataract. In his later synthesis, in *Economics and the Public Purpose* (1973), Galbraith comes down in favour of a break with the past and of what he calls the 'socialist imperative'. He repudiates the global means of economic management and control, especially monetary policy. He is aware of the grave limitation of the neo-Keynesian approach and explicit in his demand for direct controls and the need to enforce a much greater degree of equality than ever before, in order to achieve by conscious consent the economic preconditions for stability.

Put simply, the task before us – and it has gone by default now for a quarter of a century or more – is one of political education and economic reform. The trade unions, both in the leadership and the rank and file, should appreciate that their altered status and strength, and the immense advances that they have secured, require the acceptance on their part of concomitant duties and responsibilities to the community.

It must be recognized that the trade unions are no longer the weak representatives of the underprivileged masses, and that free collective bargaining is no longer the desperate effort of the weak and the hungry, holding together against fearful odds and largely unaided by social services, to secure their rightful share of the national product. The unions, on the contrary, constitute one of the most powerful vested interests in the State, and herein lies the problem, for as presently organized, the pattern of trade unionism in Britain comprises perhaps the most serious threat to economic and social stability.

This instability may arise in a number of ways. First, despite the process of amalgamation, the number of individual unions in Britain is still large. Many unions may coexist in the same industry or plant, and the interests and bargaining tactics of these unions, representing different segments of the same labour force, will often clash, as in the case of demarcation disputes. This lack of cohesion among the unions has also been a major cause of the uncoordinated pressure on wages which underlies the upward spiral of costs and prices. But herein lies the second contributory source of instability. The Trades Union Congress, unlike some of its counterparts on the Continent, is a rather loose confederation, whose authority is severely limited by the basic autonomy of the individual unions. Clearly, a major source of instability would be eliminated were an organ such as the TUC to be able to lead organized labour towards a more coherent bargaining approach; such has long been the case in the United States. Industrial action and wage bargaining are no longer isolated, atomistic phenomena – their repercussions, even those of individual, perhaps small, unions, may be far-reaching. This being the case, it becomes increasingly important that the elemental requirements of the modern economy should be recognized. But despite the relative autonomy of the individual unions vis-à-vis the TUC, the official leadership of those unions is under constant threat of erosion, and herein lies a third source of instability: the increasing power of shop stewards and convenors. If these latter can evoke the militancy of the members, or if the members themselves feel that their elected spokesmen on the shop floor are responding more sympathetically and energetically to their claims than their official union representatives, the forces for decentralization will continue to strengthen and the prospects for a coherent approach to this gravest of problems will recede further. Leapfrogging claims and petty inter-union rivalries will continue, as will the increasingly vicious and divisive circle of rising prices and costs. Such a situation is clearly worse from the social point of view than one in which labour were to be firmly organized under a single monopoly structure.

The success of any attempt at achieving some form of social consensus, then, will depend crucially on whether a rational framework of wage negotiation can be created in which considerable sections of the population will not feel themselves to be done down. It must become evident to the people affected by the new negotiating arrangements that their cooperation would benefit not only themselves, but also the country.

Any such new machinery for wage negotiation must meet two essential conditions. First, there must be an equitable means of determining wage and salary incomes, or rather income differentials, extending to the very highest levels in the professions and top management. Secondly, of course, any system which is devised must be accepted as equitable and capable of effectively implementing policy.

More broadly, the success of any prices and incomes policy will be more likely the faster the domestic product grows and the more equally it is distributed. It is at this point, in our view, that conventional Keynesian optimism founders, and where, if we are to create a workable mixed economy, it is essential to introduce socialist measures such as to bring about a basic change in social power relationships. Apart from the moral imperative, economic considerations alone demand that justice be seen to be done.

On the one hand, then, an effective prices and incomes policy requires a very much greater degree of government intervention than would have been acceptable hitherto. This, because if the government is to obtain the willing cooperation of the trade unions they will have to be given a reasonable assurance not only that their sacrifice will be temporary, but that it will not be in vain; that wage restraint, on which the success of the exercise depends, will in the not too distant future bring about positive results in terms of accelerating the increase in standards of living. Such an assurance however will have no credibility in the absence of comprehensive institutional arrangements for putting some coherent and self-consistent plan into effect. This goes far beyond anything contemplated by liberal Keynesians. To expect the trade unions to accept wages pegged to productivity increases, no matter how badly managements behave, however backward or unwilling they are to increase their commitments and to study and introduce new methods of production, would be absurd. It would be equally absurd to expect the trade unions to acquiesce in the hardship of lower-paid workers or to accept changes in taxation which impinged on the worker proportionately more severely than they did on the affluent, in the name of restoring incentives and rewarding efficiency, however well meant.

The establishment of a steady advance towards a better life in our Western industrial societies therefore depends more on a change in attitudes and institutions than on economic management. There is no evidence that the limits of taxation have yet been reached; income inequality and conspicuous consumption, on the other hand, are very much in evidence, whose flagrant injustice renders the economy so vulnerable to ever-increasing wage demands and the omnipresent risk of deliberate, punishing doses of deflation.

The important questions, then, are: how to distribute the national income more equitably; how to modernize the wages structure; and how to preserve monetary stability and our relative competitive position without creating unemployment. To all these, the answer certainly does not lie in industrial action. Nonetheless, the fate of the West depends to a large extent on the quality of the trade union leadership and on the degree of enlightenment of governments.

CHAPTER EIGHT

Backwards to Monetarism

1. The failure of Keynesian management

The extraordinary revival of monetarism followed from the neo-classical Keynesian failure to understand and avert the new inflation. The briefest reminder of the reasons for that failure will serve to introduce the subject.

When it was accepted that there was nothing in the economic system which could guarantee an automatic full employment equilibrium, a majority of the profession responded in three conservative ways. They set out to 'freeze' the new idea into a structure of equations as rigid and therefore nearly as unreal and unreliable as the old scheme had been. They hoped to manage the level of aggregate demand by indirect fiscal and monetary measures which seemed easy to apply and politically acceptable – so plenty of 'Keynesians' joined in cheering on the 'bonfire of controls' in the early postwar years. And they neglected as too hard, or put off as unproven, the early warnings of the 'left Keynesians' about the inflationary potential of a system of indirectly managed full employment in a world in which oligopoly and union power were combining to replace more and more 'market forces' by market power.

For a while the compromise seemed to be justified: the postwar years began well. There was a quarter of a century of impressive growth with unprecedented full employment and, at first, very moderate inflation. As wartime direct controls were progressively dismantled, and the accompanying psychology and expectation of restraint dissolved more slowly, the first signs of a return to some other and nastier characteristics of prewar 'normalcy' were unobtrusive. For example, the stop-and-go fluctuations were on a minor scale. Except briefly in the Korean crisis, national output never actually fell, or ceased to grow. So it was easy not to notice that after each setback the following level of unemployment was a little higher than before. By 1970 or so, the rate of inflation was higher too, and by then it was obvious to all (or should have been) that the best efforts at fine-tuning aggregate demand were powerless to prevent prices and unemployment from rising *together*, in defiance of all conventional theoretical expectation.

Then came some major shocks. The sudden and sharp increase in oil prices in 1973-4, following upon a general speculative boom in commodities and physical and financial assets, accelerated the rise of consumer prices in the industrialized countries. This in turn precipitated wage demands in most countries quite out of line with productivity growth. Thus in all countries, inflation received an unprecedented boost.

Faced with that, what should the economics profession have done? It might have listened at last to those of its members who had been predicting these effects for decades: for example the writings of Joan Robinson and Kalecki and myself in Britain, Galbraith and latterly Lester Thurow in the US. It should have studied hard to see what further modifications of Keynesian management, what further instruments of control, were needed to conserve the priceless social achievement of full employment while avoiding the accompanying problem of destabilization. It should have accepted what seem to me to be the inescapable conclusions of such a study and worked thereafter to develop a fair and consensual social contract.

2. The backslide into monetarism

Instead of that constructive response, what was the actual response of our 'science' to the neoclassical Keynesian failure with inflation?

It conformed fully to its character as analysed in the first and third of these chapters. It went back to the economics of the 1920s: balanced budgets, fixed or upward drifting exchanges, and their use in combating inflation; reluctance to create sufficient liquidity. Above all, it went back to the Quantity Theory of Money. The recrudescence of monetarism now stands out as an incomprehensible aberration, which may be likened only to the Lysenko episode in biology. But Lysenko had some potent persuasive arguments, in the labour camps of the Gulag Archipelago. Western economists and journalists, like Humbert Wolfe's British journalist, swallowed monetarism unbribed and unfrightened. However it is not difficult to see why economists as well as trade unionists and politicians have embraced this credo with such enthusiasm. It depersonalizes the economic problem. Apart from cutting public expenditure and taxation its motto is: 'Keep the money supply growing at a (low) steady rate and all will be well.' It washes its hands of short-run influences and their more permanent impact and concentrates on the never-never land of long-term adjustment, while freely issuing current, often quantified, advice.[1] What more comfort could be derived from any doctrine? It absolves everyone of all direct responsibility.

Since so much loose talk is to be heard on the subject, it is essential to be clear as to what exactly is implied by 'monetarism'. A mere acknowledgement that there is *some* connection between money and prices is not monetarism. Of course there is *some* connection between money and prices; we live in an economy where transactions are conducted through the medium of money. Prices are therefore expressed in terms of money (though paper money can be and, especially after wars, has been displaced by commodity money in the form of, e.g., cigarettes or bully-beef as means of exchange). It is therefore self-evident that prices or incomes should affect the volume and/or velocity of money in circulation, and be affected by them. Monetarism is distinguished by insisting on a fundamental causal relation between money and prices, from the former to the latter. It implies a stable two-way reversible relationship strong enough to be usable for strategic policy purposes, in particular for controlling inflation. Monetary policy is therefore held to be not merely a necessary but also a sufficient instrument for regulating prices and incomes.

All parties have long understood that public sector deficits could, on occasion, cause trouble by contributing to excessive monetary demand. Monetarists are distinguished by claiming that the relation is certain, and holds exclusively in all cases; and that there is a definite limit to the size of the public sector, beyond which democracy will break down.[2]

In fact monetary instability can originate also in the private sector as a consequence of excessive bank lending to finance either investment or consumption (for example, the financing of the stock exchange boom in 1927–9 allowed vast capital gains to sustain consumption). In such cases of *demand* inflation, prices are likely to rise ahead of costs to the benefit of profits, though under modern conditions, as we shall see, a primary rise in profit is not involved. If the process persists, other income-earners will exert pressure to capture (some of) the loot: anticipatory defensive increases in wages, interest rates and, at first more sluggishly, salaries and pensions will follow. If this continues, it will accelerate and hyper-inflation will set in. Prices will rise, and exchange rates fall, faster than the increase of the volume of money.[3] The velocity of circu-lation rises astronomically and the real value of the monetary circulation shrinks precipitately.

In principle we ought to be able to distinguish between as many types of cost-induced inflation as there are types of costs. The existence of profit-induced increases in prices will, of course, pro-voke instant denial: in a competitive system profits are convention-ally supposed to represent the minimum residue which needs to be earned to keep supply adjusted to demand. As we have seen, the postulated framework no longer exists in a vast range of manufac-tures and services. Price-leadership and information agreements have enabled dominant firms to adjust prices so as to safeguard revenues. This is confirmed, as we have already discussed, by the 'perverse'[4] movement of prices of manufactures in the mild set-backs suffered since the beginning of the 1950s and in the more serious recession in 1974-5. The increase in the price of steel in 1956 in the United States was a total vindication of the view that profits can play an actuating positive role in inflationary move-ments. The revolution in oil prices is another example. The resist-ance of politicians, bankers, industrialists and professors of eco-nomics to accepting this conclusion has been paralleled by an equally fierce repudiation by trade union leaders and their followers of the notion that wage demands have much, if anything at all, to do with consequential movements in prices.

It was for this reason that all and sundry were delighted with the discovery of the so-called Phillips curve, a 'proof' that a stable up-and-down relationship existed between the increase in wage levels and unemployment. Decision-makers could be handed a 'menu' from which to choose the politically acceptable levels of each. Unemployment could be reconciled with the 'optimum' working of the system. Unfortunately for the liberal (conservative) Keynesian, this curve vanished[5] at the end of the 1960s (if it ever existed as more than a coincidence).

The whole scene has since been bedevilled by this wholly unexpected but easily explicable rebirth of the neoclassical monetarist school. It has revived and carried to absurd lengths the doctrines of the 'old' pre-Keynesian propagandists of a do-nothing policy. Thus was revived the original neoclassical dream that the economic system, provided it is left to itself, will secure an optimum allocation of resources including a minimum 'natural' (i.e. inescapable?) rate of unemployment. Professor Friedman's account of that natural rate being 'ground out by the Walrasian system of general equilibrium equations' has been quoted earlier (in note 21 to Chapter 3).

Thus the Walrasian system is revived and its rehabilitation is said to be completed by finding a substitute for perfect foresight through the Rational Expectations Hypothesis. This, the monetarists claim, is sufficient evidence to render State intervention harmful a priori. Given the sharp fluctuations of the stock exchange and commodity markets, as well as of investment nowadays, one is not inclined to accept this further refinement of the discredited neoclassical micro-economic faith as a useful basis for the diagnosis of modern problems. However, the new version tries to differentiate itself from the old. It purports to cope with the awkward problems of bilateral monopoly and growing oligopoly, and the importance of increasing returns in the markets for goods and services, by 'absorbing' these difficulties, that is correcting the conclusions to take care of them (rather in the way that 'free trade' authors dealing with foreign trade or growth 'absorb' problems of unemployment or distribution of income). Unfortunately for this school, such acceptance of a need for such correction in fact makes it impossible to 'grind out determinate Walrasian answers'.

Friedman disregards these difficulties in a cavalier way. He accepts, at least implicitly, a model in which basically there are so many (small) units (including wage-earners) that they are unable to influence prices (including wages) as in a Walrasian system of perfect competition, while he incorporates contrary elements (as 'imperfections' reducing employment) without acknowledging that these rob the model of a determinate solution.

Just as they have neglected the macro-economic developments of the last century and a half, the crises and long-run unemployment, the monetarists have also dismissed the micro-economic changes, the growth of monopolistic structures and behaviour that have so fatal an effect on macrodevelopments as to blur the distinction between the two. The growth of decision-making units on the side of both employers and labour which we stressed as the main cause of the dysfunction of the system is disregarded; so is the consequent subtle transformation of market *forces* into market *power*. As we shall see, this renders Friedman liable to grotesque mistakes in his diagnosis and forecast for the oil problem and foreign exchange fluctuations.

A good example of the influence of different past experience on organized behaviour and economic outcomes is seen in the British and German responses to increased import prices, particularly oil prices. In Britain, the accelerating rise in import prices was paralleled, indeed exceeded, by an increase in domestic costs. This ultimately forced down the rate of exchange, thus vindicating speculative anticipations that had not been justified by the basic economic situation at the time of the beginning of the attack on the currency.[6] In Germany, both the government and the trade unions were still so much influenced by their memories of monetary catastrophes that the increase in oil prices, so far from stimulating wage claims, reduced trade union pressure even in sectors where the rise in unemployment was too low to explain such a change in attitude. Germany, and especially its trade unions, had paid a terrible price for the earlier inflations and monetary collapse, although they had been in no way responsible for them. It is against this historical background that German unions have shown that they will not embark upon actions which might attract blame for another such debacle. In contrast, many British unions tried to safeguard what they believed to be their members' direct interest, and maintained or increased their money wage demands without much regard for the likely indirect effects of such pressure. In each national case past experience was decisive because the concentration of economic power enabled a uniform national policy to be followed.

3. The nature of inflation

A workable and politically acceptable solution to the most important problem facing the non-Soviet world requires a correct analysis of the inflationary process. This is not easy. A great many factors are involved, the interaction between them is intense, and their causal direction is difficult to discern. Cause and effect intermingle and the dangers of *post hoc ergo propter hoc* solutions are daunting.[7] If, as in most econometric and mathematical exercises, a neoclassical system is (mostly implicitly) taken for granted, eventually the conclusions must follow that all inflations originate on the monetary side. In such a system no single factor on the supply side can initiate a cost increase which translates itself into a sustained inflationary movement.

The fact that the great hyper-inflations of history were caused by budget deficits[8] due to wars, revolutions or despotic profligacy and exactions met by the debasement of the coinage or the printing press was taken as empirical 'proof' of the monetary origin of inflation. Too much money (in this scenario) was chasing too few goods. From these experiences was derived the quantity theory of money. The French Assignats, the old Rouble, the Reichsmark and the various astronomical Hungarian inflations attested its strength.

In its crudest form it made prices directly dependent on the volume of money.[9] The conventional formulation was that, *other things being equal*, the absolute level of prices was proportional to the volume of the money supply.[10] Now this formulation is no 'proof'. It is either trivial or untrue. It is true (and trivial) only in the case where a government changes the denomination of the monetary unit as did de Gaulle in France in the sixties (but unlike the case of the German currency reforms in 1924 and 1948, which were accompanied by a revaluation of debts, thus causing strong shifts in asset distribution). If the change in the volume of money (which the difference between the two situations implies) is meaningful (and substantial), then the difference of the method adopted for its infusion into the economy could not help but have an influence on prices and output, and other things could not possibly be 'equal'.

The monetarists ride roughshod over these arguments. They combine, as we have seen, a long-run (how long?) Walrasian 'real' model with a denial that monetary intervention can alter the outcome of its working in anything but the shortest of short runs, and translate that long-run (equilibrium) position into money terms by the old Fisherian attempt[11] to reduce the quantity theory into a 'scientific' equation. It follows that prices (and money income) are determined exclusively by the money supply. The demand for money is a stable relationship. Fiscal measures cannot permanently affect the national income. Nominal interest rates are augmented by the expected rates of inflation. Thus expansionary monetary policy ultimately produces inflationary expectations which paralyse its effectiveness. It follows that the sole strategic variable is the stock of money and its growth. As we shall see, every one of these assumptions has been shown to be fallacious and the empirical evidence questionable if not totally misinterpreted. This does not mean, however, that *a dominant belief* in the monetarist doctrine would not make it come true – for a short time, and at grave cost in unemployment and lost production. Like Pavlov's dogs, financiers would sell and lend or remain liquid, mechanically following the reported ups and downs of money supply.

Unfortunately for humanity and the economics profession, Friedman's missionary persuasions came at a time when all too many people were in urgent need for some such dispensation. There was widespread disillusion with the neoclassical Keynesian performance. The élite whose 'fine-tuning' had failed longed to be released from responsibility for it. It seemed salutary to restore financial 'discipline', that is the supremacy of the banking and financial community. Common sense and compassion should have driven them all to look for ways *forward* – for appropriate additions or replacements to the Keynesian armoury, to complete and stabilize the Keynesian achievement. But Friedman would have none of that 'New(est) Economics', and has led his flock back to a primitive neoclassical faith in the power of a self-adjusting market system to maintain the best rates of employment and growth that government meddling and other intrinsic imperfections will allow. In that view, the historic achievement of the Keynesian revolution was merely to create inflation by vain attempts to reduce unemployment below its natural level. To undo that ill effect, the proliferation of the 'public sector' must be severely cut. The high unemployment benefit must be pruned. There must be an end to all intervention which hinders the flexible interaction between price and demand and supply, which is the ideal mechanism for securing balance and prosperity.

The sooner we get back to the impersonal perfection of free markets the better, says Friedmanism. This may, of course, result in unemployment, but not as much as will follow from continuing intervention. In the long run, unemployment is caused by the imperfection of markets and by attempts at managing them. Each degree of interference has a corresponding 'natural' rate of un-employment which can be affected only temporarily by monetary manipulation and eventually only by accelerating inflation. Apart from cutting public expenditure and taxation, the only useful thing that government can do is to limit increase in the money supply strictly to a low annual rate of, say, four or five per cent.

It is true that a democratically elected government might not escape the wrath of an electorate which was forced to suffer a cut in its economic security and standard of living. But a Friedmanite approach had not really been tried in its full vigour in a democratic country until the recent elections in Israel and Britain. In the former it was overshadowed by the visit of President Sadat to Jerusalem (though it might be argued that that miraculous appar-ition was fostered by the bread riots in Cairo caused by the insist-ence of the IMF on a cut in food subsidies).[12] In Chile, Argentina and Brazil, where there are ample means of enforcing any policy however iniquitous, similar policies failed and were promptly re-pudiated by the Guru. The hesitant first steps taken by major industrial countries in that direction around 1970 merely succeeded in halting the miraculous postwar recovery. Mrs Thatcher's ex-periment however has been – at least in its first couple of years – more thoroughgoing. As economists we ought to be grateful to her – seldom have we seen so unequivocal an experiment. But the price in human misery is high. It is paid not only by those who lose their jobs but also by the mounting anxieties, and all the consequent family hesitations and uncertainties, of the much larger numbers who have to wonder whose jobs may go next.

The monetarist school entirely disregards the experiences of the century and a half before the outbreak of the Second World War. Yet those showed that left to itself the capitalist system is basically unstable. Consequently their policy recommendations are capable of catastrophic effects. On the one hand the purer monetarists believe that prices – even oil prices – behave themselves if left alone – in May 1974 Friedman famously predicted that the OPEC oil prices would soon return to 'normal'. On the other hand the remaining neoclassical ex-Keynesians who still believe that fiscal demand management, with some monetary policy aids, will suff-ice[13] now blame all troubles on 'special' price fluctuations such as those of 1973-4, instead of concluding that their own policies and preferred methods of management have been growing less and less appropriate over the years. They also try to rescue the credibility of the profession by minimizing their basic theoretical differences from the monetarists, while acknowledging the rift between their *practical* advice.[14] Cumulative movements are excluded from the analyses of both. Neither believes that 'science' can notice history, whether on the large scale of historical changes to the economic system, or in day-to-day processes of the kind in which one thing leads to another, then on to another, instead of 'back to equilibrium'. For the monetarists it is *un*anticipated changes which are seen to be the cause of disruption. The often self-justifying and self-sustaining character of sharp changes in stocks due to psychological or other shocks is not dealt with.[15]

Regulation of the 'supply of money' as the main instrument of economic policy follows therefore from the implicit assumption that the markets are perfectly competitive and self-adjusting.[16] Of course Friedman pays lip-service to the existence of imperfections; but these merely result in changes in the 'natural', i.e. irreducible, unemployment. Apart from this they do not interfere with or even modify the working of the economy.

In other words, the monetarist model is totally unfit to analyse the economy of the modern world, its constituent states and problems. It is clear that none of the assumptions which Friedman made to reach his extraordinary conclusions bears any relation to reality. They were chosen precisely because they led to the desired theoretical conclusion, that inflation is a purely monetary phenomenon, originating solely in excess monetary demand. It follows that trade union bargaining affects only the distribution of income between groups of workers, or unemployment.[17] Other lapses from 'optimality' are accounted for by malfunctions in the system induced mainly if not exclusively by government intervention. Except by the prescribed method of monetary management, government can do nothing to improve economic performance, and every attempt to improve it will in fact make it worse.

As before, the worst aspect of this extraordinary reasoning is not so much its detail as the conception of science and history that underlies it. Its explanation of price movements is actually a 'fallacy of the consequent'. It fails to see that in a dynamic and highly oligopolistic economy no Walrasian equation system can be established at all, let alone help to explain or predict the changing situation. Once the importance of the path, i.e. the series of short-run impulses and changes, is recognized, the concept of a long-run equilibrium vanishes.[18]

I shall now turn to the methodology of the quantity theory.

4. The meaningfulness of the quantity theory

We have seen that the rationale for the choice of the 'supply of money' and its rate of change as the main criterion for and instrument of economic policy is the assumption that the economy in the main works on Walrasian lines. We have argued that these underlying assumptions invalidate Friedman's conclusions because they *imply the conclusions* he wishes to establish.

The modern monetarist analysis (and the attempt to put it on an empirically testable basis) dates back to Irving Fisher.[19] Fisher tried to show that the absolute level of (money) prices was ultimately determined by the volume of money. The analysis begins modestly, with an *identity* $MV = PT$, the now-famous '*equation* of exchange'. In plain words this means that the total money spent is equal to, really identical with, the total money received. Not much illumination there. In order to be significant as a policy instrument, the identity must be transformed into an equation in which every component must be sharply defined and must refer to the same system. There must be a provable, stable relationship between the independent strategic variable and the rest of the system included in the equation. This relationship would have to hold in *both* directions, that is, be reversible.

In respect of every one of these conditions serious doubts arise. If, for example, one could be sure that (in this version) the transactions velocity of circulation (V) is constant, determined by habits and monetary institutions which, in the nature of things, vary so slowly that the resultant speed of turnover of the monetary stock can be used as a parameter, the first step would have been taken towards the successful 'testing' of the monetarist thesis. On the other hand, T, the volume of transactions, was conventionally taken to depend on the full employment level of real resources based on the usual set of Walrasian supply conditions. As evidence accumulated, however, it became obvious that these assumptions were not sustainable.[20] Far from being stable, national product (and total money transaction much more) showed marked variations (though much less in the execrated interventionist period, 1945–70, than before or after). Moreover, as we shall see, there is a close relationship between the various possible definitions of money and their respective velocities which further reduces the relevance of the 'volume or supply of money' as the basis of decision-making, or its main policy instrument.

The problems raised by the required transformation of the $MV = PT$ identity into a fully-fledged equation are not exhausted there. If M is directly and exclusively to determine P, then not only V but T also must either be constants or vary in the same proportion in the same direction all the time. The assumption that they do behave so involves grave difficulties. The economic system, as we have seen, consists of two interconnected and strongly interacting spheres: flows and stocks. The former are usually much steadier than the latter, and their investigation, since Quesnay and the French physiocrats, has stimulated the formulation of schemes of equilibrium flows. The stocks, as they are dependent on unpredictable psychological influences, have been neglected. This has given rise to grave errors in prediction and advice. Indeed, the accumulation and decumulation of stocks (whether of financial or real assets) are one of the most important causes of global economic instability. Among the financial stocks are money savings, some of which can be mobilized instantly or with only a small timelag, while others have access to markets like stock exchanges where the actual turnover is but a fraction of the stock, but where (because of the magnitude of the total) devastating impacts can originate. Astronomical international money balances are lent and re-lent on the so-called Euro-currency market, which is totally unregulated.[21] At the slightest disturbance of 'confidence' they fly from one centre to another, thus swamping the more stable income flows and often becoming both destabilizing and, ex-post, self-justifying, possibly self-aggravating. Meanwhile the highly developed consumers' credit system, by facilitating anticipatory borrowing and sudden debt repayments, can violently change the even flow of saving. Consumption and savings have in successive periods proved less stable than investment, thus weakening the basic approach of Keynesian theory and policy-making. As we have seen, all these disturbing movements are excluded from the monetarist 'equation'. Having formally eliminated them, it follows *by definition* that prices, the passive factor, must react to the active strategic factor, the independent variable money (M).[22]

As soon as we scrutinize the methodology of this procedure we encounter grave difficulties and objections.[23] It should be obvious, if we are to avoid a second fallacy of the consequent, that all ingredients of the identity/equation must refer to the same system. But they do not.

There is first of all the question of defining what is meant by the money supply. This looks straightforward. It is not. Money has a number of functions. Among them, those of means of exchange and standard of deferred payment move on the same orbit as the total volume of transactions (the accent, as we shall see, being on *total*). But these do not exhaust the functions of money: for instance, another, and most important, of its functions is as a store of value. In that function inert money becomes an asset and does not enter transactions. Variations of the volume of this inert money can be deeply destabilizing.

This failure to establish a unique definition of the money supply, or of the money that effects prices, is of great importance. One monetarist listed no fewer than seven options:

Retail M1 M1 less interest-bearing sight deposits.

M1 Notes and coin in circulation + United Kingdom sight deposits in sterling with the banks.

M2 M3 less wholesale time deposits (e.g. deposits over £50,000).

Sterling M3 M3 excluding United Kingdom residents' deposits in foreign currencies.

M3 M1 + public and private sector time deposits with the banks.

M4* Sterling M3 + private sector holdings of Treasury bills, tax instruments and commercial bills.

M5* M4 + building society deposits.

The difference between these definitions of money is that as one proceeds down the list, more and more of the existing volume of short-term *assets* are included as *money*, that is, the successive definitions include more and more money or quasi-money used as

* As defined by stockbrokers W. Greenwell. Quoted in the *Guardian*, April 1979.

a store of value. These do not have much to do with transactions except when they themselves change hands; and when this happens it may be for a variety of motives, though they may well exercise a powerful (and often destabilizing) influence on economic activity. Thus, as the definition of money is widened, its velocity falls. Indeed some store-of-value money, e.g., building society deposits, can be regarded as the residue of money of narrower definition circulating more quickly than it would have done had there been no such transfer to the building society, e.g. a cheque drawn on a bank account handed over to a building society, which re-lends it to a house-buyer, who passes it on to the builder, etc.[24] The rate at which assets change hands seems to change cumulatively as optimism wanes to pessimism and vice versa. We shall presently discuss the implication of this for the monetary control of the economy.

As a consequence of this difference in the functions, and therefore in the velocity or efficiency, of money, the assumption that V is stable and governed by long-term institutional or traditional factors is perfectly untrue. Change of time deposits into current account deposits, cross-borrowing, by way of sterling deposit certificates, or the holding of Treasury Bills by the discount market, will affect the so-called supply of money in its main definition of M3. Quicker payments (as the CBI advocates) will increase the velocity and tend to counteract restrictive monetary policy. Far worse, the large investors, such as the pension and life insurance funds, by holding off the gilt-edged market, can blackmail the Treasury by causing a (formal) increase in the money supply (though, as they will stay idle, their investment has no economic significance), forcing it to grant higher rates of interest.[25]

The difficulties do not end there. Changes in foreign sterling balances were at one stage included in, and are now excluded from, the definition relevant to policy-making by the Bank of England, M3 (sterling): not so deposits created by credit operations on their basis. For certain purposes British-owned balances in foreign currencies are not counted (though, with the appreciation of sterling, their inclusion would have contributed to the decline in the rate of expansion in 'money supply'). The main official 'indicator', M3, does not differentiate between personal and business deposits, both of which ought, moreover, to be subdivided into convenience and precautionary deposits, and into deposits held as liquid (speculative) assets. Thus, a shift in holdings towards financial institutions other than banks, and into assets other than money deposits – e.g. building societies or the issue by banks of bonds – would diminish the official money supply and thus allow expansion, or vice versa – for no good 'real' reasons. High real rates of interest would also tend to reduce the money supply as people will hasten the repayments of loans, though this effect might be somewhat offset by the flow of deposits from financial institutions towards the banks.

The very concept of 'money supply' is arbitrary and fuzzy. The 'recognized' formula has undergone startling changes. Altogether the liability of the concept to manipulation, together with the psychological impact of the changes of its volume, represent one of the most dangerous consequences of the monetarist doctrine. In the long run the bias will be against expansion because expansion, given the present structure of the economy, tends to entail inflation (though it is uncertain whether restrictive monetary policy will end inflation, even if it results in stagnation).[26] To make confusion worse confounded, money substitutes can easily be created.[27] The stricter the official definition the more likely it is that they will be created. Deposit certificates, trade credit and credit cards can be used for a number of functions which will normally be performed by money 'proper' (that is closer to the conventional concept of money).

A closer look reveals a further and greater weakness. In order to discover whether, by an alteration of whichever M we have chosen, prices alone will be directly and proportionately affected, we need to know that V applies to *all* transactions, that is to say to both the income-expenditure stream or *flow* and to the redistribution of assets, i.e. to *changes* in the ownership of *stocks*. We have seen that changes in stocks can produce sharp changes in flows, which might become self-stimulating and cumulative and destructive of the stability of flows – if indeed the latter were stable. Thus it is of the utmost importance to include all transactions, including stock exchanges and other transfers of assets, so as to be sure that the monetary balance of flows is not offset by the change in the velocity rather than the volume of money. Total turnover can certainly not be identified with a Walrasian measure of GNP. Irving Fisher tried to estimate the former – no official statistic exists because in a modern society T, the total transactions, is all but unknown.

Thus a proxy, the national income or product, has to be substituted for it. This procedure is only legitimate if there is a stable relationship between the two.[28] But it is precisely at this point that the history of business cycles points in the opposite direction. If anything stock changes seem often to have been a violently destabilizing factor. Thus the velocity (V) as now used by monetarists is an illicit hybrid concept, because it excludes all non-income transactions (house purchases, other transfers of assets, realization of paper profits etc.), though all definitions of money include money used for the transactions thus excluded, and there is no reason at all to believe that the income transactions move parallel with the non-income transactions for which they serve as proxy. The denominator *covers the whole economic system* while the numerator deals exclusively with *final (income and outlay) payments*. Thus the resultant ratio is not a measure of the true transaction velocity at all (though it is so recorded even in British official statistics). Yet these transactions can yield significant profits or losses and affect investment decisions. The true velocity of money might increase or fall violently without the sphere of income/outlay being nearly as much affected.

The monetarists' approach shows a regrettable ignorance or disregard of the actual working of the monetary system. As we have just suggested, *the statistics of the so-called 'money supply or stock' must not be used for policy-making, because of the possible destabilising effects of non-income transactions, which are excluded from the conventional concept*. A most significant example is the near-collapse and then incredible rise of sterling in 1976–80. The period is characterized by the swing in oil imports of some £4 billion in 1980. Nevertheless the current balance was expected to show a deficit and is (because of the deep depression which reduced imports) likely to show just a balance. As the rise in wages and prices was notably higher in Britain than in competing countries an import penetration took place which exerted fatal pressure on British industry. Friedman, contemplating the British case, used the purchasing power theory to explain the sterling crisis of 1976. Compared with the dollar, the pound bought fewer goods, so he predicted it must inevitably buy fewer dollars. But then – though continuing to buy less goods – the pound rose from $1.57 to over $2.40, i.e. by more than fifty per cent.

There is a further snag. It has not been shown – and is very questionable – that the motivations of giant firms can be equated with those of wage- and salary-earners, yet a considerable part of the money supply belongs to the non-personal private sector. The true or transactions velocity of circulation is not merely much higher but also more unstable than the income velocity, i.e. GNP/M, and can generate fluctuations in the non-income (stock) sphere. Changes in stocks, e.g. of inert deposits, are not caught by the traditional monetary statistics. Yet they can be activated and upset the current balance. Neither are capital gains covered, which can boost demand. In truth there is no good reason to expect a single number indicator to reflect all complicated transactions, including for example the speculative excesses of financiers. Nevertheless we have come to the pass at which even the Bank of England (not to say the central banks of the United States and, though to a lesser extent, of Germany) have fallen into the Chicago trap, and regard the 'supply of money' or 'money stock' as the main basis and instrument of monetary policy and economic management.

The same doubts attach to P (price). Which assortment of prices should be adopted? The consumer retail or even the wholesale index surely cannot perform the task: they exclude the price of assets, of securities and real estate whose price movements might interfere with, indeed destroy the balance in flows. Nevertheless these proxies are used, though they need not, and in critical moments will not, *accurately reflect* the magnitude of the basic change and its probable consequences.

The famous Quantity-Equation thus proves to be a feeble identity quite unfit to be used for policy-making, though it is being lustily used by governments and Central Banks for that very purpose, with painful consequences. Faced with these objections Friedman has proposed a different 'proof' or 'test' to show that monetary factors alone are responsible for inflation, a device somewhat like the old 'Cambridge' money equation,[29] and specially attractive because it emphasizes free individual choice. The argument is simple:

Experience has demonstrated that *people* [my italics] are pretty stubborn about how much money they want to keep in their cash boxes or bank accounts relative to their incomes. If on the average they have gotten accustomed to keeping in cash or in a bank account let us say, three months' income, and then if their cash balances go up, they will try to restore that three months' income.[30]

Experience has not demonstrated anything of the sort: even the ratio of GNP to M3 (called by the Bank of England, velocity) has, on the contrary, fluctuated very sharply.[31] It will depend on the pattern of expectations, on the degree of idle capacity, and on whether increases in demand are translated mainly into output or mainly into price increases. To assume that it will be regularly the latter is to say that inflationary expectations are irrepressible. This has been shown to be wrong between 1948 and 1966 in the US, and systems of voluntary wage and price restraint have operated successfully in a number of countries, particularly Austria, Norway and Sweden.

It clouds the issue further to talk about *people*. Who are these people? Friedman seems to suggest that they are 'ordinary people, just like you and me', who have wages or salaries and spend them. This is clear from what follows, in the same article in *The Times* (13 September 1976):

As a result, if you decide you would like to have more cash in your pocket, the only way you can get it is by inducing somebody else to have less. Now conversely if the Bank of England prints money or creates money in the form of deposits, and if that is excess money supply in the sense in which we have just described it, then you will try to reduce your cash balances. You do this by spending – but your spending is somebody else's income, so the effect of this is that the attempt doesn't change cash balances at all, but it bids up spending until everybody is satisfied to hold the new cash balances.

For example, if people want three months' income in the form of cash, and if suddenly or over a period of time they find they have four months', well then they will tend to bid up spending until the larger nominal amount of money, the larger amount of money in pounds, is the same percentage of the larger income as it was before. What happens if people spend more? To some extent it may lead other people to produce more, but that is only so long as other people are being fooled, so long as they think this is something real, not something nominal. As soon as people catch on to what's happening, the attempt by some people to spend more will bid up nominal incomes, incomes in pounds, but most of that will come out in the form of prices. That is why an increase in the quantity of money, acting through the effects on people's spending, has to end up – or tends to end up – in higher prices.

Two things need to be said. The first (of which the words 'or tends to end up' suggest that Friedman is aware) is that when there is unemployment it is by no means sure that the system will not respond, as in 1961, by an increase in production which is sustainable. There need be no 'fooling' about this: production will increase and prices might stay level, or increase but little. This is a real, not nominal, improvement.[32] Secondly, we saw that Friedman's 'money' is not a homogeneous mass, but is an arbitrary concept which can include, apart from 'active', also dormant or inert asset money. A large proportion of these balances and assets are not owned by the personal sector 'just like you or me'. They are held by the treasurers of large corporations who can go liquid or invest – alternatively in financial assets, in real estate, in stocks of raw materials, in semi- and fully-finished goods, etc., or in productive equipment or buildings. Their knowledge and motivation are far removed from Friedman's 'ordinary people like you and me'. They will try to maximize profits, including those on foreign exchange. They might, and probably will, have a decisive impact in starting a boom or a slump. The relationship of total transactions to these liquid funds is not at all stable. The most convincing proofs of the lack of constancy in these presumed economic relationships are the startlingly different results which econometric analyses produce on the basis of only slight variations in time period or in the set of variables studied.[33]

The volume of money, however defined, will of course have implications for interest rates, and through the change of the value of both physical and financial assets, will have some influence on economic activity. But even in this context monetarism has woeful effects if it means concentrating solely on the volume (supply) of money. It is inconceivable that the movements of hot money should not affect the velocity of circulation. The influx of money of the magnitude which Britain has experienced in 1977–80 must have lowered the true velocity of circulation. Through those years it consisted mainly of Arab petrodollars fleeing from 'Mr Carter's administration. Influxes of that kind are deposited and become part of the huge volume of idle short-term assets.[34] The 'average' velocity of the total money supply is then reduced. If the authorities try to reduce the rate of increase in the money stock to its pre-influx level because monetarism holds that the volume has a direct effect on prices, this will exert a strong deflationary influence because the lower overall velocity due to the expansion of inert deposits owned by foreigners will not be offset by a sufficient increase of the total money supply.[35] Interest rates will rise, investment will be depressed, while the export markets dwindle because of appreciation of the pound.

The abolition of exchange control has even worse effects. It entails a worsening liquidity position as *short-term* debts continue to accumulate (or at least not to decrease) while money is invested abroad *long-term*. We have had experience in 1930-1 and again in 1949 of the consequences of this folly. It is also to be feared that such investment abroad tends to displace investment that would (or could) have been undertaken at home. This is the more likely as the supply of competent managers seems to be the most important bottleneck in British industry. Another depressing factor is the limitation on the availability of equity capital, without which loan-capital cannot be obtained. Finally, and from a national point of view, the benefit of overseas investment accrues mainly to the foreigner in wages, employment and taxes, while in the case of domestic investment they all benefit the home economy. Measures which have the effect of diverting British investment abroad are not sound policy at a time when unemployment is at record postwar levels and the urgent need is for the promotion of domestic investment and exports.

For all these reasons it is absurd to expect that curbing the increase of the money supply, as the main measure of economic policy, will produce an optimal Walrasian solution with a balanced growth path. In reality, when combined as monetarists recommend with steady reductions of public production and income-transfer, it amounts to the worst possible kind of 'incomes policy': an attempt to restrain wages by using massive unemployment to weaken the bargaining power of those remaining employed. Not only does the policy promise unemployment and lost production on a scale unknown since the 1930s; it is also dangerously self-reinforcing. Its effects on class feelings and union militancy will make any relaxation of dear money more and more difficult, as the workforce grows more and more determined to compensate for past suffering by turning any such relaxation into higher wages. In thus deliberately setting out to base the viability of the capitalist system on the maintenance of a large 'industrial reserve army', monetarists may validate Marx's analysis.

By contrast with that, the only peaceful and productive way to deal with the instability of our real world of bilateral monopoly and oligopoly is by way of what I have for thirty years past called a new social contract. That requires patient work by all parties to build the necessary technical understanding, goodwill, and consensus. That vital political and social task is made vastly more difficult by the current confusion and misdirection of a majority of the economics profession. Some of them are now ascribing our present troubles to utterly impersonal long (or Kondratieff) cycles, at a time when the world cries out for the full use of its existing capacity – as if to prove that, outdoing the Bourbons, they have learnt nothing and forgotten everything. Taught by such teachers, governments of either party now follow monetarist policies whose effects the electorate rightly hates. The trade union leadership has not learned, or cannot convince its membership, that a free-for-all even if temporarily profitable for some winners (because the price increases lag some time behind the cost increases) is fratricidal and before long, politically suicidal.[36] If monetarism is the incomes policy of Karl Marx, free collective bargaining has become the incomes policy of the jungle. To persuade people and politicians to more intelligent and cooperative courses is a political task. But it needs to be built on realistic economic understanding, including the exposure and decisive rejection of monetarist and *laissez-faire* illusions.

Appendix to Chapter 8:
Professor Friedman and statistics

The monetarist school claims that it is built upon empirical foundations, in the sense that its predictions (or 'retrodictions') are factually true even if its formal assumptions are not – i.e., it claims to be a black box that *works*. It follows that the utmost care and scrupulousness is required in proving the accuracy and relevance of the predictions, and therefore of the policy measures based on them.[1] Yet on closer scrutiny it is clear that the technical standards of the work have often been far from perfect.

Consider the analysis of the behaviour of the American monetary system during the 1929-34 Great Depression. If the Keynesian analogy of the string and the weight is true, that is that the banking system can *repress* demand ('pull the weight') but is powerless to increase demand ('push') once a downward spiral has started, then we should find that the hard high-powered money supply would be unchanged or increasing, and the shrinkage of demand would express itself primarily in a fall of the velocity which was self-generating.

Friedman denies this and asserts that the need for public sector intervention has not been proved. According to him (together with H. Schwartz, *A Monetary History of the United States 1867-1960*, Princeton, 1963), the cause of the disaster was the *deflationary* policy of the Federal Reserve. Kaldor in his attack on monetarism (*Lloyds Bank Review*, 97, July 1970) showed that on Friedman's figures his theories could not be upheld. There was an expansion of high-powered money. Though Friedman answered Kaldor (*Lloyds Bank Review*, 98, October 1970), he never dealt with this fundamental point.

In the same confrontation Professor Friedman asked: 'If the relation between money and income is a supply response... how would he [Lord Kaldor] explain the existence of essentially the same relation between money and income for the UK after the Second World War as before the First World War, for the UK as well as the US, Yugoslavia, Greece, Israel, India, Japan, Korea, Chile and Brazil?'

Kaldor's lapidary answer in the House of Lords needs to be quoted:[2]

The answer, of course, is that I could not explain it. Nor could he. For the relationship between money and income for all these countries is not at all the same. In fact, they could not be more different, as your Lordships will see when you look at the figures. ... in Switzerland four times as much money is chasing goods as it does in Britain: in Italy, Japan and Israel nearly three times as much: and in West Germany twice as much. None of this is in the least consistent with the monetarist doctrine.

One of the basic assumptions (and fierce assertions) of monetarists, on which many of their policy recommendations rest, is that the velocity of circulation (the 'efficiency' of a unit of money to transact business) is determined by long-term and slowly-changing institutional factors and that therefore it remains for practical purposes stable. Professor Sir W. A. Lewis, in *Growth and Fluctuations, 1870-1913* (London: Allen & Unwin, 1978), Chapter 3, pp. 69-70, finds Friedman's definitions fuzzy and his conclusions consequently weak; he shows that the fluctuations in the latter part of the nineteenth and beginning of the present century can be accounted for by changes in 'velocity'.

Even so close a friend and comrade-in-arms as the late Harry Johnson had to admit, in reviewing the *Monetary History of the United States* (*Economic Journal*, June 1965, p. 395), that the defence of their view of the growth of excess reserves 'involves a very dubious attempt to reconcile the hypothesis with the facts by some intricate inferences about the lags involved', and that: 'Professor Friedman's attachment to the permanent income formulation of the demand for money, and his resistance to allowing interest rates any important influence on velocity, in spite of good theoretical reasons and a great deal of empirical evidence attesting to such an influence, is itself a rather perplexing puzzle.'

Professor Friedman's way with facts and figures is illustrated in a variety of instances by his treatment of British history.

First, his popular BBC lectures explained that in the first industrial revolution Britain made spectacular economic progress to become the world economic leader during a period of very small government and very free trade. The fact is that Britain's economic growth forged ahead of its European competitors while it was exploiting an effective monopoly of the steam engine, from about 1780 to 1840. Through most of that period the nation had a high and complicated tariff (which probably did not help the industrial revolution much), massive public investment and spending (which certainly did help) and an extensive public welfare system with wage supplements and welfare allowances indexed to basic costs of living. There were some years during the Napoleonic wars when new public capital formation almost certainly exceeded new private; and a good deal of the new private investment was created to meet government procurement orders.

There followed a long period, from about 1840 to 1931, when Britain did indeed have the freest trade and relatively speaking the cheapest government and (until 1914) the smallest public sector among the industrially developing nations. Yet, for competitiveness, that century saw the relative decline of the country. Numerous competing countries, led by the US and Germany, emerged and overtook and passed Britain in output and income per head. Every one of them had protective tariffs, and a bigger (relative) public sector than the British.

Having thus dealt with the distant past by simple historical inaccuracy, the Professor proceeds to deal with the more recent past by statistical discrimination. In *From Galbraith to Economic Freedom* (Institute of Economic Affairs Occasional Paper No. 49, 1977) he set out to discredit 'socialistic policies' by proving that they had crippled Britain's economic growth since 1945. He begins by misrepresenting the size of the public sector. In at least four places (pp. 6, 12, 46, 56), he compares national income with total government expenditure. That compares an item which includes transfer payments with one which excludes them, and probably also excludes capital consumption (though that is less clear). That is to say, he chooses a ratio which, though irrelevant, gives spurious support to his thesis. The variants are as follows:

Ratio	*1975*
Public expenditure excluding transfer/GNP at factor cost	34.3%
PE including transfers/National income plus transfer	51.7%

The consequences of socialism are then illustrated by reference to the weak economic performance of Britain in comparison with Japan and Germany since 1945. This is an odd comparison to choose when judging the impact of 'socialism' on Britain. Surely what we need is to compare the British performance during a period of sustained boom under 'Friedmanism', e.g. in the period 1900–13, with the record under 'socialism', say 1945–75.

The results are as follows:

Average annual rate of growth per head of GNP at constant factor cost:

1900–1913	0.2%
1948–1975	2.2%

When confronted with these figures, Friedman appeals to C. H. Feinstein's newer data (*National income expenditure and output of the UK 1855–1965*, Cambridge, 1972), according to which gross domestic product at constant prices grew at 1.5 per cent and then suggests that the slump year of 1893 should be used for the comparison. Even these devices only boost his prewar growth figure to 2.1 per cent, which is still below the postwar 'socialist failure' rate. Professor Sir Arthur Lewis' latest calculations show an absolute fall for the end of the pre-1914 period. It was also a period when – in 1913 – personal savings reached a maximum and fifty per cent

of new investment went overseas, while British domestic investment languished. (Besides leaving the country poorer, those facts
contradict two more of Friedman's assertions.)

In response to these objections, Friedman next asserts that the
absolutely worse British performance before the First World War
than after the Second can be attributed to Britain's industrial
supremacy in 1914. The US and Germany were able to expand
faster because they had the British to imitate. In fact the British
were by no means world leaders in the new and rapidly expanding
industries and had lost their leadership even in some of the older
ones. Their bulk exports were coal, ships and textiles, all on the
way to decline. Modern metallurgical, electrical, chemical and
optical industries were led by the US and Germany, and the 'free'
British capitalists were disastrously failing to follow. American
investigators in the 1920s found even British coal-owners mulishly
unwilling to modernize. Generally British industrial capacity was
so weak that Liberal governments were, after 1914, forced to introduce Safeguarding Duties to get heavy and light engineering,
electricity, and motorcars going. Only in overseas finance were the
British still dominant, much to the discomfort of their industries
which lacked adequate support. The British weakness in the latter
was, and is, due to bad management (especially labour management), insufficient investment at home (in contrast to investing
massively abroad), a heavy preference for property rather than
industrial investment, and a defective trade union structure.

Again in *Encounter*, in November 1976, Friedman asserts that
the British 'tipping over' to totalitarianism is due to over sixty per
cent of the national resources being used for the public sector. This
is as usual based on comparing the *GNP figure*, i.e. a figure which
excludes transfer payments, with *total public expenditure*, which
does not. In fact the use of real resources for public purposes
represents only slightly more than a third of the total. Such is
objective 'positive' economics.

It is fair also to report Friedman's brush with Professor Modigliani.[3] The latter together with A. Ando investigated data produced by Friedman showing the inferiority of the Keynesian apparatus based on the multiplier, and found that the superiority was
spurious: it was the result of mis-specification of the Keynesian
relation.

CHAPTER NINE

The International Aspect

In no field of economics has conventional thinking so tight a grip both on Academe and on policy-making as in international trade. In no field have self-serving power and prejudice pretended so successfully to strive only for the equal growth of all, as in that of international economic relations. In no field of economics has dissent from the dogmas handed down with increasing refinement from one generation of professional economists to another been more violently persecuted.[1] The free trade doctrine was, perhaps, even more pernicious in its influence on policy in weaker countries than was its twin in the domestic sphere, Say's Law of the Markets. It withstood the Keynesian revolution[2] and has now achieved new strength from the monetarist reaction. It forms the very basis of the non-agricultural sections of the Rome Treaty, which was accepted even in those member countries which might rightly have suspected that their present inferiority would be further aggravated and their prospects for employment and growth further worsened by the 'free' play of international market forces.

The basic explanation of this, and of the intolerant *odium theologicum*, is that differences in living standards between the various groups of countries are greater and less amenable to mitigation than within countries. Far from justifying the optimism of the classical and neoclassical theory in the gradual trickling down of the fruits of progress to the equal benefit of all, inequality between nations has increased. The maximization of something called world income[3] is even more vicious and meaningless than the unqualified acceptance of national income growth as a sufficient aim for all within a nation.

1. International trade in the modern world

The world economy has undergone profound changes in production and trading. The leadership has been concentrated in fewer countries and firms whose gain is cumulative while their less successful competitors are hard-pressed. Within countries the process of concentration of power has created giant corporations. These have extended their operations to a growing number of countries, and, especially in manufacturing, have come to dominate their weaker 'hosts'.[4] By orthodox Western economists these portentous changes have been, and are, dismissed or disregarded. A harmoniously balanced model was created – by applying the Walras construction to worldwide problems where it was even more illicit than in a closed developed system – a model of the world economy which reflected a non-existent harmony, and which promised automatic full employment *and* stability.

All the objections which have been ranged thus far against the neoclassical approach to economic issues apply *a fortiori* to its analysis of international trade and economic relations. For example there is in international relations no politically actuated redistribution of income[5] (except for the aid programmes which are determined by the 'donor' countries). Thus the differences in living standards are even sharper between than within countries, and remedial action much more difficult to initiate. It follows that in periods of accelerated technical change the handicap of being small and weak is heightened, for the education, research and development effort of the small and weak cannot match the formidable technical and economic advances secured by the strong.[6] The rapidity of change acts to accentuate and increase the differences among countries. A reversal (even mitigation) of this inferiority, if not impossible, is difficult to bring about. The problem is aggravated by the fact that comparative costs are constantly altering.[7] Thus the concept of 'long-run equilibrium'[8] which forms the foundation of the free trade case is either trivial or useless for application to the analysis of problems in a real world which is constantly subject to rude, often unexpected, shocks, and which is now once more threatened with mass unemployment and stagnation. A move to freer trade under these circumstances was and is likely to impede the development of (at least industrial) production in less favourably situated countries.

In this chapter I shall put forward the view that present-day problems can be dealt with satisfactorily only if we accept the fact of a widespread double oligopoly, i.e. a strong interdependence on the inter-country and inter-firm levels. This means that the conventional constructions, which disregard the path of readjustment influenced and often indeed determined by this two-tier oligopoly, will give wrong answers to the policy-makers.

2. The irrelevance of orthodoxy

Conventional theory, and particularly the traditional theory of international trade, was founded on a strictly static model of the economic system, in which resources, including technical knowledge and tastes, were assumed to be given and fully used. In that world their allocation was all-important. There must have been in the mind of its propagators some idyllic picture of a tranquil (but most profitable) system of cost-minimization in which 'given factors of production' are capable of being reallocated *between* industries instantaneously and without any difficulty. As long as this process in fact takes place in an environment of rustic simplicity – on *both* sides – such a picture might not have been a complete distortion of reality. One could see Arcadian maidens turning from the milking of cows to the spinning of wool, without the risk that 'capital' would totally lose its value in the change. So long as 'resources' are taken to be land and mobile labour, with the attribute of easy adjustment between alternative uses, this picture might have been acceptable for the analysis of current problems: Jeffersonian northern agricultural states of America were perhaps the last instance of this blissful state. An easy reallocation would then be possible without the benefits of cheaper imports being offset by losses, the most painful of which would be the elimination of entrepreneurial ability and industrial skills.

But nothing could be further from modern reality than Arcadia.[9] The problem now consists in the reciprocal influences (including trade between generally speaking unequal partners) which determine the rate and direction of growth of members of an open trading system. Trade will determine growth; and growth will determine trade. Capital accumulation, which raises the productivity of both land and labour; the advantages of large-scale production; technical progress: it is the pervasive importance of these three related factors which makes nonsense of the conventional approach.

It is easy to demonstrate, moreover, that in real life a few years' economic growth far outweighs in quantitative importance any conceivable 'improvement' resulting from a 'better allocation' of *given* resources, at any rate in 'rich' fully industrialized countries. The opening-up or liberalization of trade might lead to the underselling of the principal industries of weaker countries, so imparting a sharp deflationary shock to their economies, while the stronger countries who benefit thereby might in the process expand their own industries. The destruction of capital suffered by the poorer countries in this way might be irremediable but statistically unrecorded. Trade between unequal partners is not likely to leave factor endowments unchanged; moreover, its impact will not be symmetrical (especially if the initial discrepancy is further widened as a result of biased technical progress). Hence the position of the ultimate equilibrium will depend crucially on the antecedent historical circumstances and not merely on the values attaching to a single shift.

3. The meaningfulness of the two-commodity model

A two-country model constructed for the analysis of the consequences of international trade evades several all-important problems; analysis in terms simply of two commodities obscures most others. The relation between the two commodities *defines* rather than explains the mechanism of change. The results obtained are trivial. If it is further assumed that these commodities cannot be 'inferior', that is, 'perverse reactions' to price movements are excluded, a large area of the impact of innovation on trade is also eliminated from the scope of analysis, since the displacement of exports by innovation cannot be analysed in a two-country model. Problems of trade, especially international trade in manufactures, can hardly be investigated on these terms; far from being identical, goods change all the time and the products of the technological leaders can often show non-price advantages. Thus price comparisons can mean very little. It would, for this reason, be impossible to establish statistically with any accuracy whether the efficiency or the prices of a given country have risen relatively to another.

If the concept of 'goods' stands for aggregates, for 'bales' or baskets of products, index-number problems of the utmost difficulty arise, since any significant non-infinitesimal changes (such as need to be analysed) will distort the original comparative cost position, and change the composition of the aggregate. The consequences of this are highly pertinent. The Marshallian reciprocal demand curves in foreign trade, being *mixta composita*, obscure by their simplicity the extreme complexities underlying their 'shifts' – these being accompanied by, and inseparable from, changes in their shape. The concept of a shifted curve with an *ex-post* elasticity is even less legitimate.

If the effects of accumulation and increasing returns are excluded by assumption from the traditional approach, so is the related problem of *technical progress* by postulating a 'given state' of technical knowledge. If at all, it is treated as an external, autonomous, once-for-all change, to which there would be a slow adjustment in an otherwise completely changeless system. The model, conceived of in terms of unspecified countries, suggests a principle of symmetry whereby the impact of such a limited change is random or unbiased. No doubt it is admitted that some countries or areas could be hurt by change, but the impression most insistently conveyed is that this would be the exception rather than the rule. No emphasis is laid on the continuity of the process and on its close connection with capital accumulation. Thus the consequential disturbance of the comparative advantage of the poorer areas, which have to rely for their exports on primary products produced by primitive methods, is disregarded.

The orthodox suggestion is that new technical knowledge will spread, and thus also increase real incomes, outside the initiating focus of progress; alternatively that prices in the innovating country will fall and its partners will benefit through the improvement of their terms of trade. This view neglects the basic difference between international trade *among* unequal partners and inter-regional trade *within* modern, highly integrated societies or welfare states. In a framework of disparate economic growth and in the absence of deliberate intervention by a sovereign agency, technical progress seems not merely to have increased disparities historically, but to have acted as a positive impediment to the development of the poorer areas.

The competitive power of traditional (old-fashioned) producers is reduced by increases in technical knowledge and the consequential reduction in costs, and by the introduction of new and superior (or better-advertised) products, often more so even than as a result of the 'mere' accumulation of capital in the stronger countries. Technical progress is, in these terms, likely to bring net benefits to the initiator of change – even though *some* of the victims of change are likely to be situated within its own political boundaries. The process will follow two continuous paths:

1. refinement in the production of existing commodities and services, probably also produced by other countries; and

2. the discovery and development of new or radically improved products.

The former will enable luckier and more energetic producers to cut prices at home and abroad: the influence of the latter will be more far-reaching. It might lead to a displacement of older products and impose dangerously large price cuts or widespread structural changes on their suppliers. But if the new technique is radically different from the old (as in the case of the mechanical loom) then the displacement of existing suppliers as a result of developments discussed above might be no less damaging or violent: prices might be forced down below levels capable of providing subsistence standards for workers in industries which did not benefit from the change.

4. The impact of decreasing costs

The historical neglect of *decreasing costs* in the traditional theory can also be seen to have been inexcusable. Far from being the rare exception, economics of scale have embraced an ever-widening field – not excluding a considerable part of agriculture. Once the importance of increasing returns is admitted, however, and their nature analysed, they can be seen to be largely irreversible; in other words the historically observable relationship between output and capital is unique, in the sense of being reciprocally connected with the conjunction of capital accumulation and technical progress. On the other hand, in poor areas the difficulties and imperfections of effective decision-making, and the lack of entrepreneurial ability and capital, vitiate the assumption that potential fields of investment opened up by trade will be automatically exploited. The 'exceptional' case of infant industries expands to encompass infant *countries* and *regions*, and discriminatory policies become essential to any sane conception of maximum economic progress.

The analytical isolation of theory from the realities of the world has conduced to the neglect of continuing changes in the character of international relations: for instance the increasing importance of the multinational corporations in international trade is, of course, ignored by the conventional model, which assumes that trade is conducted by myriad atomistic units unable to influence prices. But, apart from foodstuffs and a certain (limited) number of raw materials, the micro-economics of foreign trade is, even at the level of trading units, such as between governments, one of oligopoly.[10] There exists indeed a form of double oligopoly, in which governments and multinationals have to manoeuvre with due regard to the probable and possible reactions of their competitors and the government concerned.[11] As the vicissitudes of the British balance of payments conclusively show, international price leadership can frustrate the intended results of, or the opportunity provided by, depreciation and downward floating. This is especially so, if, as in Britain, the gains from increased profits resulting from downward floating or depreciation have not been used for investment and industrial restructuring. Conversely price-leadership and improved quality, delivery and marketing can offset even a sharp up-valuation, as the German and Japanese examples have shown.

Indeed there is a danger that innovations might overshoot the mark, thus threatening to weaken the poorer areas even further. In such cases the former comparative disadvantage of the dominant country in the production of hitherto labour-intensive products will disappear. Once this happens, superior marketing techniques and other institutional factors may even result in that industry being transformed into an exporter. Not only industry, but also agriculture, may be so affected, as in the case of rice in the United States. The devastating effects of the rise of the British textiles industry on India is a good example. Apart from Japan, Hong Kong,

Taiwan and South Korea (and the southern United States) there is hardly a case where 'cheap labour', without initial protection, led to the rise of competitive industry.

On the other hand, in the rich, progressive areas, there loom the so-called pecuniary external economies – windfall profits which can be reaped by nearly all as growth accelerates. In a rapidly growing economy, the risk of mis-investment diminishes, and an increasing number benefit from the intensification of activity. The faster the rate of accumulation, the more likely to become misleading are conclusions which have been arrived at on the basis of constant factor endowments (and costs).

The possibility of recurrent obsolescence and unemployment without any compensating advantages will necessarily increase the riskiness of enterprise in the weak countries. The incentive to invest will then be further reduced, an effect which is distinct from, but additional to, the equally unfavourable deflationary pressure imposed by the greater flexibility of the more dynamic economies upon the poor and weak: this last will arise on the one hand through the non-price advantages of superior quality or technological innovation and quick deliveries, and on the other through superior credit facilities.

5. The money aspect

The origins of the conventional wisdom on 'monetary' problems in the field of international trade reach back into the eighteenth century, to Hume. By construing the balance of payments as principally a matter concerning *specie* flows initiated by transactions of individuals, which in turn led to further expenditure decisions, in the two-country context, the whole problem of dynamic adjustment was avoided. In this way was the atomistic character of international trade asserted, to which could be applied the rules of perfect competition; thus, the relationship between members of different trading countries could be subsumed under a general-equilibrium system.

Since 1967[12] – and well before the disruption caused by OPEC – the very foundations of the international banking system and capital markets have been shaken by repeated and increasingly severe currency crises. Yet conventional economic theory, whether of the neo-Keynesian or monetary school, has been quite unable to account for what has happened. This is clearly demonstrated by the wails and confessions of its principal standard-bearers. The very fact that each camp has been characterized by deepening and increasingly violent discord is added proof of the helplessness of traditional methods in the face of modern problems. Among the neo-Keynesians, the difference of opinion is between those who maintain that the balance of payments is governed by the Public Sector Borrowing Requirement and those who believe that stability can be secured at an acceptably low rate of unemployment by means of monetary and fiscal 'fine-tuning' combined with the floating rate.[13] We are back to Hume.

A country whose imports exceed its exports loses gold in financing the deficit as a result. Its prices fall. On the other hand, the surplus country receives gold and undergoes an obverse change: its prices rise. Total demand in the *system as a whole* remains unchanged. These were the terms in which the debate on the German reparation problem was conducted as late as the 1920s.[14]

The possibility, indeed probability, of a unilateral transfer resulting in a change of total demand is rather high. Both Ohlin,[15] and even more rigidly Rueff,[16] criticized Keynes within the static framework of neoclassical general equilibrium analysis. Rueff, indeed, established 'a principle of the conservation of purchasing power' in an article ironically published almost simultaneously with the 'Black Tuesday' crash of the New York Stock Exchange which ushered in the Great Depression.

The controversy, which centred on the problem of reparations, should have been concerned with the transfer of real resources from the paying country to the recipient country. This, however, depends not only, or even mainly, on the taxable capacity of the paying country, but on the ability (and willingness) of the recipient country to increase its domestic expenditure sufficiently to generate the required excess of imports in its current account. Keynes himself did not realize this in 1919 when he wrote *The Economic Consequences of the Peace*, or even in his debate with Rueff and Ohlin in 1928–9; for the issue can be correctly understood on the basis of the theory of effective demand which Keynes developed in the 1930s.

The dispute had a fleeting but most important practical interest, as the recrudescence of the pre-Keynesian analysis prevented the exaction of reparations after the Second World War.[17] It has lately assumed renewed and vital interest as a consequence of the world oil-price crisis.[18] The direct effect of that vast increase was bound to damage the Third World grievously, but it need not have been catastrophic for the OECD countries; the increase was not more than four to six per cent of their national income. What makes the OPEC squeeze really dangerous is the attempt of countries seriatim to eliminate their deficits. As the ultimate reason for these is the unrequitable surplus of the desert oil exporters, the only result of falling back to the 'classic' procedure would be to increase pressure in one country after another, causing a multiple shrinkage in demand and output until shrinkage of the equity values would lead to panic liquidation. Keynes came out of the reparations argument as the total victor and consolidated what was already a formidable reputation.

There are essentially two aspects to the problem of unilateral or unrequited transfers. First, there is the *domestic* problem of 'collection' – or of 'financing' the transfer. Secondly, there is the international problem of the consequential change in the two economies following the transfer. Both aspects, the 'collection' and the 'transfer', are complicated and cannot be treated as they usually were in the Hume-type model based on bullion movement and price changes. Both aspects – the financing and the disposal of the transfer – are likely to lead to changes in *aggregate* demand in the *system as a whole*, and this might frustrate efforts, however honest (which the Germans were not) by the debtor country to meet its obligations. Even in a world of bullion standards, where gold can be hoarded, it is possible for a deficiency of purchasing power to arise from the failure of the strongest country. With a fully developed banking system, the magnitude and likelihood of such a deficiency is increased. In short, in a decentralized individualist monetary economy there is no automatic way in which the recipient country could accept the transfer, since there is no automatic mechanism by which to increase effective demand (of the recipient) for the paying country's resources. In all likelihood in the short run planned savings will increase in the recipient country, and planned investment will decrease.

6. Managing the transfer

However, if effective demand in the recipient country can be increased sufficiently the so-called 'transfer' problem largely disappears.[19] There need be no net deflation, nor a deterioration in the terms of trade of the paying country, as was conventionally assumed. There is no more striking example of this than the ease with which Western Europe received Marshall Aid from the USA after the Second World War (the USA's terms of trade actually improved). This was in sharp contrast to the experience after the First World War and again after 1929, when general deflation made the transfer of reparations from Germany impossible. In such circumstances it is an analytical confusion to advocate changes in exchange rates as a means of promoting the transfer; both Keynes and Ohlin thought that the outcome would be determined by price elasticities of demand when the success of the transfer really depended on adequate effective demand.

There is a lesson in all this for one of the most serious of international problems of the present day. The difference in the pattern of international experience, and therefore of anticipations, has transformed a general tendency towards inflation into a serious problem of international relations among the OECD countries.

These differences in economic experience largely explain the unequal rates of inflation in these countries and the consequential serious imbalances in their external payments positions. For some time this fundamental change did not make itself felt. As time passed, these countries developed very different rates of inflation – depending on the relative strength and extent of their trade union organizations, and the rate of increase of investment and productivity, as well as on the general economic psychology. There developed a tendency for external payments imbalances to increase, and for reserve balances to grow correspondingly. By 1970 these were appreciable; by 1973, i.e. before the oil price crisis, they were very marked indeed.

By 1971 it had become clear that the Bretton Woods system, already rescued once by Marshall Aid and sustained by vast expenditure by the United States on armaments and aid, was again in crisis. In August of that year, following a persistent and cumulative loss of capital, the United States closed another chapter of

Bretton Woods history by suspending the convertibility of the dollar. In December, under the Smithsonian Agreement, there followed a 'realignment' of exchange rates which, contrary to a general belief that it could not happen, provided for a general devaluation of the dollar, both against other major currencies and against gold. It was evidently thought that a once-for-all adjustment would restore balance.[20] This self-deception did not last long. By the middle of 1972 the new value of the pound could not be sustained, and in June was effectively permitted to float down to its previous parity. At about this time the lira was also to come under pressure.

The world economy, as we have seen, had by the early 1970s begun to show signs of a return to the malfunctioning of the prewar era. Speculative fever in both real estate and shares, especially in London, was threatening the solvency of the whole financial sector. Central Banks, both in the United States and Britain, had to intervene on a large scale to stop a run which might have brought about a collapse similar to the crisis of 1931-3. The price of European raw materials and food imports showed an unwelcome increase. This effect was greatly magnified by the blow administered to the world economy in 1973-4 (and more recently) by the unprecedented oil price increase inflicted by the OPEC countries. The value of oil exports quintupled and the world was faced with the prospect that most of this vast sum would be unrequitable in the short run, in the sense that it would be impossible for the oil-importing countries to 'pay' for their oil on the basis of a higher level of exports of manufactures, since the OPEC countries, especially the Arab countries, are physically unable to absorb the required quantity of manufactured imports, notwithstanding the implementation of ambitious development plans. And perhaps in the wake of the experience of Iran, the signs are that attempts at further high rates of absorption will be curtailed, accompanied by a cutback of oil production. The only alternative to oil-importing countries accepting their counterpart deficit in the short run is massive, indeed cumulative, deflation.

7. The neoclassical model adopted by monetarists

The neoclassical approach adopted by the monetarists obviously implies that there is a market-clearing price based on 'real' factors, i.e. the inflation-discounted current balance. This was made quite clear in the passage cited (in a footnote to the previous chapter) from Friedman's *Newsweek* column of 25 October 1976. Part of it is worth repeating in the present context:

> There is no mystery why the British pound has been plummeting in price. The mystery is why the British government has been wasting its taxpayers' money in futile speculation against the decline.
>
> How much a British pound is worth in dollars depends fundamentally on how much a pound will buy in goods and services and how much a dollar will buy. If a pound will buy as much as $2 will buy, the pound is worth $2. If a pound will buy only as much as $1 will buy, the pound is worth $1.

Hardly had he unburdened himself of this wisdom than the pound shot up from $1.56 to $2.36 while cost and price inflation in Britain continued at a faster rate than in competing countries and, more especially, the real value of the yen fell by some twenty per cent.[21] The origin of the analytical failure was the complete disregard, which we have already encountered in the domestic context, of *changes in stocks* which were especially large and vulnerable in the field of foreign balances as a result of the OPEC accumulations and their private recycling through so-called Euromarkets.

The displacement of funds mainly from New York to London was the most important cause of the consistent appreciation of the pound. That appreciation flatly contradicted the neoclassical purchasing power parity theory. The 'liberal' Keynesians committed the opposite error in the postwar period. Their mistake was to ignore the psychological impact of devaluation or 'floating' on speculative anticipations and income (including wage) claims. The aim of devaluation is to cut production costs in terms of foreign currencies through cutting real wages without having to cut money wages. The need for the operation arose because the government had been unable to control costs relative to foreign competitors and, therefore, exports flagged and imports rose because of the overvaluation of the currency. Import prices rise in the home and export prices are cut in terms of foreign currency.[22] Only if wages do not rise in cumulative doses to match the *net* 'advantage' of devaluation (or depreciation), that is the advantage remaining after the previous 'overvaluation' has been made good, will devaluation 'work'. How well it will work depends on the speed and energy of entrepreneurs in making use of the opportunity vouchsafed them, and on the attitude of trade unions.

There are good examples of this. There is the British case of 1931 whose success bemused British economists of the neoclassical tradition, and even of its Keynesian variants. They ignored the fact that Britain in that period underwent a savage deflation and suffered from massive unemployment, rapidly falling prices followed by slowly declining wages, and a new tariff with a number of industrial competitors sticking to their old gold parity. 'Success' was dearly purchased. There is also the German resurgence after 1950, and France after the second devaluation of 1958 (the first having been frustrated by the Algerian war and wage inflation). In both cases real wage costs were deliberately cut. A profit inflation ensued, stimulated by exports, leading to a surge in productive investment and productivity. The 'miracle' then would yield increasing money and real wages without a deleterious impact on imports and exports. All-round satisfaction would then have been achieved.

In Britain serious doubts should have arisen about the effectiveness of either devaluation or (managed) depreciation as a deliberate and continuously or even frequently used instrument of policy. It is unlikely, first of all, that a cut in real wages could be achieved surreptitiously by monetary measures. It would be resisted by escalating wage claims, as we have seen in 1979, though part of the blame must be put on the Treasury's notion that inflation could be fought by raising prices through indirect taxes. If the resulting wage claims are rejected a bitter struggle is likely to ensue, which may well rob the measure of its stimulating influence on investment.

Without a new attitude on the part of the government and trade unions and employers, and without a consensus incomes policy, British costs are unlikely to remain sufficiently competitive to provide the external export-led lift to the economy which is needed. The relief by depreciation (or devaluation) will be increasingly transitory.

8. The asymmetry of the system

The symmetry of the price-mechanism has been destroyed. Wage movements are asymmetrically directed upwards; never downwards. Price increases, like wage and salary increases in connected or equivalent occupations, are matched or anticipated by wage and salary claims. This leads to a hyper-inflationary spiral. The 1967 devaluation, no doubt, came belatedly. But could one, without an agreed incomes policy, and with a parliamentary majority of five (rapidly reduced to three) embark on a course which necessarily implied a cut in real wages and which had to be reinforced by severe deflationary measures? The country was in no way prepared for that course.

This does not mean that parities should be sacrosanct. If, in the longer run and despite an effective incomes policy, unit costs slide out of line with those of industrial competitors; if structural changes in production or demand destroy foreign markets and new export products or markets need to be found; if full employment is threatened by a violent slump abroad, devaluation or depreciation might be a valuable adjunct to other measures.

Such a downward change of parity must be an exceptional and rare measure. If repetition is foreseen and even more if it is built into the system (i.e. automatic creeping peg – or floating), the wage-price spiral will be accelerated and the policy itself will undermine the natural 'value' of the currency. A collapse follows. Thus the success of devaluation depends on consensus on incomes, and consensus on incomes is the result of conscious agreement. It must not depend on forgetfulness or on the money illusion, because when that illusion is destroyed, inflation is transformed into hyper-inflation.

The obverse, up-valuation (or floating) of the currency because of the asymmetry of the behaviour of the unions is likely to be more effective in worsening the balance of payments[23] especially of a manufacturing country. It is highly unlikely that the anti-inflationary – or at least stabilizing – impact on the import prices especially of primary supplies will outweigh the worsening of competitiveness. As we have seen, these aspects of the foreign exchange policy were, because of its total concentration on the problem of inflation, largely neglected by the 1979 Conservative government, with dire consequences to the embattled and ailing manufacturing sector of the British economy. The authorities seemed to expect an automatic diminution of wage demands despite the acceleration of the inflation in prices. What was really beginning – contrary to vociferous assertions by ministers – was a new kind of incomes policy based on the increase in unemployment or the fear of it, together with measures to decrease the bargaining power of labour. This could only reinforce the general hostility of the unions – though it must be admitted that their mulish opposition to a consensus incomes policy had to bring on the confrontation in the first place.

The Conservative government, immersed in its perilous anti-inflationary policy, came under increasing pressure to reduce the pound by abolishing exchange control. This was done, and according to the Bank[24] the lifting of exchange control resulted in an outflow of $£\frac{3}{4}-1\frac{1}{4}$ billion, greeted by the financial press as the acquisition of foreign assets which would prove essential in the future when the oil and gas no longer came to the rescue of the British balance of payments. In my opinion this reasoning is based on false premises and socially dangerous policies. In the first place it is wrong to regard uncontrolled and therefore unknown foreign assets as valid national reserves. If there should be a confidence crisis (e.g. because of a threatened victory of a left-wing-dominated Labour party) the last thing to happen will be a repatriation of these assets. Moreover the basic argument completely disregards the actual international situation of Britain. With the current payments barely balanced after heavy deficits, the lifting of exchange control represents a repeat performance of a policy of borrowing short and investing and lending long, a process which in the past led to crises and more often than not enforced heavy losses of output and income. The obstinate refusal of the Bank to learn from past embarrassments is difficult to understand.[25]

So much for the 'macro' aspect of the monetarist policy. The micro-economic is not less reprehensible. If the export of capital facilitates production abroad instead of at home, only profits after taxation will accrue to the exporting country. Most of the value-added tax and wages will benefit the recipient country. The argument that the foreign investment need not encroach on domestic activities of the firms neglects the fact that single firms would have to keep a minimum equity ratio to total capital. Neither this nor indeed management is in unlimited supply. Thus even direct foreign investment is likely to interfere with domestic expansion.[26] All objections apply with greater force to portfolio investment. Can there be any serious doubt that the 'uncapping' of sterling played a ruinous part in the erosion of British investment at home? This was the most ominous act in the whole Thatcher experiment.

9. The political background

The dangers inherent to weak countries in an unadulterated free, or even freer, trade approach have been acutely aggravated by the change in the world political system, the 'liberation' of practically all colonies and the associated fractioning of continents. This has brought into relief the differences in size and population of the new states, as well as in their available resources, including technical knowhow and institutional arrangements. The impact of past experience on the functioning of the international economic system is far greater; motivations, in terms of policy goals and criteria, are increasingly diverse. The analysis of international relations on the basis of a model or system in which there are a great number of relatively small countries engaged in perfect competition with an infinitely large unit representing the world, is totally irrelevant to the problems of today's reality. It is necessary to the purpose, however, which demands that the interaction between countries, which in reality must pay regard to the actions of others,[27] should be reduced to a perfectly or atomistically competitive mechanism in which reactions are prompt and tend to restore the original equilibrium. However, the number of countries engaged in international relations is far from infinite; the difference in the size and power relations between the unequal partners is even more crass. The free trade argument is thus conducted in terms which are flatly contradictory to the facts and needs of the real world of inequality.

10. Prevalence of oligopoly in manufacture

Once the neoclassical assumptions are abandoned, however, the vital importance of the short-run path becomes evident. It will determine the outcome of the process of adjustment, which, if the initial shock is considerable, will almost certainly be historically unique. In such circumstances, case-by-case analysis is the only legitimate approach, since generalizations will almost certainly be misleading. The relationship between initiating disturbances and subsequent developments is at best tenuous. Much will depend, as we have said, on the immediate historical antecedents. The reactions of individual (powerful) countries and firms can no longer be disregarded. It is this growing importance of single decision-making units, with their own psychological biases, which has vitiated the conventional style of impersonal economics based on mechanistic interrelationships. Once it is admitted that the impact of a change in international trade is, first, to affect countries through their balance of payments, and that these countries will then react in different ways, the whole problem assumes a new aspect.

This oligopolistic relationship between countries is complicated, indeed aggravated, by the fact that within these countries there has grown up a variety of multinational firms controlling an increasingly important share of world trade, especially in manufactures, which has rendered the original framework and concepts of international trade theory irrelevant. It should be noted in addition that the restricted number of countries which dominate these exchanges export only a limited range of products, of which they are becoming increasingly important suppliers. Hence the conventional approach to the problem of readjustment, either in terms of 'elasticities' or 'absorption', becomes either trivial or meaningless. What matters is the psychological framework and the impact of the proposed corrective measures on the world economy, which in turn depends on the world's reactions to them, many of which must be diverse and not 'mechanically' predictable. It is on such chains of action and reaction and further action that the outcome of unique shocks and interventions will depend.

The increasing concentration of economic power, the growing importance of single units, the breakdown of determinacy, must be seen against the all-pervading background of cost-push inflation. The immense importance of this for our theme derives from the startling differences between national institutions and states of mind, and consequently between national rates of inflation. It is this difference which appears to be at the root of the continuous or recurrent difficulties in which a growing number of countries have found themselves. Here again we are faced with totally new problems, the solution of which cannot be approached successfully within the old framework.[28]

11. The determinant factors

The conclusions emerging from these considerations are tentative and make no false claims to determinacy. We may enumerate, however, certain factors, apart from those automatic price- and income-effects which impinge upon the domestic economy, which will determine the deliberate reactions of governments to, say, a deficit on the balance of payments, given the degree of freedom within which they can operate and implement policies:

1. the principles of policy; that is, whether the government, for example, wants (a) to stabilize employment, (b) to maintain reserves, or (c) to maintain price stability; or any combination that is possible;

2. the latitude of choice politically open as between policy instruments with which to carry out policy; for example, whether restricted to 'global' monetary controls or capable of implementing direct controls;

3. the degree to which the country depends on foreign trade, since substantial dependence might make compensatory policies difficult, if not impossible;

4. the availability of international reserves, and their size relative to the country's imports and payments obligations;

5. the country's relative economic power, measured by its share in world industrial output and ownership of natural resources;

6. the supply of entrepreneurial ability and technical innovative power; and

7. the institutional arrangements in labour relations.

If the initial imbalance has been considerable, the outcome of the balancing process will almost certainly be historically unique. The notional segregation of the 'long-run' or 'real' factor-allocation problem from 'short-run' or 'monetary' phenomena can only produce nonsensical results. By construing the balance of payments as principally a matter concerning specie flows initiated by individuals, which in turn led to further expenditure decisions, in the two-country context, the whole problem of dynamic adjustment was avoided by the conventional writers.

The mechanism by which equilibrium is allegedly regained after some disturbance has been formulated either in terms of elasticities, or in terms of book-keeping identities, such as savings and investment; hence the effects of devaluation or the payment of reparations are analysed on the basis of partial schedules, depicting the relationship between the demand for exports and imports and their price. Alternatively, change can be analysed in the context of simple Keynesian relations such as the marginal propensity to import or the margin of unused capacity. In neither system are the functional relationships or propensities altered as a result of the disturbance and of the adjustment to it. Yet in the case of severe disturbance that is precisely what matters. The interposition between productive units of the monetary, fiscal and commercial policies of states of vastly differing size, moreover, adds a further element in international trade relations which conflicts with the assumption of perfect competition. This would be the case even if perfect competition prevailed on the level of the individual or the firm, which, patently, it does not.

The relationship between the initial change in the balance of payments and consequential developments is, of course, of an entirely different and more attenuated nature: it will also depend on the historical position, and it will in its turn determine anticipations, that is, the reactions of the countries, producers, etc., involved. This fact is of decisive importance. The *ex-ante* 'schedule' and its elasticity are not necessarily relevant, since they are highly likely to change with developments through time; in any case, it is neither legitimate nor safe to assume a priori that they are constant. The *ex-post* schedule, on the other hand, depends on the historical sequence of events (e.g. their impact on the level and urgency of demand in each country), and on the impact of these on anticipations, all of which will influence accumulation and hence the country's competitive strength. If there exists a causal relationship between the initial change and these subsequent autonomous impulses, the latter can no longer be ignored as being of a second order of importance. The assumption that we are confronted with reversible relationships, and that therefore the comparison of final equilibrium positions can yield meaningful answers for predictive purposes, is patently wrong.

12. Indeterminacy

If the path from the original position is not uniquely determined, and if a number of final equilibria were possible, depending on what happened as a result of the first autonomous impulse or change (including consequential policies adopted), then the comparative analysis of two given final equilibrium situations will not yield *generally* acceptable conclusions.[29] Long-run equilibrium will in fact never be established, because the whole system will be undergoing continual change, the adjustments to the 'first' disturbance never being permitted fully to work themselves out.

Nor are resources 'given' in the long run. Not only does accumulation take place all the time, but trade has been, and necessarily will be, one of the main determinants of the growth of resources, especially those vital resources, capital, entrepreneurial ability and technical skill, whose importance is demonstrated by the rise of multinational corporations. Relative factor endowments and comparative costs are, therefore, continually changing as a direct result of the very trade to which their divergences as between countries allegedly (viz. Heckscher-Ohlin) give rise. Consequently the eventual outcome, the precise character and shape of any so-called equilibrium position reached after adjustment, is analytically inseparable from the path of that adjustment.

At the simplest level, and in the context of a *given* framework of policy and conjuncture, one may say that the imports and exports of a country will be determined by:

1. the relation of money-costs and incomes at home and abroad at existing exchange rates;

2. the relation of prices of goods and services entering into international trade at home and abroad;

3. the relation of demand to productive capacity at home and abroad which, in turn, will be influenced at the margin by the rate of investment; and

4. anticipations about the stability of these relationships.

However, these factors will be far from independent of each other. Changes in the terms of trade, for instance, will affect incomes, and all changes in incomes will affect prices, and possibly the sensitivity of demand to changes in price. Moreover, changes in price resulting from autonomous increases in costs will have effects totally different from those due to changes in demand. This aspect of the problem, vitally important under modern conditions, is of course ruled out a priori by the assumption of perfect (atomistic) competition in the market for goods and services both in domestic and international trade.

There is, further, a twilight zone in which increases in money incomes will have disproportionate effects, irrespective of the price changes that may occur. As full employment is approached, domestic supply comes under pressure. Imports rise. The sensitivity of demand to increases in foreign prices decreases. Thus, the development of productive capacity and the dynamism of the economy (which determine the point at which shortages arise) will play a decisive part in determining the balance of payments. If the traditional Quantity Theory is irrelevant because it cannot account for the effects of increases in productive capacity, the primitive Keynesian 'absorption' approach is no more sophisticated.

Analysis must, therefore, take into account the comparative relation between income and capacity in each country. This, however, gives rise to the possibility that secondary effects may assume a greater importance than primary changes, with the secondary in the longer run offsetting or more than offsetting the primary. It is this factor, moreover, which introduces perhaps the most hated element - indeterminacy - into this crucial part of basic economic theory, for, as a result, generalizations become precarious, if not illicit. 'Science' has to give way to history and politics, a truly shocking prospect!

It should also be recalled that relative incomes at home and abroad are inextricably related with prices. Equally, the interaction between prices, incomes and demand will differ according to the historical configuration of a particular situation: this because international trade and the money economy make prices depend not only on wants, but also on price expectations. All these factors will be decisively influenced by (a) the structure of both sides of industry and their relations with each other and with the government, and (b) their historical experience, both of which follow from the

basically oligopolistic nature of the product market and the bi-
laterally monopolistic character of the labour market. Thus, with
stability codetermined by historical antecedents, a second fundamental and multiple kind of indeterminacy pervades the system.

13. Monetarism and inflation

The victory of monetarism was to have momentous consequences.
With few exceptions, every country, whether debtor or creditor,
had experienced high rates of inflation. According to the monetarist
recipe, therefore, they each took action to curb the rate of increase
of their 'money supply'. In addition (but not necessarily connected
with the fight against inflation, though using the fear of it to
strengthen their position) there was an all-round effort to cut back
government expenditure. Both policies aggravated the deflationary
bias of the world economy as a whole stemming from the OPEC
oil price rise. The drive to eliminate deficits, i.e. Arab surpluses,
which could not be removed, created a situation in which deficits
would be transferred from one country to another, all the while
intensifying the downward spiral and sapping economic confidence. The increased dollar balances in the hands of the Desert
Arabs and torrents of this 'hot' money fleeing from one centre to
another, seeking refuge, were bound to bloat the money supply
while reducing the velocity of circulation. Any attempt to throttle
back the growth of money supply mechanically, irrespective of the
monetary situation, would therefore have a further net depressing
effect.

Originally, had the main OECD countries responded rationally
to the challenge, there need have been no severe consequences in
dealing with OPEC's unrequited transfers and the implied transfer
of real resources. At some $100 billion p.a. their value represented
no more than perhaps three per cent of the national income of the
OECD countries, a perfectly manageable amount, provided that
a cooperative effort could have been made to agree on an equitable
distribution of the resulting balances. Despite pious declarations
at a number of 'summit' and other conferences, no such agreement
was forthcoming. Indeed there was a competitive movement to
deflation. The violent increase in interest rates has not been rational. The aim should have been to neutralize the violent increase

and periodic displacement of liquid balances by concentrating them to Central Banks or the IMF. Such cooperation was never seriously discussed. Indeed, it was only at the latest of these conclaves, in Bonn and Tokyo, that the existence of a problem was recognized: it is unlikely however that the means envisaged there will be sufficient for the purpose. The Venice get-together produced even less understanding of the problem, putting the (wrongly conducted) fight against inflation as the first priority.

14. Confusion

Policy-making was further confused by the sudden agreement of the (Keynesian) new Cambridge school and the monetarists who were making notable progress in capturing influence. Both denied that short-term prediction was uncertain – though they both made bold attempts to compass the 'long or medium' future. The 'new' Cambridge school maintained that the foreign balance was determined by the public sector balance – falling back to the old fallacy in asserting that an *ex-post* outcome could be used for devising *ex-ante* policies to bring about the desired change. As their mistaken belief coincided with the political desires of the conservative circles in the City and the government, it had immediate and considerable influence. Thus the PSBR and its reduction became the priority in British policy-making and the elimination of the global imbalance was made impossible. With the change of government in Britain in 1979 this policy was very much intensified and it was claimed that (together with an unparalleled increase in interest rates) it would help to establish a firm base for a recovery by 'squeezing' inflation out of the economy. Unfortunately this process of 'elimination' of inflation has to work through a weakening of trade unions by increasing unemployment and by direct anti-union legislation. Therefore even if it succeeds it is unlikely to last: unions subdued by those means will fight hard to regain their previous standards and relativities as soon as deflation ends and employment recovers. Moreover entrepreneurial capacity may well have been weakened by the attempt to deal with union strength. Hence any policy of full employment would have to be ruled out: the Marxian theory of a permanent reserve army would have come about. This however would not stimulate investment and modernization. As most advanced competitors are investing in research and development on the one hand and improved plant on the other, the outlook for Britain is alarming.

The gravity of the problems facing countries like Britain – which have a heavy dependence on foreign trade, but which have not been able to match their rivals' competitiveness – is still not fully realized. This failure is due to insufficient appreciation of the force of decreasing costs. To change a losing trend demands sacrifice to make resources available for an increase in investment, yet the increase in the activity which it entails will itself embarrass the balance of payments. Twice since the war Britain has received fortuitous gains which could have been utilized to solve this awkward problem. The first was the sudden violent improvement in her terms of trade in 1951-2 which amounted to some £1200 million p.a. It was dissipated by decontrol and increases in consumption. The second bounty was the discovery of the vast riches in the North Sea. The fact that Britain's current international payments are just in balance, despite a contribution from oil and gas of some £6 billion at present prices, shows that the country is well on the way to missing this second, unexpected and transient opportunity. Hardly any country in the situation of Britain has managed successfully to escape from the steady worsening of her balance without some protective screen. The two most successfully reconstructed economies were ruthless in this respect. The Germans did it with subsidies, the Japanese by secret government fiat. Protection is needed because in the period of readjustment and transition the dominant foreign firms would stifle the still weak domestic producer. The British example of 1931-7 has, as we saw, encouraged the beliefs that a simple devaluation could do the job: it could subsidize exports and hinder imports uniformly. There would be, it is said by partisans, no distortion in economic structure. Unfortunately the starting position is not one corresponding to a classical equilibrium. Some industries are more backward than others. The 'new' Cambridge notion that a non-discriminatory stimulus would overcome the difficulties leaves out of account the fact, regrettable as it is, that the managements of a number of firms have patently fallen down on their jobs. A devaluation or a uniform tariff, however necessary in the present grave threat to the survival of British manufactures, will, like previous protective measures, not overcome the basic defects of the economy. A much greater accountability would have to be assured. Moreover the protection must be fitted to the specific needs of the ailing industry. It makes no sense to wait for 'new' industries to provide substitute work-places for the disappearing 'old' ones. It is the old industries which have to be reshaped to restore competitiveness and transform them into 'new' ones.

Beyond this discriminating specific protection British macro-economic policy will have to be reconsidered. We saw the arguments for a separation of a financial from a commodity pound. The latter might be separated by confining manufactures to a lower parity than the rest of the trade. This would alleviate the problem of the terms of trade and lessen the risk of price inflation in primary products. Added general measures could include quotas to ensure that no positive damage to foreign industries should invite retaliation. What is important is that the present dogmatism should be replaced by flexibility and pragmatism. It is queer that this sort of plea should be needed, of all places, in England.

15. Liquidity

The international accumulation of vast uncontrolled liquid funds resulting from the current imbalance of payments presents an extremely dangerous problem. The surplus oil-exporting states have deposited a large part of their foreign exchange earnings with OECD (mainly US) banks. However, competition between these banks, together with the ruling anti-inflationary policy, has resulted in some very high interest rates being paid on these deposits. The consequence of this is that there has been a feverish drive on their part to find borrowers at a time when demand for funds was weak as a result of depressed economic prospects. This manifested itself in a massive expansion of foreign bank loans, especially to the developing countries in search of funds to cover their increased oil bills. The brilliant Staff Report of the Subcommittee of the Foreign Affairs Committee of the US Senate has pointed to the dependence of the large US banks on their foreign loans; and, moreover, to the precariousness of the geographical distribution of these loans.[30] Even the BIS, in its Annual Report[31] for 1976, remarks acidly: 'The result [of the liquidity creating] was an intensification of interbank competition and a further compression of the banks' earning margins to levels that seemed based on the assumption of a future without problems or losses.'

I am old enough to remember the flood of bankers in the 1920s trying to persuade Hungarian banks to borrow. It ended in a general moratorium to avoid open bankruptcy. As no really comprehensive statistics exist relating to international banking flows,[32] it is extremely difficult to know whether these assets and liabilities are prudentially balanced, in respect of their maturities. The total of both US and Euro-based foreign lending has grown from an insignificant amount to a total (including redeposits) of over $1000 billion in 1979. It is hardly conceivable that such an expansion will have taken place with a future that will prove 'without problems or losses'. The existing institutions are totally insufficient to stifle a confidence crisis resulting from the failure of an important client, a giant corporation or a country.

16. Are existing precautions sufficient?

We have been deceived once before about the sufficiency of the increase of liquidity created by international agreement, and Keynes took a prominent role in that deception.[33] Far from providing 'the setting for an expansion of world trade and international investment', the addition to international reserves made available under the Bretton Woods institution was totally insufficient for a successful playing of the new rules of the game – i.e., strict non-discrimination, currency convertibility and rapid removal of direct controls over foreign trade and payments – to be sustained.

Keynes defended his brainchild, the International Monetary Fund, by pointing to the manifold safeguards built into its operations, which would force creditor (and not only debtor) countries to contribute to the process of balance of payments adjustment. Besides the ultimate alleviation permitted for debtor countries through changes in exchange parities, there were more specific escape routes:

1. The imposition of emergency quotas on imports by countries in balance of payments difficulties, in accordance with the rules laid down in the plans for the International Trade Organization (later the General Agreement on Tariffs and Trade);

2. mandatory controls over exports of capital by countries that were borrowing from the IMF; and

3. the scarce-currency clause, intended to permit debtor countries to ration payments for the exports of a country in persistent surplus and thus to restore the basic current balance of payments by direct action.

Much play was made of each of these safeguards at the time. Unfortunately for the supporters of Bretton Woods, these ingenious contrivances, which were designed not only to reduce the size of probable imbalances but also to accelerate their adjustment, turned out to be ineffectual or politically unworkable, as some of us predicted at that time. Those which were not invoked early fell into complete desuetude, not least because of the amateurishness of the British representatives at the two Bretton Woods institutions, and their masters in London.

When the first testing time came, in 1947, the resources of the Fund were quite insufficient to meet the demands upon them. Fortunately the economic crisis had occurred at a time when the Soviet Union was showing signs of aggression, thus reinforcing the urgency and the need for measures to be taken to prevent severe economic disruption in Europe, with its threat of mass unemployment and even a breakdown of the social order. In response to this need the United States injected massive quantities of resources into Europe under Marshall Aid, which represented a vastly greater amount than the original dollar resources of the IMF. Perhaps even more important, the strict rules of the Fund, and of the GATT, based as they were on an unrealistic conception of internation economic relations in a world which had yet to recover from the war, were suspended. The United States even consented to discrimination against its own exports. It was in this way that a relapse into the prewar type of business cycle was avoided at a critical juncture.

When countries acquired surpluses in recent years – the United States, Japan and especially Germany – they changed tack slowly and did not emulate that statesmanship. They continued their fight against inflation and worsened global imbalances while increasing unemployment. The German and Japanese deficits in the end provided a counter to the net surpluses, but not before severe damage was inflicted on the world economy. Indeed we must expect a cumulative deflationary pressure to continue. The fact that even those countries are moving into deficit as a result of the latest oil price rise may well increase the stimulus to deflation.

The scene has thus been set in which one country after another is trying to eradicate its deficit by stimulating exports and curtailing imports. The fact that the latter is to be achieved mainly by cutting (initially public) expenditure rather than by imposing tariff-surcharges or quotas makes no difference to the impact on foreign countries as a whole – although it increases domestic unemployment more than direct trade restrictions would.

Although some 'readjustment' is no doubt in order in debtor countries, competitive bouts of cumulative deflation, in an attempt to shift deficits from one country to another, only lead to increased unemployment and stagnation, and ultimately undermine the international monetary order and banking system. Every effort should rather be made to establish due restraint on costs in the debtor countries so as to reduce differences in inflation rates; but savage cuts in public expenditure must be avoided. It is equally essential that the industrialized creditor countries should at least move into balance, and preferably shoulder part of the structural deficit, instead of aggravating the situation in debtor countries by also running immense surpluses.

17. Conclusion

On the one hand it is important to prevent the spread of deflation as a result of shortages (or anticipated shortages) in reserves. At the same time it is equally important to ensure that any increased facility to create international reserves will not be abused, in the sense of its sustaining in certain countries an inflationary process which, in the end, would permeate the rest of the world trading system. Thus there is a pressing need for a strong central organ with the responsibility of facilitating the creation of sufficient international reserves to obviate such cumulative deflation. The severe crises experienced by the United States prior to the establishment of the Federal Reserve System – themselves the result of the very absence of such an institution – seem evidence enough to carry this point. The value of – and the need for – the accumulation of reserves by any country is immediately reduced when their creation is provided for by some central authority. At the same time, this should diminish cut-throat competition for their ownership, thereby relieving pressure on the world economy and dramatically decreasing the risk of a general liquidation of credit. On the other hand, access to such a central organ would have to be regulated. Agreed rules of conduct would have to be established.

Unfortunately the events of the last few years do not suggest that such a balanced approach to one of the most important international economic problems has yet found acceptance. There is instead a continued yearning for the extremes of ancient orthodoxy, for a return to the fallacies of the past, whereby 'perfect competition' and 'rational expectations' as a valid substitute for perfect foresight would be restored by banning 'monopolies' - especially trade unions - and restoring the general convertibility of currencies.

Notes

Chapter 1
Introduction: Hubris and After

1. *Unequal Partners* (2 vols, Oxford: Blackwell, 1963), *Economics of Poverty* (London: Weidenfeld and Nicolson, 1966, 2nd edn 1974), and (in collaboration with P. D. Balacs) *Fact and Fancy in International Economic Relations* (Oxford: Pergamon Press, 1973).
2. J. Robinson, *Essays in the Theory of Employment* (London: Macmillan, 1938).
3. N. Kaldor, 'A model of the trade cycle', *Economic Journal*, L (March 1940).
4. See Oxford Institute of Statistics, *The Economics of Full Employment*, ch. 5, and my *Unequal Partners*, esp. vol. 2, sections 3 and 4. Congratulating Kalecki on his contribution to the former, Keynes was scathing about my contribution, as he was in his last (posthumously published) article (*Economic Journal*, L V I, June 1946).
5. Contemporary monetarism is akin to a sudden reassertion of the phlogiston theory of fire or the ether theory of light or electric transmission. If any scientist were to be mad enough to attempt it he would be laughed out of court. In economics it is a daily event.
6. The new neoclassical anti-Keynesians now seem to argue that orthodox monetary management, by preventing a collapse of the US monetary circulation in 1929/33, could have mastered that crisis and made the Keynesian revolution 'unnecessary'. It is regrettable that each generation must learn by its own mistakes: the post-1935 adult has not experienced the trauma of pessimism which overtook the world after the collapse of stock exchange values and the refusal of entrepreneurs to undertake risks by borrowing. The psychologically induced fall of the velocity of circulation, which was the prime mover in the general depression, is no longer even discussed. Professor Friedman speaks of a contraction of the monetary base when according to his own statistics the volume of 'high powered money' in fact increased. The fall in bank deposits was due to hoarding, to the withdrawal of deposits. See M. Friedman and A. Schwartz, *Monetary History of the US* (Princeton: National Bureau of Economic Research, 1963); also N. Kaldor, 'The new monetarism', *Lloyds Bank Review*, 97 (July 1970). Professor Brummer's intemperate answer, 'A Monetarist view of Keynesian ideas' (ibid., 102, October 1971), seems to me to consist of assertions without arguments.

7. I learned the language before the term 'macro' became fashionable. Throughout this book 'global' refers not to the terrestrial globe but to the whole (usually national) economic system, and to measures designed to operate indiscriminately on the system's aggregates.

8. P. Samuelson, *The Problems of the American Economy* (London: Athlone Press, 1962). Despite its title, it is more of a plea for a greater use of economists in Britain and a vindication of their greater use in the US.

9. Hence the regrettable establishment by the Central Bank of Sweden of a Nobel Prize for what is essentially a political profession. Its simultaneous grant to both Myrdal and von Hayek shows the absurdity of the whole conception. The former voiced his protest publicly (*Challenge*, 1977).

10. A. M. Okun, *The Political Economy of Prosperity* (Washington DC: The Brookings Institution, 1970), p. 31. The late Dr Okun, whose death robbed the US of a balanced applied economist, recently advocated an incomes policy, unfortunately in the administratively impossible form of taxes and subsidies to 'bribe' people into acquiescence ('An efficient strategy to combat inflation', *Brookings Bulletin*, vol. 15, no. 4, 1979).

11. E. H. Phelps-Brown, 'The underdevelopment of economics', Presidential Address to the Royal Economic Society, 8 July 1971 (*Economic Journal*, LXXXII, March 1972).

12. Wassily Leontieff, 'Theoretical assumptions and non-observed facts', in *American Economic Review*, LXI (March 1971), 1–7. The failure of his 'global' model elaborated for the United Nations shows the risks involved.

13. R. M. Solow, *Times Literary Supplement* (28 March 1975), p. 347. The 'MIT-oriented' economists on the other hand want resolutely to assume simple relationships between complex collective concepts or aggregates, e.g. linear functions for the relationship between employment and national income, the so-called Okun's 'Law' or the even more hair-raisingly absurd Phillips curve. Both have been controverted by events. Yet Professor Solow claims that 'mainstream economics' (that is Cambridge, Mass.) 'are actually trying to find out something concrete about the world' while 'the British Cambridge types (with the exception of Nicholas Kaldor) seem to be fighting ghosts: if we were Cambridge economists it is a little difficult to imagine what we would be doing.' Coming from that quarter, enriching the subject with ever more unrealistic assumptions and worse results, this seems lacking in critical detachment. This article goes on to dismiss monopoly and oligopoly as *déjà vu*, and then reiterates the hoary old neoclassical explanations of profits. One must not be astonished at anything.

14. Reprinted from *Business Week* by *Economic Impact*, US Information Agency, under the title 'Theory deserts the forecasters' (no. 12, 1974/5, p. 66). This issue contains an astonishing collection of admissions by celebrated economists, including some of the most mathematical, that their writing is useless if not positively mischievous.

15. F. Hahn, 'Some adjustment problems' in *Econometrica*, 38, 1 (January 1970).
16. A. A. Walters, 'A failure of economics', *United Malayan Banking Corporation Economic Revue* 2:2 (1971), 27-8.
17. M. Friedman, 'A theoretical framework for monetary policy', *Journal of Political Economy*, 78 (March/April 1970), 193-238.
18. M. Friedman, 'Have monetary policies failed?', *American Economic Review* (May 1972), Papers and Proceedings, 11-18. Also letter to *The Times* (London), 2 May 1977, especially the penultimate paragraph.
19. R. L. Heilbroner, *Economic Impact*, cited in note 14 to this chapter.
20. Though there begin to be hopeful signs. There are now two new professional journals opposed to neoclassical doctrines – the *Cambridge Journal of Economics* and the *Journal of Post Keynesian Economics*. Also *Challenge* has begun to publish 'Post Keynesian' work, for example H. Minsky on 'The financial instability hypothesis' (March/April 1977), W. C. Peterson on 'Institutionalism, Keynes and the real world' (May/June 1977), and a dozen articles reprinted in book form as *A Guide to Post-Keynesian Economics* (London: Macmillan, 1979), edited by A. S. Eichner with an introduction by Joan Robinson.
21. Frank Hahn, 'General equilibrium theory', in *The Public Interest*, Special Issue 1980, 'The crisis in economic theory'.
22. Review article with R. Matthews, 'The theory of growth', *Economic Journal* LXXIV (December 1964), 890.

Chapter 2
The Nature of Economic Problems and Relationships

1. Letter to A. L. Bowley, 3 March 1901; A. C. Pigou (ed.), *Memorials of Alfred Marshall* (N.Y.: Kelley & Millman, 1956), p. 422.
2. It is interesting that Keynes – no mean adviser – shared this view: 'The theory of economics does not furnish a body of settled conclusions immediately applicable to policy. It is a method rather than a doctrine, an apparatus of the mind, a technique of thinking, which helps (by its possession) to draw current conclusions' (Introduction to *Cambridge Economic Handbooks*).
3. One merely has to look at any economic periodical to find it full of articles whose conclusions are irrelevant to real life because their assumptions were chosen for manipulative convenience. Even Professor Samuelson claimed to be able to contribute to the discussion of Britain's problems on the basis of a model which excluded dynamism and assumed *universal increasing* costs (hence excluded the economies of mass production) and *identical* production 'functions', itself rather a shaky concept. He concluded, drawing a practical moral from an abstract theoretical argument: 'Factor-price equalization is not only possible and probable, but in a wide variety of circumstances inevitable'

(*Economic Journal*, LVIII, June 1948, 103). My refutation of his argument is reprinted in *Unequal Partners* (vol. I, Oxford: Blackwell, 1963). I first thought that he intended his contribution to be a *reductio ad absurdum* of the assumptions which are at the base of modern trade theory. More recently the International Bank and the Institute of Development Studies at the University of Sussex published a booklet on Redistribution and Growth, in which mathematical models abounded with remarks (at the end of most chapters) that the data available excluded any immediate application of the 'model'.

4. J. M. Keynes, *The General Theory* (London: Macmillan, 1936), p. 300.

5. Even so the range and quality of statistical information is still limited in Britain, indeed Europe as a whole, compared with the United States.

6. This has been demonstrated by the reaction of London markets, supposedly the most sophisticated in the Western orbit.

7. Only a man innocent of the complication of mathematical or diagrammatical treatment could gaily write: 'If a student learns nothing else from his economics course, he should learn to distinguish a shift of demand schedule or a consumption function from a shift along the schedule. The liberal use of diagrams may help in this regard. And I would argue that, if the student fails to gain from his course in international trade a capacity to analyse, his recollections that the Corn Laws were repealed in 1846 (and that corn is really wheat), that the investment guarantees under the ECA programme covered this risk but not that, or that free trade is good, tariffs bad, will have little meaning for him.' (C. P. Kindleberger, *International Economics*, Homewood, Illinois: Irwin, 5th edition, 1973, p. ix.) That the 'schedules' might be imaginary because of the change of the relationship between observations did not seem to have bothered these 'scientists'. Their trusting belief in their own capacity to distinguish between movements 'on the curve' and those 'of the curve' itself shows a regrettable ignorance of the difficulties of their subject. Cf. T. Balogh and P. D. Balacs, *Fact and Fancy* in *International Economic Relations* (Oxford: Pergamon Press, 1973), ch. 3. It is amusing to see that Kindleberger's clumsiness with arithmetic and geometry manifested itself in his wartime record: see Solly (Lord) Zuckerman, *From Apes to Warlords* (London: Hamish Hamilton, 1978).

8. Milton Friedman, *Essays in Positive Economics* (University of Chicago Press, 1953).

9. Hence the regular resurgent revalidation of 'disproved' laws by the selection of different periods for empirical observation. A good example is Professor Hines' attempt (of which politically I heartily approve) to 'disprove' the monetarist explanation of 'world' inflation.

10. An extreme example of this was the different impact of the oil price crisis on the economies of Britain and Germany. See T. Balogh, 'Theory and policy-making', *Times Literary Supplement*, 9 July 1976.

11. E. W. Streissler, *Pitfalls in Economic Forecasting* (London: Inst. of. Econ. Affairs, 1970). Unfortunately his work has been used by the organization

which published it to try to discredit State intervention, as if in an oligopolistic framework the same problem would not arise – only grossly aggravated by short-term greed and speculative anticipation. See also Abba Lerner, 'The scramble for Keynes' mantle', *Journal of Post Keynesian Economics*, I: 1, 117-18.

12. Karl Popper, *The Logic of Scientific Discovery* (London: Routledge, 1959).

13. One of the most notorious examples is the attempted derivation of a statistical relationship between wage (or price) inflation and unemployment on the basis of data of varying coverage and reliability, projected backwards over a hundred years.

14. For an interesting review of the historical disregard of this fact in model building, see A. Lowe, *On Economic Knowledge* (New York: Harper and Row, 1965).

15. J. Tobin, 'Galbraith Redux', *Yale Law Journal*, 83 (1974). See also P. Davidson, *Money and the Real World*, 2nd edition (London: Macmillan, 1978). Neoclassical monetarists seem to deny the very existence of macroeconomics, restricting themselves to more and more complicated (and in my opinion, fallacious) models. These are in fact attempts at establishing a system of deductive logic. They are irrelevant to the analysis of reality.

16. These difficulties have been shown clearly in the so-called relationships between unemployment and wage movements, interest rates and unemployment.

17. The violent fluctuations of the pound in 1976-7 and of the dollar in 1977 and 1979 were attributed to shifts of balances and changes in the timing of payments for imports and exports (leads and lags). Cf. below on the importance of stocks and their fluctuations as compared with (regular) flows.

18. See, e.g., the orthodox position, H. Johnson and J. N. Bhagwati, *Economic Journal*, LXX (March 1960). On the interrelation between exports and imports, see T. Balogh and Paul Streeten, 'What is elasticity?', *Bulletin of the Oxford University Institute of Statistics* (March 1951) – reprinted in *Unequal Partners* (Oxford: Blackwell, 1963), vol. I, pp. 177-91.

19. Reconstruction of parallel curves of identical shape without regard to the possibility, indeed probability, of *different paths* of adjustment on the impact of a change is especially misleading in the case of large aggregate factors. These considerations condemn the so-called expectation-augmented family of Phillips curves. The drastic changes over time in the relationship of unemployment and wages is only the most blatant example.

20. Hence the desperate attempt by some members of the Chicago school to treat any change as a new productive factor, in order to save the concept of production function. See, e.g., Prof. Schultz on *Transforming Traditional Agriculture* (Newhaven and London: Yale University Press, 1964) and my review (*Economic Journal*, LXXIV, December 1964) reprinted in the first edition of my *Economics of Poverty* (London: Weidenfeld and Nicolson, 1966). Most comparative statics are built on this principle – e.g. comparing two

otherwise identical systems in which the size of the national debt or of the monetary circulation differs. The fallacy in this procedure is that in most cases the path from the original to the new situation will destroy the parallelism.

21. This is the reason why the so-called 'primitive' methods of forecasting the 'informed GNP' method (see O. Eckstein, 'Econometric models, etc.' in *Challenge*, March/April 1976, p. 13) have proven generally superior to the best equation systems.

I shall deal with the problem of overshooting and destabilization presently.

22. A striking example is furnished by the analysis by Mr Wynne Godley (*The Times*, 13 July 1976) of Mr Rees-Mogg's *Times* article on the relationship of money supply and inflation. This shows that the latter's claim to have 'scientifically tested' the theory of monetarism against British figures and found that 'the fulfilment of the prediction based on it can be observed' depends entirely on the choice of the period 1967-73. It totally fails if 1974 or 1975 are included. A number of other instances are quoted by D. Savage, *National Institute Economic Review*, 83 (February 1978), 73.

23. This deficiency is due to the impossibility of controlled experiments. Mrs Thatcher might earn high distinction by launching what is almost a scientific experiment in Britain. While her determined application of monetarist theory may wreak havoc with the British economy, economists of scientific spirit may be grateful for her obstinacy.

24. This was shown by the short-run response of British entrepreneurs to the devaluation of 1967. Asymmetry (e.g. ratchet) effects and *a fortiori* irreversibility will tend to weaken the usefulness of the policy weapon connected with it – though in certain cases it might lessen the need for intervention.

25. Cf., e.g., Prof. W. Beckerman's valuable review of 'Economists on inflation', *New Statesman*, 27 April 1973, p. 610.

26. F. Modigliani, 'The Monetarist Controversy', *American Economic Review* (March 1977).

27. The stock market, though it is self-clearing, cannot in any way be regarded as part of a neoclassical world. Existing stocks are so much greater than the flow of new issues on to the market that 'real' factors (e.g. profit) will play a subordinate role, risk and fear (or their opposite) being the most immediately important factor in determining prices, which show vast fluctuations. Excess fluctuations in the commodity markets are to some extent checked by supply adjustments.

28. The velocity of circulation in the last five years showed instability amounting to up to 50 per cent both in US and UK.

29. Under pressure from Lord Kaldor (*The Times*, 30 March and 6 May 1977), Friedman (ibid, 24 April 1977) retreated and averred that: 'many factors affect the precise rate of inflation that will follow a given rate of monetary growth, most notably, the potential for real growth, the state of expectations, the exchange rate regime, and the course of prices in the rest of the world. But no

continued and substantial inflation can occur without monetary growth that substantially exceeds the rate of real growth.' He also conceded that the two-year lag which monetarists had interposed between the monetary causes and the inflationary effects is not a natural constant, but depends on historical circumstances. The weasel words strip monetarist faith of all practical usefulness in policy-making. Yet it was so used, with catastrophic consequences.

30. For a survey and original critique of the current accepted state of the doctrine see A. K. Sen, 'Personal utilities and public judgements or what is wrong with welfare economics?', *Economic Journal*, LXXXIX (September 1979), 537-58.

31. A good example of the arbitrary value judgements underlying all these attempts are the cost-benefit study of the location of the third London airport and the systems of shadow prices or weights by which the correction of socially undesirable distribution effects are instigated. See Peter Self, *Econocrats and The Policy Process: The Politics and Philosophy of Cost-Benefit Analysis* (London: Macmillan, 1976).

32. Another example is the assumption that the growth of trade union membership can be used as a proxy for labour militancy. Similarly, there are attempts to save the traditional theory by 'assimilating' the distribution of income into aid planning by attributing different weights to incomes generated. Or the increase of the national income is attributed to various factors, e.g. education, investment, on the basis of a Cobb-Douglas function for determining the shares of industry.

33. Cf., e.g., Friedman's multiple 'Phillips' curves, all of which were formed on short-period observations. See his Nobel Prize Lecture, cited in Appendix to Chapter 8.

34. J. Bhagwati and H. G. Johnson, 'Notes on some controversies in the theory of international trade', *Economic Journal*, LXX (March 1960).

35. The increase in manufacturing output until 1971 has been uninterrupted and rapid. In Japan it was 90 per cent in five years. Western Europe achieved an expansion of 30 per cent in the same period, the Soviet Union 35 per cent. The Soviet Union and Eastern Europe increased 39 per cent in four years 1963-7.

36. Paul Streeten and I have analysed these aspects of the analysis of foreign trade problems. 'The inappropriateness of simple "elasticity" concepts in the analysis of international trade' and 'Exchange Rates and National Income', *Bulletin of the Oxford University Institute of Statistics*, 13: 2 and 3 (1951).

Chapter 3
A Story of Irrelevance

1. F. Hahn, 'Some adjustment problems', Presidential address at the December 1968 meeting of the Econometric Society, *Econometrica*, Vol. 38, No. 1, January 1970.

2. Cf., for instance, Professor Kornai's stimulating work *Anti-equilibrium* (Amsterdam: North-Holland Pub. Co.), in which he postulates the existence of a 'real science' of economics even while discussing the neoclassical theory as an irrelevant exercise in a deductive logical system of choice. It was, of course, Marx who claimed 'scientific' status for his analysis of 'Kapital' even before the bourgeois economists presented their counterclaim.

3. D. H. Robertson, *Utility and All That, and Other Essays* (London: Allen and Unwin, 1952). p. 40.

4. We have come to see the expression 'political economy' used in a pejorative sense, because it tries to go beyond the simplicity of tautological or vacuous equation systems. It was a sorry day for the profession when Walras discovered that with a little effort he could fabricate as many equations as there were unknowns.

5. J. B. Say, *Traité d'Economie Politique*, trans. C. R. Prinsep (London, 1821), book I, ch. 15, p. 167. It should be noted that Say's first formulation of his *Loi des Débouchés* dates back to the years just before 1803, to a period not very far removed from the first really disastrous hyper-inflation of an important currency, that of the French Assignats during the Revolution. In the following nine years, Europe was engaged in an almost continuous series of wars which, if they did not cause monetary collapse, left England with a sharply depreciated currency. Napoleon kept his monetary system afloat by a series of sharp reparation injections which reduced the rest of the Continent to the brink of bankruptcy. In a period of extreme instability leading to a disorganization of markets and a stage of economic development in which the great majority of the population were not far above a subsistence level, that is, where the difference between the 'liquidity' of different goods is not very considerable, Say's statement is not, perhaps, altogether meaningless. People may be said to try to secure at once what they want by offering what they produce. But Say and his successors maintained their thesis long after the days had passed in which it might have been justified.

6. J. R. Hicks and R. Allen, 'A reconsideration of the Theory of Value', *Economica*, N. S. 1 and 2 (February and May 1934).

7. Say was to admit in correspondence with Malthus that only goods that are 'wanted' could purchase other goods up to the full amount of their cost; 'unwanted' goods represented a dead loss to the community, and their production, therefore, did not prepare the way for the sale of other goods. Cf. J.-B. Say, *Lettres à M. Malthus*, trans. J. Richter (London, 1821), pp. 38, 67-70.

8. A. C. Pigou, *The Economics of Welfare* (London: Macmillan, 1920), p. vii.

9. Ibid., p. 10.

10. See Joseph Schumpeter, *History of Economic Analysis* (London: Allen and Unwin, 1954).

11. Carl Menger, *Problems of Economics and Sociology*, English edition (University of Illinois Press, 1963), p. 51.

12. Ibid.

13. See, e.g., Ralph Robey, *Roosevelt Versus Recovery* (New York and London: Harper and Bros., 1934); and May Committee Report, Cmd. 3920 (London: HMSO, 1931). See also the Treasury view, reputedly written by Hawtrey and Hopkins, and recently revived under the name 'Crowding Out Principle'. The similarity of the outlook in 1972-5 and 1930-1 is striking. The Central Banks in the last stock exchange collapse, however, were able to ward off a general price liquidation and bankruptcy, including bankruptcy of the banking system, though they were severely criticized by the monetarists for indulging in inflationary money printing. They and the Treasuries were (and are) willing to intervene to save the financial system and its institutions – but not to restore investment or employment.

14. J. Robinson, *Essays in the Theory of Employment* (London: Macmillan, 1938).

15. My own estimates of the extent of German rearmament were generally ridiculed as being impossibly high, so ingrained was the fear of inflation, especially in France. In fact they turned out to be somewhat too low, viz. RM 28 billion as against RM 34 billion. Cf. T. Balogh, 'The National Economy of Germany', *Economic Journal*, XLVIII (September 1938), 461-97. It is interesting that even Churchill did not seem interested or informed about the mechanism of rearmament. Valuable inferences could have been drawn from the German example for our effort, which lagged grievously behind even when war had been declared. But even Keynes was more worried about inflation during the phoney war than military weakness. His *How to Pay for the War* did not envisage a full mobilization in the face of a deadly menace. In the end Roosevelt's Lease-Lend lessened the importance of our own marginal effort – at the cost of making our own postwar international policy dependent on the US. See Martin Gilbert, *Winston Churchill*, vol. V: 1922-39 (London: Heinemann, 1976), pp. 901-7, 760-1.

16. Roy Harrod, *The Trade Cycle: An Essay* (Oxford University Press, 1936).

17. R. F. Kahn, 'The relation between home investment and employment', *Economic Journal*, XLI (June 1931), 173-98. Michal Kalecki quite independently came to the same results (English translation in *Selected Essays on the Dynamics of the Capitalist Economy, 1933-70*, Cambridge University Press, 1971).

18. This conceptual device soon began to turn sour, however, when the relationship between expenditure and 'second round' increases in demand proved to be much more complicated than originally outlined by Kahn (and even more so, later on, after the Keynesian classicizers had got to work). As Professor Meyer has demonstrated, the new version of *The Consumption Function* (Professor M. Friedman, Princeton: University Press 1957), while politically favourable to a liberal-conservative interpretation, has not proved itself in interpreting post-1960 developments.

19. As we have seen, the paramountcy of supply had, of course, always been

denied by 'fringe' economists, but their warnings made little headway among the professionals.

20. N. Kaldor, 'Stability and full employment', *Economic Journal*, XLVIII (December 1938), 642-57; and 'A model of the trade cycle', *Economic Journal*, L (March 1940), 78-92.

21. The Chicago school meets such criticism with stoical reiteration of its oft-disproved faith in the automatism of the system. Employment once more is determined by 'real' factors and cannot be influenced by government intervention: 'The natural rate of unemployment . . . is the level that would be ground out by the Walrasian system of general equilibrium equations, provided there is embedded in them the actual structural characteristics of the labour and commodity markets, including market imperfections, stochastic variability in demands and supplies, the cost of gathering information about job vacancies and labour availabilities, the cost of mobility, and so on.' (Friedman, 'The role of monetary policy', *American Economic Review*, LVIII (March 1968), 8.) This formulation tries to escape the awkwardness posed by bilateral monopoly and growing oligopoly, and by the importance of increasing returns in the markets for goods and services, by 'absorbing' these difficulties (much as 'free trade' authors dealing with foreign trade or growth 'absorb' them).

Unfortunately for Chicago, this acceptance in fact precludes 'the grinding out of determinate answers'. This appraisal is much like Harry Johnson's blaming the varying demand for leisure to explain regional differences in unemployment. Indeed Professor Phelps goes further: 'It would be as senselessly puritanical to wipe out unemployment as it would be to raise taxes in a depression. Today's unemployment is an investment in a better allocation of any given quantity of employed persons tomorrow; its opportunity cost, like any other investment, is present consumption'. (Phelps (ed.), *Microeconomic Foundations of Employment and Inflation Theory* (London: Macmillan, 1971), p. 17). 'We' are investing in other people's misery to obtain for ourselves a 'better allocation' of resources. Intense disutility, it seems, is no longer caused by unemployment because workers are said to be voluntarily searching for better jobs. A more despicable humbug was never invented.

22. J. Robinson, *The Economics of Imperfect Competition* (London: Macmillan, 1933). Others too were advancing simultaneously and independently along a similar path. Cf. R. F. (later Sir Roy) Harrod, 'Notes on supply', *Economic Journal*, XL (June 1930), 232-41; 'The law of decreasing costs', *Economic Journal*, XLI (December 1931), 366-76; and 'A further note on decreasing costs', *Economic Journal*, XLIII (June 1933), 337-41. Also cf. E. H. Chamberlin, *The Theory of Monopolistic Competition* (Cambridge, Mass.: Harvard Economic Studies, vol. XXXVIII, 1933); R. F. Kahn, 'Notes on ideal output', *Economic Journal*, XLV (March 1935).

23. Cf. J. M. Clark, *Competition as a Dynamic Process* (Washington: The Brookings Institution, 1961). See Hicks' formulation, p. 25, n. 1.

24. A. Young, 'Increasing returns and economic progress', *Economic Journal*, XXXVIII (December 1928), 527–42.
25. P. Sraffa, 'The laws of return under competitive conditions', *Economic Journal*, XXXVI (December 1926), 535–50.
26. J. R. Hicks, *Value and Capital* (Oxford University Press, 1939), pp. 84–5. Professor Hicks has since repudiated much of that work, in charming terms: 'Clearly I need to change my name. Let it be understood that *Value and Capital* (1939) was the work of J. R. Hicks, a "neoclassical" economist now deceased; while *Capital and Time* (1973) and *A Theory of Economic History* (1969) are the work of John Hicks, a non-neoclassic who is quite disrespectful towards his "uncle".'
27. According to J. Robinson, 'bastard'.
28. Cf. the failure of A. Crosland to appreciate the socio-economic problems of full employment, which he considered totally solved.
29. I shall always remember the explanation of the late McCord-Wright when attacked at an Oxford seminar: 'My colleagues always say I am fuzzy; I am not fuzzy; life is fuzzy.'
30. J. R. Hicks, 'Mr Keynes and the "Classics": a suggested interpretation', *Econometrica*, V (April 1937), 147–59. It was effectively with this article that the so-called neo-Keynesian synthesis began, with the general-equilibrium IS–LM curve formulation of subsequent textbook fame.
31. P. A. Samuelson, 'The general theory', in Seymour E. Harris (ed.), *The New Economics: Keynes' Influence on Theory and Public Policy* (London: Dennis Dobson, 1948), p. 148.
32. Ibid., p. 159.
33. 'The balance of payments of the United States', *Economic Journal*, LVI (June 1946), and my reply, *Bulletin of the Oxford University Institute of Statistics*, 1946, republished in *Unequal Partners* (Oxford: Blackwell, 1963), vol. II, p. 149.
34. Economics being what it is, there is of course a large neoclassical school which disputed it. First we had a quantitative denigration of the importance of the problem: this failed almost immediately. Subsequently the very existence of *in*voluntary unemployment was disputed.
35. The social democratic analysis of the post-1945 world problems – such as Mr Crosland's *The Future of Socialism* (London: Cape, 1956) and Mr Strachey's later books, e.g. *Contemporary Capitalism* (London: Gollancz, 1956) – assumed that all strictly economic problems had been solved.
36. It is worthwhile to quote at length from Keynes' critical review of Professor Tinbergen's *A Method and Its Application to Investment Activity: Statistical Testing of Business-Cycle Theories*, I (Geneva: League of Nations, 1939), where he sounds an early warning of the way things were to go:

'How far are these curves and equations meant to be no more than a piece of historical curve-fitting and description and how far do they make inductive claims with reference to the future as well as the past? I have not noticed any passage in which Professor Tinbergen himself makes any inductive claims whatever. He appears to be solely concerned with statistical description ... If the method cannot prove or disprove a qualitative theory, and if it cannot give a quantitative guide to the future, is it worthwhile? For assuredly, it is not a very lucid way of describing the past ... I have a feeling that Professor Tinbergen may agree with much of my comment, but that his reaction will be to engage another ten computers and drown his sorrows in arithmetic.' [p. 568].

(From J. M. Keynes, 'Professor Tinbergen's method', *Economic Journal*, XLIX (September 1939), 558-68.) For the positive havoc this sort of scientism can do, see also Paul Streeten's and my paper 'What is elasticity?' reprinted in *Unequal Partners* (Oxford: Basil Blackwell, 1963), vol. 1, pp. 177-90.

37. See T. Balogh, 'Fluttuazioni economiche (Business Cycles)', *Dizionario di Economia Politica* (Milan, 1961). Professor Schumpeter, op. cit.

38. Even today this still remains the attitude of a number of 'liberals' whose advocacy of shop-floor bargaining (deriving, no doubt, from their belief in the rectitude - not to say feasibility - of income distribution according to marginal productivities) unwittingly exacerbates the threat of cost inflation. Even the old Treasury principle asserting that additional employment could not be created by such intervention has been revived in the new 'crowding out' thesis.

39. Between 1922 and 1929 the index of wholesale prices (1963 = 100) fell from 41 to 35 (it had stood at 79 in 1920), reaching 26 in 1933; by 1937 the index had risen to 33. See London and Cambridge Economic Service, *The British Economy, Key Statistics, 1900-1970* (London: Times Newspapers Ltd, 1971), Table E, p. 8.

40. J. E. Meade, *The Control of Inflation* (Cambridge University Press, 1958).

41. Thus, even as late as 1972, Professor Johnson could still write: 'The evolution of Keynesian theory since the immediate post-war period has in fact produced only one significant contribution to monetary analysis - the Phillips curve ...' H. G. Johnson, *Inflation and the Monetarist Controversy*, Professor Dr F. de Vries Lectures (Amsterdam: North-Holland, 1972), p. 58.

42. For the best in a bad lot see the National Institute's quarterly forecasts, especially of the balance of payments. They at least had the intellectual courage to analyse the relative success in prediction of these models and found that a random forecast would have given no worse results.

43. On this issue, see Mr Worswick's and my own memoranda to the Cohen Council: T. Balogh, 'Productivity and inflation', and G. D. N. Worswick, 'Prices, productivity and incomes', *Oxford Economic Papers* (new series), vol. X (June 1958), pp. 220-45, 246-64.

44. In a study, Dr Bray suggests that the Treasury model suffers from wide

margins of error in predicting unemployment from Gross Domestic Product. Thus, policies based on it might be (and, in fact, were) quite erroneous. Of this very important conclusion there can be no doubt. Far more doubtful, however, is his most significant positive conclusion that unemployment would, after a lag of three years, stabilize at an 'equilibrium' level at various rates of growth: for example, 580,000 at 2 per cent or 280,000 at 5 per cent. Thus, a policy which aimed at higher unemployment would be as self-justifying as one that aimed at a higher rate of growth. But the latter conclusion is a *non sequitur*. The effects of a fall in unemployment on incomes and the balance of payments might be fatal to its stability. Moreover, increases in productivity cannot be plucked out of the air by 'shifts' in the 'pattern of [manpower] flows towards productivity-increasing flows'. Managerial and structural reorganization and a change in the use of resources towards well-chosen investment would be needed. The figures available can hardly sustain Dr Bray's manipulative skill. See J. Bray, 'The road to faster growth', *The Economist*, 235 (30 May 1970), 58-9.

45. The opening salvo in the debate is in M. Friedman, 'The quantity theory of money: a restatement', in M. Friedman (ed.), *Studies in the Quantity Theory of Money* (Chicago University Press, 1956). The ensuing debate, carried on in various journals, was to be increasingly esoteric and acrimonious; as the competing orthodoxies became more and more factiously entrenched, so did the relevance of economic discussion evaporate. The wasteful abuse of Keynes' liberating vision could hardly have been more ironic. Cf. M. Friedman and D. Meiselman, 'The relative stability of monetary velocity and the investment multiplier in the United States, 1897-1958', in E. C. Brown *et al.*, *Stabilization Policies*, Commission on Money and Credit Research Series (Englewood Cliffs: Prentice-Hall, 1963), pp. 165-268; A. Ando and F. Modigliani, 'The relative stability of monetary velocity and the investment multiplier', *American Economic Review*, LV (September 1965), 693-728; M. Friedman and D. Meiselman, 'Reply', ibid., 735-85; A. Ando and F. Modigliani, 'Rejoinder', ibid., 786-90. And more recently, N. Kaldor, 'The new monetarism', *Lloyds Bank Review*, 97 (July 1970), 1-18; M. Friedman, 'The new monetarism: comment', *Lloyds Bank Review*, 98 (October 1970), 52-3; and N. Kaldor, 'Reply', ibid., 54-5. See also Friedman's letter to *The Times*, 12 December 1972, and his *Monetary History of the US* (with Schwartz) (Princeton University Press, 1963).

46. This has been acknowledged by Professor Friedman, *The Times*, 2 May 1977.

47. Committee on the Working of the Monetary System (Radcliffe) Cmnd. 827 (London: HMSO, 1959), esp. ch. 6, pp. 381-529 and ch. 12, pp. 979-85.

48. This passivity was based on the notorious 'Treasury Principle', lately revived as the 'crowding out process'. Any increase in public sector activity would inexorably reduce private demand.

49. Professor Pigou was the first to emphasize the importance of these psychological changes and the anticipating actions to which they gave rise. The

'global' monetary policies acted, as we said before, through inducing these brusque changes in sentiment and then outlay. We shall return to this central problem which is besetting the non-Soviet world.

50. Professor F. W. Paish and M. Hennessy, 'Policy for incomes' in Hobart Papers No. 29 (London: Institute of Economic Affairs, 1969).

51. Professor R. G. Lipsey and M. Parkin, 'Incomes policy: a re-appraisal', *Economica*, 1970. What is somewhat less comprehensible is that this sort of study should not have been answered together with a rectification of the 'Survey' by Professors Laidler and Parkin, *Economic Journal*, LXXXV (December 1975), jointly sponsored by the Royal Economics Society and the Social Science Research Council). A more one-sided exposition could hardly be imagined.

52. See Kaldor's paper in *Lloyds Bank Review*, 97 (July 1970).

53. *The Times*, 22 January 1974. My answer was printed on 28 January 1974.

54. It was just such arguments that Keynes attacked. Despite the fact that the general equilibrium approach tried to avoid the shortcomings of Marshallian partial analysis by acknowledging the interdependence of supply and demand factors, the mistake still continued to be made of rationalizing the workings of the economy in terms of an enormous firm. In such a model there could be no problem of effective demand. The lower the wage rate, *ceteris paribus* the higher the reward to capital: the workers would merely consume less and property-owners would consume more. But the only way to cut real wages was, effectively, to cut money wages. However money wages are as much an element of income as they are of costs: the fall in money wages would merely induce a fall in aggregate demand. Business prospects would tend to be revised downwards and investment plans curtailed: unemployment, instead of being reduced, would be increased. In logic – not a strong suit among the economics profession – this is called a fallacy of composition.

55. Most surprisingly Hicks, as we saw, also joined the band and has come under fire. Galbraith, in *Economics and the Public Purpose* (London: Deutsch, 1974), differentiated between the planning and the market sector. In analysing the international implications I preferred to stick by the expression 'oligopoly' even in the case of countries (*Fact and Fancy*, Oxford: Pergamon, 1973). Stuart Holland has also adopted this dichotomy, calling it mid-economy.

56. See, for instance, James Tobin's 'Galbraith Redux', *Yale Law Journal*, 83 (1974), 1291-1303.

57. Ibid., p. 1291.

58. The escape route suggested by Patinkin has proved to be irrelevant. See D. Patinkin, *Money, Interest and Prices* (New York: Harper and Row, 1956). The oil crisis (and its complete misdiagnosis by Friedman) has conclusively shown the intimate connection between large scale micro-economic developments and the macrosystem.

Chapter 4
Evaluating Policy

1. G. Myrdal, *The Political Element in the Development of Economic Theory*, 1930, trans. and with introduction by P. P. Streeten (London: Routledge & Kegan Paul, 1953); N. Kaldor, 'Welfare propositions of economics and interpersonal comparisons of utility', *Economic Journal*, XLIX (September 1939), 549–52; A. P. Lerner, *The Economics of Control* (New York: Macmillan, 1946).

2. P. P. Streeten, 'Programs and prognoses', *Quarterly Journal of Economics*, LXVIII (August 1954), 355–76, and Appendix to G. Myrdal (1930), op. cit.; J. de V. Graaf, *Theoretical Welfare Economics* (Cambridge University Press, 1957); K. J. Arrow, *Social Choice and Individual Values*, Cowles Commission Monograph No. 12 (New York: John Wiley, 1951).

3. This sort of approach is seen especially in attempts to isolate the contribution of selected variables (e.g. human capital) in the development process, and in cost-benefit calculations designed to estimate the welfare effects of certain measures (e.g. the siting of airports or motorways) on the basis of an income distribution which is widely felt to be unjust.

4. A typical instance is the impact of devaluation on competitiveness.

5. Critical voices are beginning to be heard. See especially Kaldor's urgent article in which he attacks the whole system of equilibrium economics – N. Kaldor, 'The irrelevance of equilibrium economics', *Economic Journal*, LXXXII (December 1972), 1237–55; also J. Kornai, *Anti-Equilibrium* (Amsterdam and London: North-Holland Pub. Co., 1971).

6. J. K. Galbraith, *The Affluent Society* (London: Hamish Hamilton, 1958); *The New Industrial State* (London: Hamish Hamilton, 1967); and *Economics and the Public Purpose* (Boston: Houghton Mifflin, 1973). See for a typical reaction Professor Tobin's review article, already quoted, in *Yale Law Journal*, 83 (1974).

7. In this connection the so-called cost-benefit studies are seen to be no more than a means of rationalizing the status quo and hence securing its implicit political acceptance and maintenance. In studies like those of the third London airport, or under the Little-Mirrlees approach to project appraisal, implicit assumptions mix with politically motivated and arbitrarily quantified factors to produce covertly value-structured results. See, e.g., F. Stewart and P. P. Streeten, 'Little-Mirrlees methods and project appraisal', *Bulletin of the Oxford University Institute of Economics and Statistics*, 34 (February 1972), 75–91. Mishan, for instance, seems to want to quantify both the quantifiable and the unquantifiable; when the latter eludes him, however, guesswork has to be substituted. See E. J. Mishan, *Cost-Benefit Analysis* (London: George Allen and Unwin, 1972). Marshall already has condemned this chicanery. See also F. Stewart, 'Social Cost Benefit Analysis in Practice', *World Development*, 6: 2 (1978), esp. pp. 163–4, and Peter Self, *Econocrats and the Policy Process* (London: Macmillan, 1975).

8. This explains the persistent efforts on the part of conventional economists to assert the purity or neutrality of their political values, and their attempts to convict of inconsistency authors such as Professor Galbraith, who have accepted the need for the overt integration of these two aspects of policy-making. There is, however (*pace* Professor Galbraith), no contradiction between this viewpoint and the effort to conduct a technical analysis of institutions and policies such as I have undertaken *before* deriving *political* conclusions in my evidence to the Radcliffe Committee. Cf. Committee on the Working of the Monetary System, Principal Memoranda of Evidence (London: HMSO, 1960), vol. III, pp. 31-47.

9. Cf. P. P. Streeten, 'Programs and prognoses', cited in note 2 to this chapter.

10. As is customary in economics, there has recently been a violent change of attitude on this topic, not merely for environmental reasons, but also on the basis of distributional and employment criteria. I have deprecated 'growth-manship' for a score of years or more (see my book *Unequal Partners*, 2 vols, Oxford: Blackwell, 1963); but the present revulsion seems to have gone too far, so far as the peaceful uses of nuclear energy are concerned.

11. In fact the assumptions required make such an exercise extremely hazardous. More generally the whole question of what is susceptible of quantification in the social sphere is a highly contentious issue. The notorious 'intelligence quotient' is a case in point. Clearly that which can be measured by the criterion of intelligence testing - IQ - need bear no relation whatever to what is generally conceived of as intelligence, or needed for intellectual success; it is strictly limited to the abilities required to pass the test, including confidence and composure, which are strongly influenced by class.

12. This includes those goods and services supplied by government. Such a view is disputed by those who think that, since government services have not 'stood the test of the market', they should not be included in the measure, or only partially. As President Eisenhower said: 'Our federal money will never be spent so intelligently and in so useful a fashion for the economy as will the expenditures that would be made by the private taxpayer, if he hadn't had so much of it funneled off into the federal government' (Arthur Schlesinger Jr., *The Big Decision*, 1960, pp. 5-6). Even Professor Kuznets has done this in his evaluation of war-output so as not to give support to those who maintain that full utilization of resources is only possible through war or rearmament: see Simon Kuznets, *National Product, War and Prewar* (New York: NBER Occasional Paper 17, 1944); *National Product in Wartime* (New York: NBER, 1945).

13. In a review of Professor Samuelson's *Collected Scientific Papers of Paul A. Samuelson*, edited by Joseph E. Stiglitz (2 vols, Cambridge, Mass.: MIT Press, 1966), Professor Arrow states: 'Samuelson enunciates a strong set of sufficient conditions for the validity of the competitive hypothesis, notes how incredible it is that the conditions are satisfied in the real world, and then suggests that, by some miracle, the real world is not totally different from the

competitive picture (p. 1422). But there is no indication to what extent and in what directions his price-theoretic theorems should be modified in applications to the real world.' (K. J. Arrow, 'Samuelson collected', *Journal of Political Economy*, 75 (October 1967), 234).

14. It is interesting to note that so eminent an adversary of 'bourgeois' economics as the late Maurice Dobb, in his book *Welfare Economics and the Economics of Socialism: Towards a Commonsense Critique* (Cambridge University Press, 1969), seems to accept this fundamentally unsound approach (or at least criticizes it in its own terms); 'common sense' would attack the basic assumptions. On all this see P. P. Streeten's papers cited in notes 1 and 2 to this chapter.

15. See below and Isaiah Berlin, *Four Essays on Liberty* (Oxford University Press, 1969; Revised edn 1973). I shall return to this important point.

16. A. C. Pigou, *The Economics of Welfare*, 3rd edition (London: Macmillan, 1929), pp. 10-11.

17. Ibid., p. 11.

18. Ibid., p. 12.

19. Ibid., p. 8.

20. Ibid., p. 20.

21. T. Scitovsky, *Welfare and Competition* (London: Allen and Unwin, 1952), p. 30. Italics added. He (not unlike Hicks) totally changed his approach in *The Joyless Economy* (New York: Oxford University Press, 1976).

22. Ibid., p. 40. Italics added.

23. Professor Kornai (op. cit., note 5 above) has elegantly formulated this important distinction by differentiating between economics and the logical theory of consistent choice.

24. Professor Pigou had a sound instinct from the point of view of economics as the handmaiden of policy when he groped after a definition of the national income which would depend on measureable quantities of goods alone and not on something subjective like tastes or needs. This is obviously impossible, as national income changes in composition and goods have to be valued somehow to be weighed. He therefore with some distaste settled for a less stringent test. Considering a single individual whose tastes are taken as fixed we say that his dividend in period II is greater than in period I if the items that are added to it in period II are items that he wants more than the items that we have taken away from it in period II ... Passing to a group of individuals (of given numbers) whose tastes are taken as fixed, and among whom the distribution of purchasing power is also taken as fixed, we say that the dividend in period II is greater than in period I if the items that are added to it in period II are items to conserve which they would be willing to give more money than they would be willing to give to conserve the items that are taken away from it in period II. Thus $\sum p2q2$ will be greater than $\sum p2q1$. Nothing is said of any attendant conditions. Man is considered as a consumer alone and his economic behaviour is held to be exhausted in this definition.

I submit that this (even if it were feasible as a definition, which, as we shall demonstrate, it is not) can only be accepted in the case of minute changes of no importance. It certainly has no meaning in the field of foreign trade or economic development, where the attendant changes in the non-consumers' sphere are often substantial.

25. Cf. J. Kornai, *Rush versus Harmonic Growth* (Amsterdam: North-Holland Publishing Co., 1972), Lecture II.

26. Pigou, op. cit., pp. 17-18.

27. In Pigou's treatment a bare three pages (op. cit., pp. 14-17) are devoted to the implications for welfare of the manner in which incomes are earned.

28. This aspect of the problem seems to be left wholly out of account by certain 'social-democratic' theorists who look to economic 'growth' as a source of finance with which to expand the social services without encountering class resistance. See, for example, C. A. R. Crosland, *A Social Democratic Britain*, Tract No. 404 (London: Fabian Society, 1971). In fact, American experience shows persuasively that demand-oriented growth might not provide an increase in 'free margins' for social purposes. Indeed, it is for the very reason that growth is demand-oriented that it pre-empts the uses to which any increase in output is put.

29. The attempts by 'growth' protagonists to brush this problem aside by demanding that producers should pay compensation or have their activities taxed have no meaning, of course, unless spelled out in terms of the 'cost' involved to consumers, that is, to the present and future members of the community. The very unequal geographic incidence of the harm caused renders this approach inapplicable. An increase of direct pollution controls is obviously in order.

30. This represents the basic problem of Britain. See 'British Malaise', a review article in *Books and Bookmen* (June 1976).

31. D. H. Robertson, *Utility and All That, and other Essays* (London: Allen and Unwin, 1952), pp. 14-15. Italics added. Two years earlier, Dr Little had proposed only two (as contrasted with Robertson's four) criteria for an improvement in welfare, viz. (a) that national output should have increased, that is, that the Scitovsky double-criterion be fulfilled, and (b) that the distribution of income should not have deteriorated. See I. M. D. Little, *A Critique of Welfare Economics* (Oxford: Clarendon Press, 1950). Even so, determinate solutions to problems of policy would still be fortuitous. The possibility of conflict, as Professor Robertson recognized, is not eliminated if more than one criterion requires to be satisfied. Yet even with one criterion, national income, as we have mentioned, any increase would still have to be measured in terms of a set of prices thrown up by some given income distribution. Nor can such a criterion help in determining the best allocation of output between consumption and investment, since again the social rate of discount will be affected by the distribution of income. Ultimately the policy decision must rest on a political value judgement.

32. Robertson, op. cit., p. 37.

33. Ibid., p. 40.

34. That is, according to the familiar criteria and assumptions associated with the name of Pareto, the welfare of individuals is best served if market forces are permitted to respond freely to the pattern of consumers' demand. But there is not one but an infinite number of Pareto-optima – 'efficient' points – and the final outcome will be determined by the initial distribution of income and, hence, pattern of demand and prices; whether one such optimum point constitutes a higher or lower level of social welfare than another must therefore be a matter of political judgement with regard to that distribution. Far from denying this to be the case, no effort has been spared by some to prove that, given the initial supply of resources, nothing 'positive' can be said about the superiority in terms of welfare of any optimum position *vis-à-vis* another, within any 'feasible' range of distribution. Cf. P. A. Samuelson, 'Evaluating real national income', *Oxford Economic Papers* (NS), II (January 1950), 1-29. Thus, through the back door, so to speak, the 'do-nothing' policy was implicitly vindicated again: if one cannot be sure that one situation is better than another, there can be no a priori reason for altering the status quo. The amount of ink that has been spilt on this subject, since Professor Kaldor's most jestful demonstration that interpersonal comparisons of utility could be circumvented by postulating notional compensatory payments to 'losers' in any change, is remarkable. Kaldor was specifically concerned with evaluating the effects of a move from protection to free trade on real income – not on total welfare. Indeed he states quite clearly: 'Whether landlords, in the free-trade case, should in fact be given compensation or not, is a political question on which the economist, *qua* economist, could hardly pronounce an opinion ... For it is quite impossible to decide on economic grounds what particular pattern of income-distribution maximizes social welfare ... All that the economist can, and should, do in this field, is to show, given the pattern of income distribution desired, which is the most convenient way of bringing it about.' (N. Kaldor, 'Welfare propositions of economics', *Economic Journal*, XLIX (September 1939), 549-52). Whether or not compensation is due or losses should be avoided depends on political considerations, as Kaldor clearly acknowledged.

35. Nor is it mere coincidence that they have, almost to a man, favoured Britain's entry into the Common Market, implying their acceptance of the do-nothing principles embodied in the Treaty of Rome. Recently they have also tended to accept a monetarist approach – a deflationary policy causing mass unemployment and endangering steady expansion – instead of introducing direct controls to enable a restructuring of British industry. They have always been naïvely hopeful that this 'liberalizing' policy pattern, dotted with some nationalization, would produce acceptable rates of progress and inflation.

36. J. R. Hicks, *Essays in World Economics* (Oxford University Press, 1959).

37. It is also closely related to the notion that there exists a stable and reversible

relation between unemployment and wages or prices. As with so many other 'economic' relations, it has been found to be extremely unstable and crucially dependent on political and psychological factors.

Chapter 5
The Individual and the Group

1. That is to say, the satisfaction derived from the consumption of the good must not be impaired if the consumption of some other good is diminished; hence, items of consumption which may require a certain combination of goods (e.g. tea, milk and sugar; whisky and soda) cannot be included.

2. This is of special importance when it comes to the matter of choice from among different paths of development in poor countries. A country which opts for the motorcar, so to speak, also imposes upon itself certain constraints in matters of town planning and transport investment. This applies as much to the USSR as to Brazil.

3. One notable attempt to escape from the restrictions of the traditional commodity-oriented theory of consumer behaviour has been made by Professor Lancaster, who hypothesizes that it is not commodities *per se* which enter into individuals' preference or utility functions, but their inherent 'characteristics'. (K. Lancaster, *Consumer Demand: A New Approach*, New York and London: Columbia University Press, 1971.) Thus, it is not in relation to relative commodity prices that the rationality of consumer behaviour should be judged, but to the imputed relative prices of their 'characteristics'. Yet it is doubtful whether Lancaster's 'consumer' is much more of a plausible figure than of old. He must still be aware of the full range of products and their prices; his preferences must be fully articulated; there must be no externalities in consumption (although it is the commodity's characteristics which are now the focus of the consumer's attention, there should be no kudos attaching to its consumption); optimization still requires continuous divisibility in commodities. Furthermore, the consumer must now be assumed to have knowledge of the characteristics inherent in all commodities; or rather, given the list of characteristics entering his preference function, he must be aware of all those commodities in which they occur, and in what degree. Now, apart from the conceptual and practical problems of measurement, the question arises as to which set of characteristics our consumer will use in selecting from any given bundle of commodities. What 'kind' of characteristics are legitimate? Thus, in selecting between items of food, say, is no weight to be given to the 'appleness' of apples and the 'pearness' of pears, regardless of the relative imputed 'prices' of their constituent characteristics in terms of vitamins, calories or whatever? If this point is given, it follows that choice cannot be construed as the outcome of a rational comparison of commodities with

commonly held characteristics. As long as a commodity (or a brand of commodity) is desired for its own sake, it will dominate any other in the relevant consumption set. This in turn will tend to undermine such support as the 'characteristics model' may have lent to the concept of consumer sovereignty, since there is no reason to suppose that preferences in terms of characteristics will be any the less susceptible of distortion and manipulation through advertising than is the case with preferences between commodities.

4. The theory of imperfect competition is mainly concerned with the consequences of market imperfection on the behaviour of the *firm*; the consumer with brand- or shop-loyalties is not exactly a respectable figure in orthodox analysis.

5. W. S. and E. S. Woytinsky, *World Population and Production: Trends and Outlook* (New York: Twentieth Century Fund, 1953), p. 267. The efforts of banks to attract student accounts are a similar phenomenon. It is very rarely that customers will change their bank, so it is important to influence their initial (and largely irrational) choice, and it seems that the banks are prepared to incur losses in the attempt to secure what are initially quite small deposits.

6. J. K. Galbraith, *The Affluent Society* (London: Hamish Hamilton, 1958), p. 124.

7. As we have seen, the hope that a faster increase in national production will bring with it more contentment, a higher degree of social integration and greater scope for the fulfilment of collective needs is an illusion which has gained wide acceptance in Britain as a result of the failure to secure a 'satisfactory' rate of growth since the war. In view of Professor Friedman's propaganda suggesting that this failure was due to high taxation and the crippling weight of government expenditure, it must be emphasized that the rate of growth after 1945 was higher than between 1874 and 1913.

8. Cf. A. Marshall, *Principles of Economics*, seventh edn (London: Macmillan, 1916), p. 89.

9. See, e.g., Richard Wollheim, *Socialism and Culture*, Tract No. 331 (London: Fabian Society, 1961), pp. 23–5.

10. Ibid., p. 47.

11. This system - which produced the monolithic ruling class to oversee the Victorian empire - has been one of the most totalitarian or 'directive' educational experiments ever witnessed.

12. On the power of conditioning an apt instance is quoted by the *New Yorker* of 21 April 1951, p. 24, from *Sound Tract*, a well-known US trade magazine:

'Speaking of surveys, we tried an experiment the other evening. The result was not what Nimo Roper would call "significant". But it may lead you or your favourite researcher into further inquiry.

'To a curly-headed four year old being tucked under the covers, we posed this question: "Susie, which product brushes teeth whiter?" "Colgate, of course, Gramp." We couldn't resist another. "Which product washes clothes cleaner?" Without a moment's hesitation: "Tide." We tried once more. "Which coffee gives the best value?" When she replied "A & B and now good night Gramp," we hurried out of the child's room with other questions beating at our brain.'

13. Out-and-out advocates of *laissez-faire* think they have found an answer in providing parents with educational vouchers which can be spent at their will. The scheme promoters conveniently forget that this would merely add to inequality, as the rich could always supplement the vouchers with their own means.

14. This would appear to be wholly acceptable not only to Conservatives, but also to the theoreticians on the right of progressive parties in Britain and overseas. Thus, Mr Crosland: 'But the popular mood is one of intense resentment of high taxation and of certain forms of public spending such as family allowances and supplementary benefits.' (C. A. R. Crosland, *A Social Democratic Britain*, Tract No. 404 (London: Fabian Society, 1971), p. 3.) It is not altogether surprising that Mr Crosland classed these transfer payments as public *spending*. Mr Jenkins, when Chancellor, put the jingle of the pennies in private pockets higher on the priority list.

15. So-called diseconomies of consumption; see J. K. Galbraith, *The New Industrial State* (London: Hamish Hamilton, 1967).

16. Cf. E. J. Mishan, *The Costs of Economic Growth* (London: Staples Press, 1967).

17. It is interesting that the Soviet Union has now committed itself to a pattern of development in imitation of the United States, thus signalling one important loss of faith in the potential superiority, in this important respect, of a centrally planned economy.

18. The underprivileged and impoverished of the world cannot be expected to accept zero growth before a completely new attitude has been established. This applies also, of course, to those countries which by some fluke (or as a result of the protection of one of the superpowers) have acquired great wealth, especially the oil-producing countries. The latter's attitude to their erstwhile comrades in poverty shows less sensitivity than has been displayed, at least since the last war, by their capitalist exploiters.

19. C. A. R. Crosland, *A Social Democratic Britain*, op. cit.

20. See, e.g., W. Beckerman, 'Economic development and the environment: a false dilemma', in *Environment and Development* (The Founex Report), *International Conciliation*, No. 586 (January 1972), 57-71.

21. The boom between 1926 and 1929 in the United States is the most striking recent case; history is littered with such examples.

22. Any such disapproval could not, of course, manifest itself in effective action until the working classes had acquired the necessary economic power to transform their protest into industrial paralysis. With this came a fear for the very basis of democracy, and in a number of countries the assertion of workers'

rights provoked violent countermeasures on the part of the propertied class; on the consequences of full employment, see Chs 7 and 8 below.

23. Cf. Friedrich von Wieser, *Social Economics* (London: George Allen and Unwin, 1927), p. 9.

24. As Professor Haberler once put it, correctly: 'In an individualistically organized economy ... what is to be regarded as a better position, a larger national income or a superior welfare position, must be defined in terms of individual incomes and welfare positions' (G. Haberler, 'Some problems in the pure theory of international trade', *Economic Journal*, LX (June 1950), 226). He went on, however, to define an 'improvement' solely by reference to *physical* output, valued on the basis of *arbitrary* weights, that is, based on prices and exchange rates determined by the *existing* distribution of income. Thus, he could not avoid dealing with income distribution. He merely selected his weights arbitrarily:

> 'Modern welfare economics had, however, shown that in the following sense the situation after trade can be said to be better off than before. *It is not necessary* that income will actually be redistributed so that everybody will in fact be better off. There will practically always be some individuals who are worse off than before. But it is sufficient that everybody *could* be better off. That is the definition of what is meant by saying that one situation is better and constitutes a larger national income' [loc. cit., pp. 226-7].

25. This seems to have been the import of Professor Robertson's dictum (p. 74, above).

26. This fact becomes of paramount importance in the power-concentrated stage of industrial development at full employment. Interestingly enough, it is ignored by socialist or communist writers (e.g. J. Kornai, in *Rush Versus Harmonic Growth*, cited in note 25 to the preceding chapter).

27. Late refinements such as that elaborated by the World Bank and the Sussex Institute of Development Studies (*Redistribution with Growth*, Oxford University Press, 1974), or the Beckerman/Atkinson approach ('Reflections on Redistribution and Growth', *World Development*, 5: 8 (August 1977), or *Economics of Inequality*, Oxford University Press, 1975) do not alter the fact that all measurements are made on the basis of existing prices or a political decision on 'shadow' prices. The unfavourable impact of relative prices on inequality has been stressed by Beckerman. Thus the result is based on value judgements still. These exercises may be of some value for persuasion. For decision-making they might present additional problems.

28. It is one of the more blatant fictions of the theory of demand that the consumer is assumed to know how he would distribute his income between various goods and services at all levels of income. Moreover, the analysis is couched in such terms that he will always consume *some* of every good at any given

price-ratio. This derives from the curious way in which the element of choice is brought into the picture; for the goods from amongst which he builds up his bundle of consumption only exist (are produced) *because* there is a demand for them (their availability presupposes demand). Zero consumption of any item is therefore precluded by assumption. The highly plausible condition that both below and above certain levels of income the consumption of some goods may be zero (the former through necessity – because of indivisibilities, or because some goods or services may have value only above a certain quantity – and the latter through choice) is completely excluded from purview.

29. It is of interest sociologically to speculate as to why the later representatives of the classical Utilitarian school explicitly considered the effect of economic policies (such as free trade) on the distribution of income; whereas the neoclassical approach was to brush such awkward problems aside as queer exceptions to the general rule.

30. Indeed, Pareto himself emphasized that 'the whole theory of economic equilibrium is ... independent of the notions of (economic) utility, value in use, or ophelimity ... A complete treatise of pure economics could be written [without such concepts], and one day it may be convenient to do so' (V. Pareto, *Manuel D'Economie Politique*, 2nd edition (Paris, 1927), p. 543). Indeed, it was convenient: all traces of utility, ordinal or otherwise, were to be ruthlessly excised by Hicks in his book *Value and Capital* (Oxford: Clarendon Press, 1939).

31. Cf. L. Robbins, *Essays on the Nature and Significance of Economic Science* (London: Macmillan, 2nd edn. 1935).

32. Ibid.

33. Cf. N. Kaldor, 'Welfare propositions of economics and interpersonal comparisons of utility', *Economic Journal*, XLIX (September 1939), 549-52 (reprinted in N. Kaldor, *Essays on Value and Distribution* (London: Duckworth, 1960), pp. 143-6).

34. Cf. T. Scitovsky, 'A note on Welfare propositions in economics', *Review of Economic Studies*, IX: 1 (1941-2), 77-88 (reprinted in T. Scitovsky, *Welfare and Growth* (London: Allen & Unwin, 1964), pp. 123-38).

35. Cf. J. R. Hicks, 'The foundations of welfare economics', *Economic Journal*, XLIX (December 1939), 696-712.

36. Cf. Robin Marris, *The Machinery of Economic Policy*, Research Pamphlet No. 168 (London: Fabian Society, 1954), pp. 18-19. Italics added.

37. See I. M. D. Little, *A Critique of Welfare Economics* (Oxford: Clarendon Press, 1950).

38. On the other hand, such 'model developers' as Pakistan, Colombia or Korea provide sad examples to the contrary. Cf. K. Griffin, *Underdevelopment in Spanish America: an Interpretation* (London: Allen and Unwin, 1969).

39. It is astonishing, in this connection, that Professor Kornai, a confirmed supporter of education, should hold that the costs and sacrifices incurred in

education justify inequality in income distribution. One would have thought that the burden of not having to work as an unskilled labourer would be none too oppressive. Cf. J. Kornai, *Rush versus Harmonic Growth* (Amsterdam: North-Holland Publishing Co., 1972), p. 37.

40. This has always seemed a rather spurious argument, so far as the higher managerial or intellectual positions are concerned. Above a certain level of material satisfaction, power and status are a sufficient element in providing the stimulus to work. Yet it is here that the gravest offences against the principle occur. For instance, the attempt to implement an incomes policy in Britain after 1965 was morally and politically undermined by the ill-fated report of the National Board on Prices and Incomes on top salaries in the nationalized industries, which recommended large absolute increases in salary after a number of other privileged professions (the Civil Service and judiciary) had received similar increases. The same mistake was made in December 1973, when the salaries of Principals and Assistant Secretaries were increased. It was once more repeated in 1978. It is no use pleading in such cases that a large proportion of the increment goes in taxes, or that no increase has been awarded for some time.

41. Cf. A Bergson, 'A reformulation of certain aspects of welfare economics', *Quarterly Journal of Economics*, LII (February 1938), 310–34.

42. Cf. K. J. Arrow, 'Samuelson collected', *Journal of Political Economy*, LXXV (October 1967), 236.

43. Cf. J. Tinbergen, 'Some thoughts on mature socialism', Jawaharlal Nehru Memorial Lecture, *Eastern Economist* (Annual Number 1971), 25 December 1970, 1113–26 (1117).

44. This was acutely recognized by writers such as Knut Wicksell and Henry Sidgwick, but wholly lost sight of later by the mechanistically-minded neo-classical economists. Cf. H. Sidgwick, *Principles of Political Economy* (London: Macmillan, 1883), bk. III, ch. 5, and K. Wicksell, *Finanztheoretische Untersuchungen* (Jena, 1896), pp. 62–3.

45. Keith Griffin has shown that at any rate in Asia 'development' (as measured by the 'growth' of GNP) can and usually does entail such regressive redistribution of income as to naturally increase poverty. Among a number of contributions the latest is (in collaboration with A. Rahman Khan) 'Poverty in the Third World: Ugly Facts and Fancy Models', *World Development*, 6, 3 (March 1978).

46. Even Pigou restricted the validity of his welfare analysis to those nations 'with a stable general culture'. Cf. A. C. Pigou, *The Economics of Welfare* (London: Macmillan, 1920), p. 21.

Chapter 6
Production: Freedom and Efficiency?

1. *The American Individual Enterprise System. Its Nature, Evolution, and Future.* By the Economic Principles Commission of the National Association of Manufacturers (New York: McGraw-Hill, 1946), p. 1019. Quoted by K. Galbraith, *American Capitalism* (1952) at p. 43 of the revised edition (London: Penguin Books, 1963).

2. Socialist writers from Barone to Lange, overwhelmed by the crystalline beauty and majesty of the claims on behalf of the mathematical system which assured this perfection, were reduced to claiming rather feebly that a centrally owned and controlled economy could be made to imitate this mechanism. The absurdity of the basic assumptions on which these proud claims rested was never exposed. Recently a social democratic writer (always more logically articulate than Conservative authors) asserted that new consumption goods, such as new children's toys, could not have been invented and introduced by a totally planned system. The alarm caused by less innocent inventions of the Soviet can no longer be attributed (analogously) to spies.

3. At times perfect mobility of the factors was also assumed, that is, absolute ease and capacity to shift from one employment to another – the resistance to change might be less if this were true.

4. I have dealt with the mechanism of subterfuge in that field in a different context (*Unequal Partners*, 2 vols, Oxford: Blackwell, 1963).

5. J. M. Clark, 'Toward a concept of workable competition', *American Economic Review*, xxx (June 1940), subsequently enlarged as *Competition as a Dynamic Process* (Washington, D.C.: The Brookings Institution, 1961).

6. Adam Smith, *The Wealth of Nations* (London, 1776), bk. IV, ch. 2.

7. A. C. Pigou (ed.), *Memorials of Alfred Marshall* (London: Macmillan, 1925), pp. 338, 339.

8. The convention by which economists differentiate between increasing investment 'with a given state of technical knowledge' and 'an increase in technical knowledge' is quite illicit. Technical progress only has significance when incorporated in new investment; but new investment will not necessarily embody the most recent technical advances. It is for this reason that the notions of reversibility and of the substitutability of techniques have to be rejected as plausible representations of the productive process. (See N. Kaldor, 'Economic growth and the problem of inflation', *Economica*, (new series), XXV (August 1959), 212-26.)

But no sooner does Professor Kaldor expose these bogus distinctions than he himself proceeds to postulate the existence of a stable long-run relationship between the rate of accumulation of capital and the rate of growth of output, where the crucial factor is 'the rate at which [a society] adopts improvements in productive techniques' (ibid., p. 221). That is the 'relationship expresses the "technical dynamics" of the economy, since the more "dynamic" are the people in control of production (the entrepreneurs), the readier they are to change techniques and to introduce innovations, the faster will productivity increase and the faster will capital be accumulated' (ibid., p. 222). Unfortunately, this capacity to make use of technical innovations is not an immutable characteristic. It depends on the anticipations of entrepreneurs; it will change, and change significantly, through time. Indeed, it is one of the more important tasks of development planning to induce such change. We know hardly anything about the relationship which Professor Kaldor wishes to formalize, and his attempt to explain development through time on the basis of its constancy is not convincing.

9. P. S. Florence, *The Logic of British and American Industry*, 3rd edition (London: Routledge and Kegan Paul, 1972).

10. G. J. Stigler, *The Theory of Price* (New York: The Macmillan Company, 1942). His further attempt to establish the prevalence of competition (*The Behaviour of Industrial Prices*, National Bureau of Economic Research, 1970) was equally forced. See G. C. Means, 'The Administered Price Thesis Reconfirmed', *American Economic Review*, LXII (June 1972), 292-306. Dr Means established the prevalence of oligopoly. These findings were reinforced by John M. Blair, 'Market power and inflation', *Journal of Economic Issues*, VII: 2 (June 1974). The relentless trend towards concentration is confirmed by, among others, A. P. Jacquemin, *Size, Structure and Performance of the Largest European Firms*, National and Commercial Banking Group; and S. J. Prais, *The Evolution of Giant Firms in Britain* (Cambridge University Press, 1976).

11. See J. M. Clark (1961), op. cit., p. 426.

12. On the question of the welfare implications of monopolistic influences in international trade, see the polemical exchange stimulated by Professor Haberler's paper, 'Some problems in the pure theory of international trade', *Economic Journal*, LX (June 1950), 223-40; T. Balogh, 'Welfare and freer trade - a reply', *Economic Journal*, LXI (March 1951), 72-82; G. Haberler, 'Rejoinder', *Economic Journal*, LXI (December 1951), 777-84.

13. As we have mentioned, Professor Galbraith saw this clearly at the first stages of his intellectual apostasy when he attempted to substitute a 'second-best' solution that would still be favourable to private enterprise - that of 'countervailing power' - to replace the inevitable dominance of impersonal forces. In *American Capitalism* he depicted the homeopathic opposition of two evolutionary monopoly forces, that of capital now confronted by labour. Although preferable to a position of unopposed power, it is by no means necessary that such a regime will furnish a best or even second-best solution. These problems are themselves influenced by historical forces and institutional arrangements which differ from country to country and occasion to occasion. The crucial inconsistency in the bilateral monopoly solution is that, on its own, it cannot provide a solution because of its implications for monetary imbalance. As we have seen, this led Galbraith for a time to an ultimate solution essentially at

odds with his initial vision – a diminution of labour's countervailing power, that is large-scale (albeit well-paid) unemployment – and certainly one which could in no way correspond to any moral ideal of economic optimum. See Chapter 7 on Full Employment.

14. Any attempts to re-create deliberately yet indirectly through fiscal or monetary means the conditions in which a 'harmony of interests' or rather a subduing of working-class ambitions might prevail between capital and labour, as suggested by Professor Galbraith and propagated by 'liberal' economists, must fail because they implicitly discriminate against labour and are incidentally harmful to expansion. In the circumstances it is to be expected that direct intervention may produce better results from a number of possible political points of view.

15. Cf. below on the 'un-neoclassical', i.e. mainly psychological, impact of monetary policy on activity and prices. The monetarist school ignores this problem by claiming that prices are (perfect) market-tested, but there is no presumption that the market corresponds to their model.

16. This refers, of course, to the 'full cost' principle under which firms are assumed to add a certain percentage margin over and above average variable and overhead costs. Such a firm would not be a profit-maximizer in the conventional short-term sense. With capacity to spare (as we have mentioned) the perfectly competitive firm could, of course, increase profits by raising output as long as costs were constant. Alternatively, if the firm was operating under less than perfect conditions (downward-sloping demand curve), by definition the conventional profit-maximizing conditions are not being met: although average revenue equals 'average cost', marginal revenue is less than marginal cost. Profits, according to these criteria, could be increased by restricting output and increasing the unit profit margin.

17. For each feasible size of plant there is assumed to exist a short-run average cost curve; and for any given plant size, the optimum point on the relevant short-run average cost curve at which the firm is producing will be tangential to the firm's long-run average cost curve. That is to say, the long-run curve forms an 'envelope' around the family of short-run curves. It is, in effect, a locus of optimum points, whose shape is strictly dependent on current technology and cost conditions. All this has little relevance.

18. 'The recreation of scarcity' (in Hungarian). Inaugural lecture. *Economic Review of the Academy of Science*, Budapest.

19. The British attitude to this problem is schizophrenic: imitating the US with its vast territory and market, antimonopoly legislation was enacted based on the much smaller British market shares, thus accentuating the handicap against them. At the same time amalgamations were also encouraged. The establishment of a Department for Prices and Consumer Protection created a new empire-building organ unlikely to be objective in its attitude, if only for self-justificatory reasons. The typical (Cmnd. 7198, London: HMSO,

1978) Review of Monopolies and Mergers Policy does not deal with the all-important international aspects of the problem.

20. J.M. Clark (1961), op. cit., ch. 4.

21. See A.C. Pigou, *Socialism v. Capitalism* (London: Macmillan, 1937), pp. 87-9.

22. This has been conclusively demonstrated by the increasing reliance placed on government finance before the war by the railways, and after it by private steel companies in Britain during the period of denationalization. Even in the US a number of industries (e.g. railways, aircraft) have come to depend directly or indirectly on State finance.

23. Sidney and Beatrice Webb, *The Decay of Capitalist Civilization* (New York: Harcourt, Brace, 1923), pp. 72-3.

24. Pigou, *Socialism v. Capitalism*, pp. 85-6.

25. As we shall see below, experience in Britain was different and much inferior to that either in the US or the Continent.

26. Although Professor Galbraith does not refer to bankers and banking in discussing the metamorphosis of capitalism, he would no doubt consider them to be a part of the technostructure itself. In our view, however, the motives, aims and business methods of bankers are quite different from those of industrial managers.

27. See T. Balogh, 'The British élite', *The Listener*, LXXXIX (15 March 1973), 333-4.

28. See T. Balogh, 'The apotheosis of the dilettante: the establishment of mandarins', in Hugh Thomas (ed.), *Crisis in the Civil Service* (London: Anthony Blond, 1968), pp. 11-52.

Chapter 7
Full Employment and the Distribution of Income

1. J. S. Mill, *Principles of Political Economy*, edited by W. J. Ashley (London: Longmans, Green, 1920), p. 372.

2. Intimately connected with the neoclassical theory of distribution is the notorious 'adding-up' problem, originating effectively with P. H. Wicksteed's *Essay on the Co-ordination of the Laws of Distribution* (1894). Here Wicksteed tried to prove that, given constant returns to scale in production, total product would be completely exhausted if each factor received a reward equal to its marginal product. For a discussion of this inherently trivial proposition, and of what transpires to be no 'problem' at all, see Joan Robinson, 'Euler's theorem and the problem of distribution', *Economic Journal*, XLIV (September 1934), 398-414.

3. This is not to imply, of course, that Marx alone was politically motivated in his economic writings. Thus, whereas Malthus had tried to defend rent,

Ricardo sought to condemn it as a drain on profits, the true engine of growth. In his turn, Marx, of course, condemned profits (and other unearned incomes) as being nothing more than unpaid labour-time. The neoclassical counter-attack in defence of profits (and interest), however, was swift to establish itself as the new orthodoxy, although the prospect of an upward trend in real wages was offered as a *douceur* to social consciences. After more than a hundred years, there is little evidence of change in this fundamental position.

4. The extent of the improvement is difficult to establish in view of the increasingly insidious avoidance and evasion of taxes, especially in the higher income ranges. Indeed it is questionable whether certain *costs* should not be deemed *incomes*, or at least capital gains.

5. The Welfare State, direct State intervention and progressive taxation were the main means by which the Marxist prediction was refuted. As we shall see their work has not yet been completed: the body of the 'affluent society' is still disfigured by spots of individual misery.

6. Cf. Arthur M. Schlesinger Jr, *The Age of Roosevelt* (London: Heinemann, 1961), vol. III: *The Politics of Upheaval*, p. 297.

7. See my essay on 'The Crisis of Capitalism', *New Hungarian Quarterly*, Budapest (1974).

8. In classical terminology there was a 'tendency' to price stability, much as there was a tendency to full employment. With the domestic price level directly connected to the quantity of money, those employers who submitted to 'excessive' wage demands did so at the risk of their competitive positions. Since full employment was the norm, output could not be increased (in the short term); hence, either prices would tend to rise or the demand for imports would increase, or a combination of the two. At all events, the country's international competitiveness would deteriorate; but forces would be at work to restore the status quo. As gold flowed out to finance the balance of payments deficit, the 'quantity' of the domestic money stock would decline, thereby imposing a deflationary pressure on internal prices; the consequent squeeze on profits would depress the money-wage rate at which entrepreneurs would be willing to 'offer employment'. Whatever the resulting level of employment (as we have already seen, it will be by definition voluntary), the classical internal and external adjustment mechanisms will preclude secular inflation because it is impossible within such an analytical framework.

9. Cf. F. W. Paish, *The Rise and Fall of Incomes Policy*, Hobart Papers, No. 47 (London: Institute of Economic Affairs, 1969).

10. Cf., e.g., J. A. Kregel, 'Post-Keynesian Theory: Income Distribution', *Challenge* (September–October 1978), p. 37.

11. The shift in favour of profits, of course, depends on the assumption that the propensity to save out of profits exceeds the propensity to save out of wages; moreover, the greater the difference between these propensities, the smaller the required redistribution, until in the limit where all profits are saved and all wages consumed, the required fall in real wages is simply equal to the

projected increase in investment. (In a more realistic setting, where foreign trade is brought into the model, the impact on wages and consumption may be mitigated - depending on the relative import-contents of investment *vis-à-vis* consumption expenditure - but this would, of course, demand a consideration of the attendant adverse effects on the balance of payments.) But clearly, if labour refused to accept the consequent cut in real wages (and if we are to assume the savings parameters unchanged) the result would be a continuous and probably accelerating spiral of profit and wage inflation or, in breach of the initial assumption, the emergence of unemployment, depending on what was happening to the money supply and on how entrepreneurs reacted to the consequent behaviour of interest rates.

At all events, such a theory cannot go very far in explaining what *determines* the distribution of income. Nonetheless, its usefulness is not altogether lost. It can, for example, offer some insight into the problems of raising the investment ratio, *given* the existing distribution of income and savings propensities, since these, taken separately, determine the maximum feasible value of the ratio. The above remarks, moreover, have a close bearing on the recently popularized notion of 'export-led growth': to the extent that this entails increasing the ratio of exports (and, by derived process, investment) to national income, and hence an adverse impact on consumption and wages, such a prescription for accelerating growth might incur political resistance. Keynes himself refused to regard the problem of nominal wages as monetary or economic: he rightly saw it as a political problem, the determinacy of the answer to which was destroyed: 'I do not doubt that a serious problem will arise when we have a combination of collective bargaining and full employment. But I am not sure how much light the analytical (economic) method you apply can throw on this essentially political problem.' Aubrey Jones, 'Inflation as an Industrial Problem', in R. Skidelsky, *The End of the Keynesian Era* (London: Macmillan, 1977), p. 53.

12. See also K. Griffin and A. Rahman Khan, 'Poverty in the Third World: Ugly Facts and Fancy Models', *World Development*, 6:3 (March 1978), and the extensive literature quoted. For an analysis of the politics and economics of the failure of these efforts, see 'Failure in the Strategies against Poverty', *World Development*, 6:1 (1978).

13. The problem of the widening gap between rich and poor countries and the worsening income distribution within the poor countries is discussed in T. Balogh, *The Economics of Poverty*, 2nd edition (London: Weidenfeld and Nicolson, 1974). This sharpening of the traditional free trade case was based on assumptions of full employment, universally constant or increasing costs, and no technical innovations or dynamism. It was put forward in B. Ohlin's *Interregional and International Trade* (Cambridge University Press, 1935), incorporating arguments from F. E. Heckscher's earlier article 'The Effects of Foreign Trade on the Distribution of Income' (reprinted in *Readings in the Theory of International Trade* (Philadelphia, 1949), pp. 272-300). Further

'rigour' (and the suggestion that inequality would be totally eliminated) came from P. Samuelson and was based on the hypothesis that in addition to the preceding absurd assumptions, production functions would be identical in all countries ('International Trade and the Equalization of Factor Prices'). He followed it up a year later in *Economic Journal*, LIX (June 1949), 181-97.

14. Cf. my *Economics of Poverty*, 2nd edition, esp. pp. 23-4. On the basis of the above unworldly assumptions Prof. Samuelson contended that the equalization would be complete. This surprising conclusion was then used to make practical suggestions on British economic policy. As I explained in a contemporary article (reprinted in my *Unequal Partners* (Oxford: Blackwell, 1973), vol. I, ch. 15), this is obviously illicit. Yet when he was asked by a Harvard mathematician to name 'one proposition in all of the social sciences which is both true and non-trivial', he confessed that this was a test at which he always failed. 'But now, some thirty years later, on the staircase, so to speak, an appropriate answer occurs to me: the Ricardian theory of comparative advantage; the demonstration that trade is mutually profitable even when one country is absolutely more or less productive in terms of every commodity.' This theorem depends on the same nonsensical assumptions. It still haunts the textbooks and university classes.

15. The differences in the organisation of the markets of primary, especially agricultural products, the existence of a large number of all producers combined with the much greater importance of inter-trade of industrialized countries and a general cost-push tendency which is met by restricted monetary measures, explains the tendency towards a worsening of the terms of trade and retarded progress of these countries. Some of these problems, and especially those arising out of the unequal spread of oligopoly, are discussed in T. Balogh (with P. D. Balacs), *Fact and Fancy in International Economic Relations* (Oxford: Pergamon Press, 1973), esp. pp. 63-4.

16. Some progress towards the preconditions of restoring order in the labour market has sometimes been made, as evidenced by the pamphlet signed by six leading trade union general secretaries, *A Better Way*, and the sharp criticism of some of the strike tactics followed by some. But as late as the autumn of 1970, at the Labour Conference, I was harshly attacked by both Jack Jones and Hugh Scanlon for my Fabian Pamphlet *Labour and Inflation* for advocating a permanent National Incomes and Prices Board within a new '*Contrat Social*'. *The Economist* (3 October 1970, pp. 21-2) devoted a leader to this unhappy interlude:

'There were those who blamed Tommy Balogh for the whole business, although that was pushing it too far. Still there he was, turning up at Blackpool on Saturday saturnine as ever, newly married, chairman of the Fabians and putting out a new pamphlet of his, *Labour and Inflation*. In it he gave low marks to both Keynes and Friedman, and advocated instead: The establishment of an independent review body on prices and incomes, to which increases above a certain sum would automatically be referred.

'The rest of the Balogh package was unexceptionable to the trade union leaders. He wanted industrial reorganisation, more investment, "new vigour in taxation and social services", and an extension of public ownership. But this terrible idea of an incomes policy, which the union leaders had thought they had killed, was loose in the Labour party again, and it was not just Lord Balogh....

'So just after lunch on Monday, Mr Jack Jones, grey-suited, bespectacled, normally a sort of severe-looking Eric Morecambe, went to the rostrum and boiled over. He was not going to take criticism of the unions from anyone, least of all from professors and journalists who know nothing about wage claims, "as frankly they've never worked in their lives".'

Alas, this was the spirit (in conjunction with Mr Jenkins' Budget and the President of the Board of Trade's boob in allowing idle Boeing 747 Jumbo aircraft to be imported just before the election) that destroyed the Wilson government in 1970. The astonishing fact is that this problem was foreseen by Joan Robinson and Michal Kalecki in 1938 and 1943 respectively. Writing on 'The Trade Unions and the Future' (*Left News*, 1943), I put forward a case to which I adhere and which has been vindicated by events: see my *Labour and Inflation* (London: Fabian Society, 1970), pp. 29-30.

17. For a discussion in greater detail of the view that consecutive exchange rate changes might in the longer run harmonize differences in wage movements in various countries, see Chapter 9 below and Balogh (with Balacs), *Fact and Fancy in International Economic Relations*, op. cit.

Chapter 8
Backwards to Monetarism

1. See Mr Biffen's interview in *The Guardian*, 7 October 1980 and my reply, ibid., 13 October 1980.

2. M. Friedman, letter to *The Times*, 2 May 1977. See the Appendix to this chapter for the utilization of statistics in monetarist writings.

3. As we shall see, the velocity of monetary circulation is difficult if not impossible to define accurately. In extreme cases this does not make any appreciable difference because the acceleration is so great.

4. This is an *increase* or a disproportionately *small fall* in prices during a shrinkage of demand and income. See Gardner Means, 'The Administered Price Thesis Reconfirmed', *American Economic Review*, LXII (June 1972), 292-306.

5. See S. Brittan and P. Lilley, *The Delusion of Incomes Policy* (London: Temple Smith, 1977). Mr Brittan previously talked about a 'family' of short-term Phillips curves leading a vertical 'long-run' curve, i.e. a situation where easy money could no longer induce increases in output but exhausted itself in price

(wage) increases. Since the Conservative victory in May 1979 he has begun to hedge against failure.

6. See further discussion of this matter in the Appendix to this chapter.

7. See James Tobin, 'Money and Income: post hoc ergo propter hoc', *Quarterly Journal of Economics*, 80 (May 1970).

8. The Spanish extravagances which started secular depreciation in real terms of all currencies in the sixteenth to seventeenth century was of course financed by the gold looted from America by the Spanish Conquistadors.

9. But in its subtle form not necessarily proportionately: so long as money illusion still prevailed, the increase in prices was more sluggish than money; when it faded, prices ran ahead of the money supply: the velocity of circulation changed, impelled by psychology.

10. Cf., e.g., A. C. Pigou, *The Veil of Money* (London: Macmillan, reprinted 1949).

11. I. Fisher, *The Purchasing Power of Money* (New York, 1922).

12. There were also riots and industrial conflicts in Israel, where inflation continued while the well-to-do exported their capital.

13. See, e.g., F. Modigliani's Presidential address to the AEA in 1976: 'The Monetarist Controversy or, Should we forsake Stabilisation Policies?' *American Economic Review*, Supplement (March 1977).

14. Ibid., and the oddly self-satisfied encomium by Samuelson on Friedman (*Newsweek*, 11 October 1976).

15. Friedman's propensity to select data without reference to the actual economic framework excelled in his treatment (*Newsweek*, 25 October 1976) of the British currency crisis. Once more tablets were produced direct from Sinai and once more the prophet was ludicrously wrong. He stated:

> 'There is no mystery why the British pound has been plummeting in price. The mystery is why the British government has been wasting its taxpayers' money in futile speculation against the decline.
>
> 'How much a British pound is worth in dollars depends fundamentally on how much a pound will buy in goods and services and how much a dollar will buy. If a pound will buy as much as $2 will buy, the pound is worth $2. If the pound will buy only as much as $1 will buy, the pound is worth $1.'

There were then some cautious qualifications, which did not however prevent him from predicting roughly the opposite of the future course of events:

> 'Of course, this principle is easier to state than to apply. Some goods and services may cost three times as much in the US in dollars as they cost in Britain: others may cost less in dollars than in pounds. The mythical average is not readily observed – except in the dollar value that the market sets on the pound. Given the dollar value of the pound at any time, if British prices in pounds rise faster than US prices in dollars, the dollar value of the pound will go down.'

The summing up did not take into account these severe qualifications. The vast movement of funds which caused these disturbances (as they did the attack on the dollar) had nothing to do with the actual as against the (wrongly) expected flow of incomes and outlay, or the supply and demand for goods and services. They represented the speculative displacement of large monetary stocks, the total of which is now between $400–500,000 million, a displacement the analysis of which is far beyond the limited and artificial framework in which he operates. In the real world speculative attacks can be self-justifying and exacerbate the basic ill. The more permanent (and destructive) rise of the pound has been due to the speculative flows, the redirection of Arab money from New York to London, and the incomes from the North Sea. The basic competitive position worsened and there was no surplus on the current account.

16. Von Hayek (letter to the Editor of *The Times*, 12 June 1980) gives the game away by 'agreeing with Friedman that there cannot be a cost-push inflation'. This is not true of an oligopolistic system.

17. Friedman, 'The Role of Monetary Policy', *American Economic Review*, LVIII (March 1968), 8.

18. Dr E. F. Dennison's attempt ('Explanations of declining productivity growth', Brookings Reprint No. 354) to explain the share of factors which contributed to the slowing down of the increase in productivity disregards short-term impact and is based on a model which implicitly assumes free competition and a very special (and implausible) Cobb-Douglas production function which has disappeared from view presumably because of its implausibility. (For a general dismissal of this device see Kaldor, *Oxford Economic Papers*, February 1952.) I attacked the use made of these approaches in 'Education and Economic Growth', *Kyklos* (1964), 264–6. Having earnestly gone through seventeen explanations, Dr Dennison forgets what is possibly the most important, namely Friedman's victory, and the general conventional methods of fighting inflation and the consequential creeping depression.

19. *The Purchasing Power of Money*, op. cit. Fisher limited his argument to positions of balance (equilibrium). This robs it of all policy relevance.

20. See Prof. Sir A. Lewis, op. cit., p. 69, note 308. Between the first quarter of 1970 and of 1979, M3 rose at an annual rate of 10 per cent per annum; GNP in the same period at an annual rate of 17.3 per cent. The velocity of circulation must have risen substantially.

21. Characteristically the Governor of the Bank of England, in sharp contrast to the Chairman of the US Federal Reserve, has set his face against central regulation through IMF or the BIS. He has further set the scene for confidence crises which need to be 'cured' by restrictive monetary policy and the restoring and strengthening of the hold over the economy of finance (*Guardian*, 29 May 1979). There are no compulsory reserve ratios nor any published rules about the requirements for the minimum correspondence of curbing loans and deposits.

22. Friedman has an alternative approach based on the stability of the real cash holdings of individuals. This is also fallacious, as argued later in this chapter.

23. These are, of course, old-hat. Most of the mis-statements and bad advice could have been avoided if monetarist writers had consulted Keynes' *Treatise on Money*, especially vol. II.

24. K. Wicksell (*Lectures* (London: Routledge, 1961), vol. 2) regarded bank deposits in his basic analysis as a manifestation of the velocity of circulation of cash proper.

25. This has happened several times. Once the terms were so nonsensically favourable that it led applicants to indulge in unseemly physical assaults on each other in the rush.

26. The sonorous phrases of the Governor of the Bank of England (speech to the Guildhall Banquet 1979 reprinted in the *Bank of England Quarterly Bulletin*, December 1979) imply that in his view a once-for-all defeat of inflation can be achieved by high rates of interest and restrictive budget manipulation. There can be no doubt that the inflation can be halted with deflationary policies. Whether such policies of the needed intensity are feasible in a democratic society is, however, open to doubt. It would take a long period of deep stagnation to alter the basic attitudes to income claims so strongly that an expansion could be carried without cost inflation reviving. Only a voluntary (but stronger than hitherto) incomes policy could harmonize stability and full expansion. What is threatening is an attempt at coercive incomes policy which might well be defeated by strongly entrenched unions.

27. A typical instance is the evasion of the so-called 'corset', which manifested itself in a brusque increase in M3 when it was abolished. This proved that the effective M3 was much bigger than the officially published figure.

28. Historically, an extreme and therefore interesting case is represented by the so-called brokers' loans on account of others by which stock exchange bears financed the bulls by their deposits, in as much as banks had to keep a prescribed percentage of their deposits as reserves while brokers' loans (and deposits) were not so restricted. This made the boom possible. Stock exchange profits (and losses) boosted (or annihilated) demand, thus contributing to the violence of fluctuations.

29. Cf. D. H. Robertson, *Money* (Cambridge: Cambridge Handbooks, revised 1930), Appendix B, p. 182. The monetarist school would do well to return to Cambridge (England) and read a few books of half a century ago. No primitive fetish there about the reversible stable relationship between money and prices.

30. Friedman, *The Times* (London), 13 September 1976.

31. Both in the past, see, e.g., Prof. Sir A. Lewis, op. cit, and since 1970, cf. *Bank of England Quarterly Bulletin*.

32. See the sharp attacks on Friedman's paper 'The relative stability of monetary velocity and the investment multiplier in the US 1897–1958', in *Stabilisation Policies, Commission on Money and Credit* (Englewood Cliffs, N. J.: Prentice-Hall, 1963).

33. A good example of this is provided by the debate between Friedman and F. Modigliani referred to in the Appendix. See also Okun's bibliography of the literature on money and interest (A. M. Okun, *The Political Economy of Prosperity*, The Brookings Institution, Washington D.C., 1970, pp. 146-7), where the isolation of Friedman is clearly demonstrated: among twenty-one authors he is the single one not to have found a strong negative relationship between the demand for money and the rate of interest. See below, Appendix, on Friedman's empiricism.

34. They include deposits, but deposit accounts can without delay be shifted to current accounts or used even without that formality.

35. The Radcliffe Committee – Committee on the working of the monetary system, Cmnd 827, (London: HMSO, 1959), esp. pp. 389-97 – recognised the importance of liquidity in general but came to *similar* views to those that I had expressed to it and now reiterate. Monetary policy to be effective needs to be one of a *number* of policy weapons.

36. The education in economics of Mr Jack Jones and Lord Scanlon, who violently denounced me for advocating an incomes policy in 1970, cost the country two coal strikes and a loss of vast resources (not the least through the monstrous fourth licensing round favouring US transnational oil companies). The cost of the education of Alan Fisher, Moss Evans and Clive Jenkins etc. can as yet not be quantified. It threatens even larger damage to our society and economy.

Appendix:
Professor Friedman and Statistics

1. See Friedman's Nobel Prize Lecture, where he points to the need for 'positive' analysis before 'normative' advice is given. 'Inflation and unemployment: the new dimension of politics', Institute of Economic Studies, Occasional Paper 51.

2. House of Lords Official Report, 16 April 1980.

3. A. Ando and F. Modigliani, 'The relative stability of monetary velocity and the investment multiplier', *American Economic Review*, LV, 4 (September 1965), and F. Modigliani, 'The monetarist controversy, or Should we forsake stabilization policies?', 1976 Presidential address to the American Economic Association, *American Economic Review*, 67, 2 (March 1977).

Chapter 9
The International Aspect

1. F. List, the author of *Das Nationale System der Politischen Oekonomie* (Gotha, 1841), which demonstrated the evil impact on the weaker partners in any

trading exchange, was imprisoned for criticizing the 'orthodox' views of his country's bureaucracy.

2. See Keynes' defence in the House of Lords of Bretton Woods Final Act and the 'Diktat' of the US Reconstruction Loan (House of Lords' *Hansard*, 23 May 1944, cols 839-42).

3. Not noticeably relieved by technical assistance and resource aid. A quotation from an Indian leader at the height of the dominance of Britain is revealing. 'Of course, I know that it was pure philanthropy which flooded India with English-made goods, and surely, if slowly, killed out every indigenous industry – pure philanthropy which, to facilitate this, repealed the import duties and flung away three crores a year of revenue which the rich paid, and to balance this wicked sacrifice raised the Salt Tax, which the poor pay; ... Free Trade, fair play between nations, how I hate the sham! What fair play in trade can there be between impoverished India and the bloated capitalist England? As well as talk of a fair fight between an infant and a strong man – a rabbit and a boa-constrictor. No doubt it is all in accordance with high economic science, but, my friends, remember this – this, too, is starving your brethren.' Lala Murlidhar, Speech to the 1891 Session of the Indian National Congress.

The need for discrimination in favour of the 'less developed' areas ('infant industries') has in the last decade or so been accepted. The advance made in this respect has been largely nullified by the special protection against low-wage competition and the international impact of wage inflation in the industrial sphere. The rise in the price of oil engineered by the OPEC countries has been a unique phenomenon.

4. Only the oil-producing countries were able to turn the tables on the OECD countries, and then only because military intervention would result in the destruction of the oil wells and might precipitate Russian intervention.

5. This applies of course also to entities like the European Economic Community. The harsh rule of the supremacy of market forces, of non-discrimination, and the outlawing of protective intervention actuated by political pressures, has inevitably worked against the poorer members. The differences in living standards between member countries were far greater than in internal trade, where welfare measures and other ways of redistributing income mitigated the prejudicial impact of *laissez-faire*. Only in agriculture has there been a total rupture of the 'system', with terrible consequences for Britain both in respect to taxation (because investment is not liable to VAT) and because Britain imports more food than its partners. British policy-making was dominated by conventional experts.

6. As in all matters economic there are exceptions to this proposition. As the newly industrializing territories (e.g. Hong Kong, South Korea and, of course, Japan) show, the combination of cheap labour with advanced management can overcome these handicaps, especially if the multinational corporations take a hand. The introduction of automated or semi-automated plant renders training quicker, more effective and cheaper.

7. I have dealt with this problem in greater detail in *Unequal Partners*, vol. 1, secs 4 and 5.

8. See, e.g., Viner, *The Long View and the Short* (New York: Glencoe Free Press, 1958), esp. pp. 57-8. He postulates changes in output involving time while admitting that 'long run equilibrium once established will continue only for an instant of time'. It is interesting to note that Viner, in the midst of the worst crisis, asserted the relevance to economic analysis of this vacuous concept, pleading that it explained the direction in which the system would return to the next (momentary) long-run equilibrium.

9. Evidence is accumulating of a steady increase towards a dominating position of the multinational corporations' intertrade in international economic relations, cf. M. Panic and P. L. Joyce, 'UK Manufacturing Industry, International Integration and Trade Performance', *Bank of England Quarterly Bulletin*, 20, 1 (March 1980), p. 42.

10. In collaboration with P. D. Balacs, I have discussed this problem in greater detail in *Fact and Fancy in International Economic Relations* (Oxford: Pergamon, 1793), esp. chs 2 and 3, and *Economics of Poverty* (London: Weidenfeld and Nicolson, 2nd edn 1974), esp. ch. 8. Nothing better illustrates the futility of the (neo-) classical approach than the persistent tendency – in the absence of government intervention or severe failures of crops – of the terms of trade of primary producers to come under pressure as a result of the combined effect of the centralization of power in manufacturing industry and the existence of world markets in primary commodities.

11. I did not go far enough in the appreciation of the importance of this double oligopoly in *Fact and Fancy*, esp. Chs 2.1 and 2.2. I did try to take into account the asymmetry of changes in wage costs and therefore the advantages for 'readjustment' of currency up-valuation rather than devaluation. What I failed to emphasize sufficiently is the importance of *internal* oligopolistic practices.

12. Strenuous efforts continue on the part of neoclassical economists (both Keynesian and monetarist) to picture the general agreements as the basis of a steady postwar reconstruction and expansion, and to fix the date of the breakdown of these arrangements to Mr Nixon's suspension of the convertibility of the dollar in 1972. Nothing can be further from the truth. The Bretton Woods arrangements broke down in 1947/8 a score of days after the compliance by the UK with the US conditions for the Loan (see my *Unequal Partners*, vol. 2, secs 3 and 5). In the ensuing reconstruction period, lasting until the Suez crisis, the Fund remained totally quiescent (incidentally this resulted in the tacit abandonment by the European debtors of the so-called 'scarce currency' clause which might have served as a potent weapon in the period of scarcity of the Deutschmark and Yen.) For a detailed account see my *Fact and Fancy*, op. cit., and *The Dollar Crisis* (Oxford: Blackwell, 1949).

13. Some of those, who at one time maintained that the balance of payments is a simple mirror image of the state of public sector financing, seem to have

turned fatalist, and lost faith in any government capacity to rectify short-term imbalances. Their preference for non-selective protection (however great their superiority in argument over the monetarists) shows the subconscious fallback to classical assumptions, in particular that the propensity to import is low and that the price-mechanism optimizes production. In fact under oligopoly neither is true, and it is unlikely that without close supervision, import quota auction or a uniform tariff, i.e. market conformable measures, would allow a rehabilitation of industry.

14. Yet Keynes himself accepted this framework and argued (wrongly in my opinion) that it was the inelasticity of demand for German goods that would prevent the transfer of the reparations (see three articles in *Economic Journal*, XXXIX, 1929). Keynes at that point was no Keynesian. Lately a reversion to the pre-Keynes-Harrod approach (McIntosh, 'Mantoux versus Keynes', *Economic Journal*, 88, December 1978) took place. A. Graham and myself tried to answer it but the *Economic Journal* refused to publish our criticism and it was published in the *Bulletin of the Oxford Institute of Economics and Statistics*, 41 (August 1979).

15. B. Ohlin, 'The Reparation Problem: A Discussion: I. Transfer Difficulties Real and Imagined', *Economic Journal*, XXXIX (June 1929), 172-8, and 'Mr Keynes' Views on the Transfer Problem: II. A Rejoinder', *Economic Journal*, XXXIX (September 1929), 400-4.

16. J. Rueff, 'Mr Keynes' Views on the Transfer Problem: I. A Criticism', *Economic Journal*, XXXIX (September 1929), 388-99.

17. Unfortunately, however, many people in Britain, particularly in the period following the 1929 crash and the rise of Hitler, thought that Keynes' original arguments had been proved right. Keynes himself, according to D. E. Moggridge (*Keynes*, London: Fontana, 1976, pp. 144-6), seems to have been alert to the problem in 1942, but did not take an active interest when Allied discussions went wrong, mainly as the result of pastoralization proposals of Harry Dexter White, that very inscrutable individual whose stupid or malicious influence did such damage to the non-communist world by insisting on rules of the game which were bound to damage the weaker war-torn or weakened countries. Keynes, even then, did not consider the mechanism of expansion in the 'creditor' countries which would have allowed the transfer without the consequential exports of the 'debtor' bringing ruin to the former's industries. In the end, the prewar Keynesian analysis led to a total loss of reparations after the Second World War. As a result, at the end of the war it was widely believed that reparations from current production would necessarily lead to the disorganization of the world economy and unemployment. These beliefs are the main reason why Britain backed the proposals to extract reparation from Germany purely by the dismantling of her industry. This in effect would have resulted in the 'pastoralizing' of Germany – and it should have been clear to all experts that this would have been unacceptable to the US and UK public even if the Cold War had not begun. (Even more fatuous

from the British viewpoint was the failure to secure a German contribution for the upkeep of the British Army on the Rhine when the West German Federal Republic was granted sovereignty.)

18. The old error reappears in Forsyth and Kay, 'The Economic Implications of the North Sea Oil Revenues' (*Fiscal Studies*, July 1980), when they argue that benefit from the discoveries of gas and oil can only be derived by a shrinkage of manufacture. If this conclusion was warranted, the 'benefit' would represent serious welfare problems as employment would shrink. For a more comprehensive discussion see my article 'Oil Recycling – The Need for a New Lending Facility?', *Lloyds Bank Review*, 137 (July 1980).

19. Problems of 'collection' might still exist if a nation were very impoverished and problems of 'transfer' might exist if a nation's production was extremely specialized.

20. For a more detailed discussion of these issues see my *Fact and Fancy*, op. cit., pp. 39ff.

21. An even more egregious failure overtook the international monetarists of the London Business School who based their determination of the exchange rate on the comparative rates of money supply growth. In this view the manipulation of the exchange rate was bound to fail as the consequential changes in domestic costs quickly negated any advantage gained by depreciation or downward floating. Mr A. Budd in fact admitted the failure of international monetarism (*The Times*, 25 June 1980). They made a 20 per cent mistake in their projection of the rate of exchange. He stated lamely: 'We do not believe in a "high" exchange rate, whatever that may be, any more than we believe in a "low" one.'

22. The monetarists developed a 'law of one price', trying to argue that producers cannot but keep their prices as they were before the devaluation. This contention is not borne out by actual experience.

23. For a detailed discussion, see *Fact and Fancy*, op. cit. The upward float of the pound is a good example.

24. *Quarterly Bulletin* (March 1980), pp. 13-14. It has been admitted that this measure necessarily limits the effectiveness of monetary policy as it enables British banks to operate through their foreign branches against the wishes of the Bank of England. Much higher estimates have been made since.

25. For a detailed discussion see Streeten and Balogh, 'Domestic versus Foreign Investment', reprinted in *Unequal Partners*, op. cit., vol. I, ch. 19.

26. The increase in primary production which improved Britain's terms of trade in the nineteenth century is a case where foreign investment was of general benefit to the foreign lender/investor.

27. This is one reason why the monetarist conquest of financial bureaucracies is so dangerous. It gives added edge to unbalancing cumulative movements because in their dream world cumulative movements are not possible, and all readjustment is assumed to be equilibrating.

28. This was true even before the oil crisis further contorted the world economic

system, blowing up an already dangerously large expansion of unwarranted speculative credit to almost catastrophic dimensions.

29. Cf. the criticism of the Forsyth and Kay methodology above, note 18 to this chapter.

30. *International Debt, the Banks and US Foreign Policy* (Washington, August 1977).

31. 49th Report, 1978/9, p. 103.

32. Much the best, especially as far as lending to 'developing' countries is concerned, are the Reports to the World Bank on New Issues and Public Debt Outstanding, but these are by no means complete.

33. For a detailed discussion see *Unequal Partners*, vol. II, sec. 3, especially chs 7 and 8.

Index

accumulation, theory of, 110-11
advertising, 83-6, 126
Allen, R., 220
Ando, A., 182, 225, 249
anti-anti-growth propagandists, 94
'anti-growth brigade', 93
Arrow, K., 65, 237; *quoted*, 102-3, 228-9

Balacs, P. D., 213, 216, 244, 245, 251
balance of payments, 190-8, 201-2,.251-2;
    deficit, 56
Balogh, T., 159, 216, 217, 221, 223, 224,
    226, 238-53 *passim*
banks, 138-9
Beckerman, W., 94, 234
Bergson, A., 102, 237
Berle, Professor, 134, 139
Berlin, I., 229
Bhagwati, J., 25, 217, 219
Biffen, J., 245
Blair, J. M., 239
Bowley, A. L., 215
Bray, J., 224-5
Bretton Woods, 193-4, 209, 210, 251
Britain: industrial performance, 139;
    postwar performance, 5-6, 158-9
Brittan, S., 245
Brown, E. C., 225
Brummer, Professor, 213
Budd, A., 253
Burnham, Professor, 134, 136
business cycle, 40, 178

capital accumulation, 115
capital gains, 127
capitalist system, instability of, 166
cardinal utility, 97
causation, direction of, 20
censuses of production, 129
ceteris paribus clauses, 9, 16, 104, 108-9,
    115
Chamberlin, E. H., 124, 222
cheap labour, 190

Chicago School, 222
Churchill, W., 146
circulation of money, *see* velocity of
    circulation
Civil Service, 137, 138; private industry
    and, 136
Clark, J. B., 4, 78
Clark, J. M., 117, 120, 126, 129, 222, 238,
    239, 241
classical economics (*see also* neoclassical
    economics), income distribution in,
    141-2
'classlessness', 88
clock analogy (Edgeworth), 25
collective enterprise, 114
collective needs, bias against, 89-92, 93
collusion, 126
compensation principle, 99-101
competition: atomistic, 116; perfect, 40-2,
    57-8, 59, 82, 106-13, 118, 128, 132, 165;
    international perfect, 199, 202;
    monopolistic, 124; 'workable', 112
concentration of economic power, 115-17,
    118-21
conditioning, 233-4
Confederation of British Industries (CBI),
    171
consensus economics (*see also* neoclassical
    Keynesian synthesis), 5, 59, 60
consumer: in formal economics, 72; 'ideal',
    79, 95; individual as, 78-87
consumer credit, 23, 51
consumer interests, national interest and,
    101
consumer needs, change in urgency of,
    92-4
consumer sovereignty, 66-7, 72, 78, 81,
    107, 120
consuming power, distribution of, 95-104
consumption: 'characteristics' model, 232-
    3; collective, 119; conspicuous, 157;
    conventional assumptions, 71

255

consumption function, 44, 221
controls: direct, 130; wartime, 150-1
convenors, union, 155
corporate legislation, 115
corporate management, risk and, 128-30
corporations, large, 116-17, 132, 133-4, 135, 140; motivations of, 174; multinational, 189; opposition to state encroachment, 90
cost-benefit studies, 227
cost-inflation, 54, 55
costs: decreasing, impact on foreign trade, 188-90; increase with production, 111; output and, 121
Cripps, F., 55
criteria for economic performance: choice of, as political act, 77; conflict of, 73-5; kinds of, 75-7
Crosland, C. A. R., 94, 223, 230, 234
'crowding out principle' (see also Treasury doctrine), 221, 224, 225
currency crises, 173, 191
curves, mathematical, 17-19, 24; 'moves along' and 'shifts of', 19, 27; shifted, 187

Davidson, P., 217
decentralized decision-making, 113, 128, 134; improved management under, 131; limitations of, 129-31
decision, quality of, 113-18
demand, output and, 39-40
demand and supply: curves, 17-18; interdependence of, 25
demand management, 22-3, 130, 166
demarcation disputes, 155
Dennison, E. F., 247
Depression, Great, 145, 191
devaluation, 197
distribution of consuming power, 95-104; classical case for, 97
distribution of income (see also redistribution of income), 73, 157, 242-3; classical view, 141-2, 236; deterioration of, 153; full employment and, 141-57; international, 148-9; Marxist view, 143-5; neoclassical view, 142-3, 236; 'new province of law and order', 151-2
Dobb, M., 229
dollar, devaluation of, 194
domestic credit expansion, 43
Drucker, P., 134

Eckstein, O., 218
economic advice, basis of, 13-17
economic advisers, 12
economic analysis, pure; as arbiter of policy, 103-4
economic crises (see also currency crises), increasing severity of, 145
economic flair, 12
economic growth: discontinuity of, 87-8; as policy objective, 120
economics: as an art, 15-16, 62; fashions in, 2-3; limitations of, 13, 215; Marxian, 4; status of, 15-16, 204; see also politics, economics and
Edgeworth, F. Y., 25
education: and transformation of needs, 85; and values, 87
educational facilities, production capacity and, 89
efficiency of economic system, 36, 105-40 passim
Eichner, A. S., 215
Eisenhower, President, 228
emergent nations (see also poor countries), 149
employment (see also unemployment): full, see full employment; pressure on governments to provide, 72-3
employment multiplier, 39
'endowment' postulate, 97, 98
entrepreneurs, 131, 132-3; role of, 16-17, 106-7
equilibrium, 25-8, 29, 40, 108, 227; dependence on path of readjustment, 25, 203; general theory of, 9-10, 65, 96-7, 110, 226; international trade, 202; long-run, 184; social optimality and, 98-9; under-employment, 18; Walrasian, see Walrasian model
equity capital, limited availability of, 177
Euro-currency market, 169
European Economic Community, 250
European Social Democrats, 52
ex-ante schedule, 26, 202
ex-post schedule, 26-7, 202
excellence, criterion of, 66
excess capacity, 124-6
exchange, equation of, 168-9, 174; factors excluded from, 169-70
exchange control, 177, 198
exchange rate, fluctuations in, 18
exports, factors governing, 203-4

fashions: consumer, 81; in economics, 2-3
Federal Reserve System, 211
Feinstein, C. H., 181
firms, large, see corporations, large
fiscal decay/creep, 89
Fisher, I., 168, 246
Florence, P. S., 116, 239
flows and stocks, 169
foreign exchange, interest on deposits, 208
foreign trade, see international trade
Forsyth, P. J., 253
free collective bargaining, 152-3, 178;
  changed status of, 154
free competition, 107
free-market system, 105-6
free trade, 183; dangers of, to weak
  countries, 199
freedom, 105-40 passim
Friedman, M., 9-10, 14, 20, 35, 54, 162-3,
  165, 173, 213-25 passim, 241; and
  statistics, 178-82; quoted, 174, 175, 195
'full cost' principle, 240
full employment, 61, 141-57 passim, 223;
  consequences of, 87-8, 204; devaluation
  and, 197; disadvantages of, 52;
  distribution of income and, 141-57;
  growth with, 147; importance of, 47, 76;
  incompatibility with stability, 153;
  inflation and, 4; 'managed', 4; in postwar
  decades, 150-2; price stability and, 52;
  psychological significance of, 151;
  redefinition of, 76, 148

G-demands, elastic, 27
Gaitskellites, 75
Galbraith, J. K., 8, 10, 16, 59, 65, 72, 75,
  83, 84, 125, 134, 135, 138, 139, 154, 159,
  226-41 passim
games, theory of, 69
General Agreements on Tariffs and Trade
  (GATT), 209, 210
'global', meaning of term, 214
'global measures', 46
'global methods', 45
Godley, W., 55, 218
Gold Standard, 108
Graaf, J. de V., 65, 227
Graham, A., 252
Great Depression, 145, 191
Greenwell, W., 170n
Gregory, T., 146
Griffin, K., 236, 237, 243
growth models, 116

Haberler, G., 235, 239
Hahn, F., 10-11, 98, 215, 219; quoted, 9,
  10, 29
Harrod, R. F., 221, 222
Hawtrey, R., 53
Heckscher, F. E., 243
Heilbroner, R. L., 1, 215; quoted, 10
Henderson, H., 146
Hennessy, M., 226
Hicks, J. R., 44, 75, 99, 220, 223, 226, 236;
  quoted, 42
Hines, Professor, 216
historical factors, 22; lack of in Walrasian
  model, 57
hoarding, 33-4
hot money, 18, 24, 176, 205
Hume, D., 190
hyperinflation, 161, 164, 220
hypotheses in economics, 14

'image' of product, 83
imports, factors governing, 203-4
income(s): consensus on, 197; distribution
  of, see distribution of income; factors
  producing rise in, 144; national, see
  national income; real, 96; 'real world',
  104; redistribution of, see redistribution
  of income
income-savings ratio, 23
incomes policy, 152-3, 177, 198, 237, 249
indeterminacy, 203-5
India, British, 250
individual as consumer, 78-87
individual enterprise, see private enterprise
inductive method, 14
'Industrial Reserve Army', 67, 177, 206
inflation (see also hyperinflation; price
  stability), 39, 47-8, 89, 147, 148, 159;
  control of, 248; cost, 54, 55; cost-
  induced, 161; as criterion of welfare, 76;
  demand, 160-1; and failure of
  Keynesianism, 52, 61; full employment
  and, 4; interest rates and, 248;
  international differences, 200;
  monetarism and, 205-6; monetarist
  explanation of, 89, 159-60; nature of,
  163-8; profit, 148, 196; stagnation and,
  150-7; unemployment and, 48, 206;
  wage-price, 153
inflation-discounted current balance, 195
'informed GNP', 218
insurance companies, 139

interest rates, 51, 145; inflation and, 248;
money supply and, 53, 176
interests, harmony of, 96, 240
international distribution of income, 148-9
International Monetary Fund (IMF), 209,
210
international trade: equilibrium, 202;
modern, 184-5; monetarist micro-
economic policy and, 198-9; oligopoly in
manufacture and, 199-201; perfect
competition and, 202; reciprocal demand
curves, 24-5, 187; traditional theory of,
185-6; two-commodity model of, 186-8
International Trade Organization, 209
investment, influence of risk on, 119
investment trusts, 139

Jacquemin, A. P., 239
Jenkins, R., 234, 245
Jevons, W., 78
Johnson, H., 25, 217, 219, 222; quoted, 180
Jones, A., 243
Jones, H., 134
Jones, J., 244, 245, 249
Joseph, K., 90

Kahn, R. F., 39-40, 221, 222
Kaldor, N., 2, 5, 40, 65, 99, 179, 213-27
passim, 238-9, 247; quoted, 179
Kalecki, M., 159, 221
Kay, J. A., 253
Keynes, J. M., 2, 38-40, 42, 49, 53, 145,
146, 191, 193, 209, 213, 221, 226, 250,
252; quoted, 13, 49, 215
Keynesian revolution (see also neoclassical
Keynesian synthesis), 4-6, 39, 146, 213;
classicization of, 43-4, 50-1; failure of,
50-2, 61
Khan, A. R., 237, 243
Kindleberger, C. P., 216; quoted, 216
Knight, F. H., 84
Kondratieff cycles, 178
Kornai, J., 125, 220, 227, 229, 230, 235,
236-7
Kregel, J. A., 242
Kuznets, S., 228

labour market, 33, 38-9; Keynes on, 38-9
Labour Party, 152
Laidler, Professor, 226
laissez-faire economics: complacency of,
62-3; defence of, 86, 131, 132;
educational, 234; failure of, 146, 147;

international, 250; liberty and, 52, 114-
15; micro-economics and, 60;
neoclassical support for, 119; neo-
Keynesian support for, 46; revival of,
130; and socialist 'postwar failure', 5-6
Lancaster, K., 232
large numbers, law of, 54
Lauderdale, E., 34
Lenin, V. I., 101
Leontieff, W., 214; quoted, 8
Lerner, A. P., 65, 217, 227
Lewis, W. A., 179, 181, 247, 248
liberal reformer, dilemma of, 87
libertarian authors, 'brainwashing' of, 86-7
Lilley, P., 245
Lipsey, R. G., 226
liquidity, 206, 208-9
liquidity preference, 35
List, F., 249
Little, I. M. D., 230, 236
living standards, qualitative changes in,
91-2
long run and short run, 121-4
long-run equilibrium, 184
Lowe, A., 217

McCord-Wright, W., 223
McIntosh, R., 252
macro- and micro-economics, 34
mainstream economics (see also neoclassical
Keynesian synthesis), 5
Malthus, T., 34, 220
managerial revolution, 131-40
managerial salaries, 127
managers: lack of competent, 177; modern,
132-40; public-sector, 140
marginal utility, Marshallian theory of, 97
market mechanism, 4, 66, 70-1; limitations
of, 130-1; Marshallian partial analysis,
58; see also Say's Law
Marris, Robin, 236
Marshall, A., 4, 19, 25, 72, 74, 84, 92, 112,
114, 131, 132, 233; quoted, 12
Marshall Aid, 193, 210
Marx, K., 33, 64, 78, 107, 142, 144-5, 178,
241-2
Marxian economics, 4
Marxism: and distribution of income, 143-
5; 'Industrial Reserve Army', 67, 175,
206
mass production, 112, 115-16
mathematical methods, 6-7, 8-11, 12-14,
15-16, 20, 24

Matthews, R., 215
Mead, J. E., 50, 224
Means, G. C., 134, 139, 239, 245
Meiselman, D., 225
Menger, C., 4, 78, 220; *quoted*, 37-8
merchant banks, 138
Meyer, Professor, 221
micro-economic revolution, 42, 60
micro-economics, 40-2, 65, 111; macro-economics and, 34; neoclassical, *see* neoclassical micro-economics
Mill, J. S., 241; *quoted*, 142
Minsky, H., 215
Mishan, E. J., 93, 227, 234
misplaced concreteness, fallacy of, 96
models, economic, 12-13, 15, 62; assumptions of, 108; 'evenly rotating', 108; 'economic growth', 116; 'large', 19-20
Modigliani, F., 21, 22, 182, 218, 225, 246, 249
Moggridge, D. E., 252
monetarism, 44, 158-82, 213; basis of, 55; contemporary, 42-3; depersonalizes economics, 160; explanation of inflation, 89; indirect controls, 130; inflation and, 205-6; international trade, 195-9; neoclassical model, 195-6; revival of, 53-6, 159-63; technical standards of, 178-82; theory of thrift, 110; unemployment and, 147, 165-6
monetary system, elasticity of, 56
money: as store of value, 57, 170-1; 'neutrality' of, 35; quantity theory of, *see* quantity theory of money; velocity of circulation, *see* velocity of circulation; volume of, *see* money supply
money supply, 35, 43, 54-5, 164-5, 167, 168-78, 205; definition of, 170; interest rates and, 53, 176
monopoly, 112, 117, 126
multi-product firms, 121
multinational corporations, 189, 200
multiplier, 148
Myrdal, G., 10, 65, 75, 214, 227

national income, 101; quantitative definition of, 229-30; total turnover and, 173
National Incomes and Prices Board, 244
national interest, consumer interests and, 101
national ownership, 128-9

national product, variations in, 169
nationalization, moral aim of, 137
nationalized industries, 136-7; managers of, 140
needs, transformation of, 84-5
neoclassical economics, 32-8; macro-monetarist revival, 53-6; micro-economic revival, 56-60; pervasiveness of, 65-6; replies to criticisms, 59; view of Keynesian revolution, 165
neoclassical Keynesian synthesis, 2, 3-6, 22, 61
New Deal, 146
New Welfare Economics, 97-8, 99, 102
Nobel prize for economics, absurdity of, 214
North Sea oil, 207

objectivization, 66
OECD countries, 192, 193, 205, 208
Ohlin, B., 191, 193, 243, 252
oil-price crisis, 192
oil-price increase, 194
Okun, A. M., 7, 214, 249
oligopoly: characteristics of, 126; economic growth and, 118-21; economic theory and, 59-60, 162; in international trade, 189, 199-201; in markets, 16, 204-5; rise of, 47, 115-17
optimum production, 106-13
Organization of Petroleum Exporting Countries (OPEC), 190, 192, 194, 205
output: aggregate, and availability of resources, 39-40; costs and, 121; demand and, 39-40
ownership: alleged unimportance of, 134-5; and control, 136

Paish, F. W., 55, 226, 242
Panic, M., 251
Pareto, V., 4, 231, 236
Parkin, M., 55, 226
Patinkin, D., 226
Peterson, W. C., 215
Phelps-Brown, E. H., 214, 222; *quoted*, 8
Phillips curve, 55, 161, 217, 219, 245
Pigou, A. C., 4, 70, 132, 146, 215, 220, 225-6, 229, 230, 237-46 *passim*; *quoted*, 37, 70
Pigou effect, 49
Point of No Return (Marquand), 81-2
political choices, need for, 104

political economy, 10, 30-1, 141, 220
political suffrage, expanding, 144
politics, economics and, 14, 36-8, 67, 68,
    150-7
poor countries (see also emergent nations),
    104, 149, 234; effects of free trade on,
    186
Popper, K., 15, 20, 217
population growth, 107-8
positive economics, 29-30, 36, 65;
    unemployment and, 41-2
pound, financial and commodity pound,
    208
predictions, economic, 14-15
price: determination, 17-18; indices, 174;
    as measure of quality, 82; wars, 117
price leadership, international, 189
price mechanism, 71-2, 119, 134;
    asymmetry of, 197-9; signalling system,
    123-4, 128
price stability (see also inflation), 148, 242;
    as criterion of welfare, 76; full
    employment and, 52
prices: dependence on price expectations,
    204; import, 163; volume of money and,
    55; see also inflation
Prices and Consumer Protection,
    Department for, 240
Prices and Incomes Board, 117
prices and incomes policy, 156
private enterprise, 106, 113-14, 239;
    compared with public ownership, 139;
    freedom and, 119
private industry, Civil Service and, 136
private ownership: of capital, 41; of natural
    resources, 126
private property, 106
production, 105-40; censuses of, 129;
    conventional assumptions about, 71;
    deliberate limitation of, 123; expansion
    of, 115, 156 (and unemployment, 175-
    6); optimum, 106-13
.production capacity, education facilities
    and, 89
profit inflation, 148, 196
profit maximization, blurring of concept of,
    133
profiteering, 126-8
property rights, 95
protection, 207-8
psychological factors, 20, 22, 23, 26, 32, 48,
    59, 167, 172
psychology, modern, 72

public expenditure, monetarist policy on,
    89, 90, 205
public ownership (see also nationalization;
    nationalized industries), 94; compared
    with private enterprise, 139
public sector, national resources used for,
    182
Public Sector Borrowing Requirement,
    191, 206
purchasing power: conservation of, 191;
    parity theory, 195

quantification in economics, 6-7, 17-20,
    24, 147-8; insoluble problems, 23-8;
    misleading nature of, 12, 19; weakened
    Keynesian revolution, 43-4
quantity theory of money, 35, 49, 61, 159-
    60, 164, 168-78, 204

Radcliffe committee, 249
rational expectation hypothesis (ratex), 19,
    21-2, 162; political motivation of, 22
reciprocal demand curves, 24-5, 187
redistribution of income (see also
    distribution of income), 64, 99;
    compensation principle, 99-101; costs
    of, 102
Rees-Mogg, W., 218
REH, see rational expectation hypothesis
reparations, war, 191
reserve capacity, 123
resources, assumption of unchanging, 108,
    109
restrictive practices, 126
risk: corporate management and, 128-30;
    as influence on investment, 119
Robbins, L., 40, 99, 236
Robertson, D. H., 30, 220, 230, 231, 235,
    248; quoted, 73-4
Robey, Ralph, 221
Robinson, J., 2, 4, 5, 40, 58, 153, 159,
    213-23 passim, 241
Rome Treaty, 183
Roosevelt, President, 146
Rueff, J., 191, 252

Sadat, President, 166
Samuelson, P. A., 6-7, 51, 214, 215, 223,
    228, 231; quoted, 7, 45-6, 244
savings, change in structure of, 138
savings-income ratio, 23
Say, J. B., 33-5, 40, 220; quoted, 33
Say's Law, 4, 33, 38, 48

Say-Walrasian system, 21
Scanlon, H., 244, 249
schedules, 17; *ex-ante*, 26, 202; *ex-post*, 26-7, 202
Schlesinger, A., 228, 242
Schultz, Professor, 217
Schumpeter, J., 37, 125, 220
Schwartz, A., 213
Schwartz, H., 179
scientific status: importance to economists, 6-7; *see also* mathematical methods
scientism, 30, 32, 45
Scitovsky, T., 99, 100, 229; *quoted*, 70-1
Self, P., 219, 227
Sen, A. K., 219
shareholders, 135
shifted curves, 187
shop stewards, 155
short and long run, 121-4, 201
Sidgwick, H., 237
signalling system, *see under* price mechanism
simplifying assumptions, 68-70, 113
Sismondi, 34
Skidelsky, R., 243
Smith, Adam, 44, 119, 238
Smithsonian agreement, 194
social complacency, 91
social contract, new, 177-8
social justice, full employment and, 87-8
social mobility, 136
social welfare function, 24, 102-3
socialism, impact on Britain of, 181
'socialist' countries, inequality of income in, 101-2
sociological investigations, necessity for, 16-17
sociopolitical factors, 20
Solow, R. M., 8-9, 214; *quoted*, 9
Sraffa, P., 41, 58; *quoted*, 9
stagnation, inflation and, 150-7
static analysis, 9, 32, 108, 110, 115, 116, 185-6
Sterling crisis (1976), 173
Stewart, F., 227
Stigler, G. J., 239
stock market, 218
stocks: changes in, 195; and flows, 169; money circulation and, 172
Strachey, J., 223
Streeten, P., 65, 217, 219, 224, 227, 228, 229, 253
Streissler, E. W., 216-17; *quoted*, 15

supply and demand: abandonment of simple concept, 122; interdependence of, 25; state interference with, 108; supply creating demand, 34

tastes: community, cyclical pattern in, 88; manipulation of, 83-4, 90
technical progress, 30-1, 115, 187-8; and rise in incomes, 144
technostructure, 138
Thatcher, M., 90, 166, 218
Thomas, H., 241
thrift, monetarist theory of, 110
Thurow, L., 159
Tinbergen, J., 103, 223, 224, 237
Tobin, J., 217, 226, 227, 246
trade unions, 144, 151, 152-3, 196; changed status of, 154-5; German, 163; lack of cohesion among, 155; legislation, 206
Trades Union Congress, 155
transfers, unilateral, 192-4, 205
Treasury doctrine (*see also* 'crowding out principle'), 146, 225
turnover, total, 172-3; and national income, 173; and Walrasian measure of GNP, 172
two-commodity model, 186-8

unchanging resources, assumption of, 108, 109
under-employment equilibrium, 18
unemployment, 4, 31-2; increase in production and, 175-6; inflation and, 48, 206; irreducible, 167; monetarism and, 43, 147, 165-6; 'natural' rate of, 55; neo-orthodox view of, 34; neoclassical neglect of, 61; positive economics and, 41-2; 'reserve army' of unemployed, 67, 177, 206; suffering due to, 67; wages and, 50, 55, 161
unions, *see* trade unions
United Kingdom, *see* Britain
utilitarian philosophy, 64
utility: interpersonal comparisons of, 99; measurable, *see* cardinal utility

Value Added Tax, 55
values, 68; education and, 87; policies and, 67; social welfare function and, 103
Veblen, T., 4, 84
'veil' of money, 32, 57

velocity of circulation of money, 34, 35, 54, 168, 213, 218; and changes in ownership of stocks, 172; dependence on definition of money, 171; hot money and, 176; monetarist concept, 173; stability of, 179; true, versus income, 174
Viner, J., 251
volume of money, *see* money supply
von Hayek, F., 214, 247
von Wieser, F., 96, 235

wage controls, 50
wage freezes, 152-3
wage negotiation, machinery for, 156
wage-price inflation, 153, 197
wages: pegged to productivity increases, 156; unemployment and, 50, 55, 161
wages rate, 18
Walras, L., 4, 78
Walrasian model, 21, 167-8; equilibrium in, 49, 54, 58, 61, 98, 162, 222; money in, 57; supply conditions, 168
Walters, A. A., 215; *quoted*, 9-10
wants, manipulation of, 83-4, 90

ways of life, choice between, 80, 82, 103
Webb B., 132, 241
Webb, S., 132, 241
welfare: economic, misleading index of, 91-2; economics and, 64-6, 68-73; indivisibility of, 70; optimum, 98; policy criteria, 75-7; production and consumption effects on, 93
Welfare Economics, 66, 235
welfare estimates, imponderable elements in, 92-4
Welfare State, 144, 242
White, H. D., 252
Wicksell, K., 237, 248
Wicksteed, P. H., 241
Weiner, N., 7
Wieser, F. von, 96, 235
Wollheim, R., 86, 233; *quoted*, 86
worker-appointed directors, 137
Worswick, G. D. N., 224
Woytinsky, E. S., 233
Woytinsky, W. S., 233

Young, A., 41, 58, 223